FamilyFun's
Crafts

Thumbs Up,
page 139

FamilyFun's Crafts

EDITED BY DEANNA F. COOK

AND THE EXPERTS AT FamilyFun MAGAZINE

HYPERION

NEW YORK

This book is dedicated to
the readers of *FamilyFun* magazine

Most of the crafts and photographs in this book were previously published in *FamilyFun* magazine.

FamilyFun magazine is a division of the Walt Disney Publishing Group.
To order a subscription, call 800-289-4849.

FamilyFun's Crafts

BOOK EDITORS: Rani M. Arbo, Deanna F. Cook, Ann Hallock, Alexandra Kennedy, and Cindy A. Littlefield
MANAGING EDITOR: Priscilla Totten
ART DIRECTOR: David Kendrick
ASSOCIATE ART DIRECTOR: Ginger Barr Heafey
ASSOCIATE PICTURE EDITOR: Mark Mantegna
CRAFT DEVELOPERS: Janet Street, Maryellen Sullivan
COPY EDITORS: Paula Noonan, Mike Trotman
EDITORIAL ASSISTANTS: Grace Ganssle, Susan Roberts
ART ASSISTANTS: Lynn Carrier, Sage Dillon, and Catherine McGrady
PRODUCTION DIRECTOR: Jennifer Mayer
PRODUCTION ASSISTANT: Martha Jenkins
EDITORIAL INTERNS: Debra Liebson, Danielle Zerbonne
TECHNOLOGY COORDINATOR: Luke Jaeger
COVER PHOTOGRAPH: Jade Albert

Impress, Inc.
DESIGNERS: Howard Klein, Hans Teensma

The staffs of *FamilyFun* and **Impress, Inc.**
conceived and produced *FamilyFun's Crafts* at
244 Main Street, Northampton, MA 01060

In collaboration with
Hyperion, 114 Fifth Avenue, New York, NY 10011

Prepress production at Aurora Graphics, Portsmouth, NH
Printed by Worzalla Publishing Co., Stevens Point, WI

Library of Congress Cataloging-in-Publication Data

ISBN 0-7868-6304-8
First Edition
3 5 7 9 10 8 6 4

Acknowledgments

FamilyFun Contributors

Special thanks to the following *FamilyFun* magazine writers for their wonderful crafts: Steve Bennett, Susan Biesiada, Karen Bigler, Cynthia Caldwell, Laurie Winn Carlson, Colleen Carroll, Carol Case, Bradley Clark, Tobye Cook, Tania Cowling, Katie Craig, Deborah Cramer, Dede Cummings, Rhonda Spatz Darnell, Katherine Eastman, Jill Elkins, Marie Faust Evitt, Adrienne Fawcett, Susan Gelotte, Joan Goldberg, Janet Goldstein, Donne Green, Leslie Hamilton, Cathryn Harding, Joni Hilton, Teri Keough, Heidi King, Valerie Kohn, Kathleen Peelen Krebs, Drew Kristofik, Brad Lemley, Mary Magnan, Vivi Mannuzza, Shoshana Marchand, Maggie Megaw, Susan Milord, Karen Modrzejewski, Julie Niederkorn, Joy Overbeck, Jodi Picoult, Mary Purpura, Curtis Rist, Julie Rose, Barbara Rowley, Mary-Jo Rulick, Laura Purdie Salas, Mary Beth Sammons, Jonathan Sapers, Sheila Seifert, Jeanne Skvarla, Penelope U. Smith, Cindy Loop Snyder, Shannon Summers, Barbara Theisen, Emily B. Todd, Elise Webb, Katherine Whittemore, Nancy Winningham, and Lee M. Woodruff.

Especially to the following major contributors:

Rani M. Arbo, an editor of *FamilyFun's Crafts* and a former editor of *FamilyFun* magazine, lives in South Deerfield, Massachusetts, where she crafts and plays the fiddle.

Lynne Bertrand, a *FamilyFun* contributing editor, writes frequently on crafts. She is the mother of two children, Nick and Georgie, and the author of five children's books.

Janet Street has developed more than two hundred crafts for *FamilyFun* magazine since 1994. She is the illustrator of ten children's books, including *The Gingham Dog* and *The Calico Cat* (Philomel) and *One Day, Two Dragons* (Clarkson Potter).

FamilyFun Readers

Special thanks to the following *FamilyFun* readers who shared the priceless ideas that have been a success with their families: Margi Ackerman, Eileen Allen, Jean Alston, Angie Ball, Nancy Barnett, Barbara Beach, Lisa Burmester, Debbie Failinger Buskirk, Marianne Cashman, Mireille Church, Cheryl Critcher, Anne D. Driskill, Lil Eastman, Judi Ensler, Judy Bacarisse Evans, Betsy B. Gengras, Alice Giarrusso, Janet Goldstein, Elizabeth Hagner, Kimberly Hardy-Johns, Annette Hayes, Lynda Jammer, Toni Kelley, Janna Kuklis, Fredda Parish Lake, Emily Larsen, Ivy Delon Lee, Jessica Leggett, Katie Leto, Susan Lill, Ann McDonald, Lauren MacDonald, Arlene Mayer, Patty Meldrum, Darlene Mihaloew, Cathy Moore, Nancy Ojeda, Maureen O'Meara, Angie O'Toole, Lisa Pace, Susan M. Paprocki, Mary Parker, Cynthia Pegado, Joellen Pisarczyk, Shelby Powell, Karen Rich, Debra Roach, Mary Lou Scarbrough, Rachel Schwartz, Gayle Selsback, Christine Silveira, Robin Taplitsky, Julie Troester, Ann Van Dort, Jean Whitlinger, Susan Wieser, Terry Wright, and Dale Zarella.

FamilyFun Staff

With gratitude to the following staff members of *FamilyFun's* art and editorial departments, who directed much of the original work: Jonathan Adolph, Deborah Geigis Berry, Susan Clare Ellis, Grace Ganssle, Pamela Glaven, Jean Graham, Luke Jaeger, David Kendrick, Alexandra Kennedy, Ed Kohn, Gregory Lauzon, Catherine McGrady, Mark Mantegna, Dan Mishkind, Paula Noonan, Susan Roberts, Priscilla Totten, Mike Trotman, and Sandra L. Wickland. Especially to the following staff members who were instrumental in developing crafts for *FamilyFun* magazine:

Deanna F. Cook, Senior Editor of *FamilyFun* magazine, edits food and crafts for *FamilyFun* magazine. She is the author of *Disney's Family Cookbook* (Hyperion) and the *Kid's Multicultural Cookbook* (Williamson). She lives in Northampton, Massachusetts, with her husband and daughter.

Ann Hallock, Executive Editor of *FamilyFun* magazine, edits many of the magazine's craft features and oversees the annual Crafts and Holidays special issues. She lives with her husband in Northampton, Massachusetts.

Ginger Barr Heafey, Associate Art Director of *FamilyFun* magazine, lives in Leeds, Massachusetts, with her husband and two children. Ginger creates and tests crafts and art-directs many of the craft photo shoots.

Cindy A. Littlefield, Associate Editor of *FamilyFun* magazine, lives in Conway, Massachusetts, with her two children, Ian and Jade, who help her create and test many of the popular crafts that appear in the Family Almanac section of *FamilyFun.*

Maryellen Sullivan hails from Northampton, Massachusetts, where she works with construction paper and glue to create crafts for *FamilyFun* — and her cubicle, car, and apartment.

Special thanks to all the photographers, stylists, and models for their excellent work, which first appeared in *FamilyFun* magazine.

This book would not have been possible without the help of the staff at Impress, Inc., especially Hans Teensma and Howard Klein, and the staff at Hyperion, especially Bob Miller, Wendy Lefkon, Kris Kliemann, Lisa Kitei, Robin Friedman, Vincent Stanley, and David Lott.

Contents

Milk Jug Dollhouse,
page 42

Spooky Spiders,
page 230

Farm Animal Puppets, page 140

Pencil Toppers, page 25

Box of Chalk, page 35

Splatter Shirts, page 163

Chapter One

Setting Up

O F ALL THE activities we publish in *FamilyFun* magazine, our crafts generate the most mail from readers. Every day, our mailbox offers up handwritten letters with snapshots of kids proudly displaying craft projects from the magazine's pages: clay bead necklaces, clothespin Christmas ornaments, or homemade finger puppets. Seeing these photos and reading the letters remind us what crafting is all about — the chance to spend time together as a family and, in the process, create lasting memories for our children.

Since we started *FamilyFun* in 1991, readers have turned to us for craft ideas to help make the most of a rainy afternoon, a Scouting event, a birthday party, or a holiday celebration. They have clipped and saved and spilled glue all over our directions — and some have even organized their own filing systems for favorite projects. So we decided it was time to gather our crafts in one book.

That way, our readers would no longer have to rustle through back issues to find that paper wind sock or those Thanksgiving decorations they want to make *right now*.

We've hit upon a tried-and-true method for developing crafts: we look to our families, to our regular contributors, and to our readers for inspiration. What crafts have been the most impressive? The most fun for the kids? The answers, which lie in the pages of this book, range from easy drawing games to homemade play doughs to holiday keepsakes. Some are as simple as a paper chain; others are as grand as a giant playhouse. But they all have one thing in common: they have been tested by families like yours — and are proven winners with both parents and kids.

For every craft in this book, we've kept the directions as straightforward as possible. For almost all of them, we've used materials that are readily available and inexpensive (an entire chapter, in fact, is devoted to art made from recyclables). Most importantly, every project passes the kid test: children must be able to complete

A Child's Craft Corner

A special craft area in the basement, garage, or in a corner of your child's room can make art sessions positively habit-forming. Here are a few helpful hints for setting up.

Work surface: Start with a comfortable seat, good lighting, and an uncluttered surface, such as a table, desk, low closet shelf, easel, or even a breakfast tray.

Storage and supplies: A small bookcase keeps supplies out of the way yet accessible. The following ideas will help you organize:

✂ Shoe boxes and plastic containers filled with crayons, paints, and glue.

✂ Markers, pencils, scissors, and paintbrushes can stand upright in coffee cans or plastic jars or lie flat in plastic silverware trays.

✂ Egg cartons are just right for holding buttons, stickers, glitter, and odds and ends.

✂ A cardboard box can become a "collage container" for storing feathers, fabric, yarn, pinecones, shells, and other treasures.

✂ Stow paper supplies (newsprint pads, a roll of butcher block paper) on a shelf, along with a large envelope that holds loose sheets of paper, doilies, and old magazines.

✂ Save some shelf space for favorite craft books (see page 248 for a list of our favorites) and a notebook of art ideas.

the craft with only a little help from a patient adult — and have room to add their own embellishments to the design.

Doing crafts with kids does take time, but it's worth the effort. Hands-on activities hold a child's attention and develop creativity, dexterity, problem-solving skills, and confidence. With art budgets dwindling in many American schools, it's becoming more important than ever for parents to encourage and participate in art at home. Maybe that's one reason why arts and crafts are on the rise — ninety percent of all U.S. households now have at least one crafter.

So the next time you are looking for a quick activity, just open this book. Don't worry about getting a little paint on the pages. You may discover, as many of our readers have, that even if the craft turns out slightly lopsided or the tail is in the wrong place, your child will be pleased with his creation. And if you happen to take a photo of him holding up his project,

by all means send it along — your pictures are a continuing inspiration to us.

Planning a Craft Project

If you wonder what parent has the time and energy to choose a craft project, set it up, help the kids complete it, and clean up, take heart: you and your children can pull it off like pros. Here are tips to get you started, and a promise that the more you do it, the easier it gets.

Set up a work space. Since craft projects do make somewhat of a mess, set yours up in an easy-to-clean place, such as a utility room, a back porch or garage, or a corner of the kitchen. Ideally, the room should be well ventilated, especially if you are working with spray paints and sealers. Even better, reserve a spot exclusively for crafting, where art materials can be stored within arm's reach (see A Child's Craft Corner, at left, for ideas).

Choose age-appropriate projects. Try to pick crafts your children have the motor skills for — and set aside

time enough to complete the task. For a kindergartner, choose a project with very few steps or be prepared to take over when he loses interest. Older kids should be able to handle a larger-scale endeavor (say, the seven-step papier-mâché piñata on page 90). Let them go for it, but you can also encourage them to spread it out over a week of after-school time or over two weekend days.

Gather materials before you begin. There's nothing worse than realizing halfway through a project that you're out of tempera paint or construction paper. In this book, we've pulled the art materials into recipe-style lists so you can plan ahead and stock up on supplies.

Put on smocks. Before you launch into any messy craft, you're smart to dress your child in a smock. You don't need to buy an expensive one — instead, try an oversize oxford, a big T-shirt, an old apron, or anything else that's loose enough to let your child move freely yet still keep him relatively clean.

Make cleanup part of the project. Cleaning up as you go will help preserve order in your work space, and it may also save art supplies from an early demise (uncapped markers and open containers of paint or glue, for example). Start this habit early, and it will become a part of your child's regular craft ritual. For Cleanup Tips, see page 14.

Encouraging Creativity

As you approach any craft project, be sure to give your children creative license. The more room you give them, the more their art will reflect their personalities and experiences. To help them enjoy the creative process — and feel good about their artwork when it's complete — follow the tips below.

Steer toward a finished product, but emphasize the process. It's fine to have an end result in mind — older kids, particularly, like closure and are proud of finished projects. But make sure you aren't so determined to follow directions that your child can't add her own flair. The end result, after all, is no more important than the steps that lead up to it. So when you're

Setting Up

The Rules of Crafting

✂ Artists must put on smocks or aprons before they start.

✂ Tables and floors must be covered with newspaper.

✂ Wet, droopy art needs to dry before it is carried around to be admired.

✂ Art supplies must be handled properly — caps go back on markers, brushes get washed, scissors cut only paper.

✂ Artists must respect one another. No crafters should make uncaring remarks.

Safety First

✂ Always read the labels to make sure materials are nontoxic (that is, when entering the body through the mouth, skin, or eyes, it is not poisonous) and don't use them after the expiration date. See page 247 for tips on buying non-toxic materials.

✂ Remind kids to keep their hands away from their mouths and to work in a well-ventilated area.

✂ When working with young kids, keep small objects, such as beads, paper clips, and uninflated balloons, out of reach.

✂ Using an iron, a glue gun, a craft knife, and other sharp or hot objects should be a parent's job.

trying a new project, always ask yourself, "Can my child be creative with what we're doing here, or am I running an arts and crafts assembly line?"

Offer help, but not too much of it. To make your crafting time a bit more efficient, you may be tempted to lay out precut pieces of fabric or construction paper for your child to assemble. But be careful of doing too much. All that organizing, measuring, folding, cutting, and shaping can be part of the fun for your kids — and it teaches valuable lessons.

Set ground rules. Contrary to what Jackson Pollock's mother might have thought, childhood creativity rarely thrives when paint is being strewn with abandon. As in most pleasurable situations with children, an adult needs to create an environment where kids feel free because they understand the limits. After all, they don't instinctively know that the blue paintbrush goes back in the blue paint pot or that markers shouldn't be pounded down on paper. Laying down a few guidelines won't squelch your child's imagination, and it will put you more at

ease. Just be sure you limit disorder, not creativity. See The Rules of Crafting, left, for some basic guidelines.

Don't rush your child. Encourage your kids to take their time when working with scissors, markers, crayons, and other art tools that require fine motor skills. These skills are not developed overnight, so try not to get impatient just because you'd like to move on to more interesting projects. The fun of making things withers if the learner is held to impossible standards of maturity. Let your kids proceed at their own pace; they will let you know when they're ready for something more complicated.

Expose kids to art. Take your kids to arts and crafts museums, check out books from the library, and look in your local paper for special exhibits or art classes in your area to inspire your crafters to be more creative.

Choosing Good Materials

All of us have felt the irritation of working with unresponsive materials (wallpapering comes to mind). Imagine, then, how frustrating it is for a child to use

paper that rips when wet, scissors that chew rather than cut, or crayons that crumble. Good materials are worth the investment. Consider stocking up on the following basics — and if you are unfamiliar with any of them, turn to our glossary on page 246.

Paint. Although liquid tempera is handy to have, we recommend buying the bottles of tempera powder, available at most office or school supply stores, because they last for ages. Mix the powder with a little water in a clear jar, put the lid on, and shake. Add more powder or water if the paint is too thick or runny. Add 1 teaspoon of dish detergent for every ½ cup of paint and it will wash out of clothes more readily. You will also need acrylic paint, a longer-lasting paint that's available at art stores, for some of the finer crafts in this book, and fabric paint, for jazzing up T-shirts, sneakers, and other wearables in Chapter Eight.

Paper. For drawing with markers or crayons, buy copier paper or pads of watercolor, construction, or drawing paper. Or, try a roll of white butch-er paper, available inexpensively at paper or food service supply stores. Cheaper paper, such as newsprint, is okay for scribbling with pens and pencils, but it soaks up markers and paints in a most unsatisfying way. Some projects in this book also call for tissue paper, card stock, and poster board. And of course, you can never have too much scrap paper on hand.

Paintbrushes. Stockpile a few easy-to-hold brushes. Inexpensive 1-inch or ¾-inch ones, available at hardware stores, make good brushes for glue or paint. Avoid the truly cheap ones because their bristles fall out, and always rinse the brushes to prolong their lives.

Glue. White glue goes further and is neater when kids apply it with brushes. If you buy a big tub of white glue, pour it into jars that can be capped for storage. Glue sticks are ideal for kids, especially young ones. Superglue and some brands of rubber cement are toxic, so use them with caution. A hot glue gun is suggested for several activities in this book, but it should be used by parents

Setting Up

How to Respond to a Child's Artwork

Instead of interpreting your child's artwork, ask questions or talk about the effort that's gone into the art. Some good phrases to try are:

"What bright colors you used here!"

"Look at all the different kinds of lines you drew."

"I can see you've been working very hard on this picture."

"Can you tell me what is going on here?"

"This picture makes me feel happy."

Or, write down your child's own description of their art on the bottom or back of the paper.

only and should be stored out of kids' reach.

Crayons and colored pencils. For young kids, invest in good crayons; cheap ones leave weak colors and snap easily. We recommend the large Crayola box with the built-in sharpener. For older kids, use sharpened colored pencils.

Markers. Art teacher and *FamilyFun* contributor Elise Webb especially loves Mr. Sketch markers; they are broad-tipped, come in nice colors, and last. They, and other good (and more washable) markers, can be found in toy, art supply, and discount stores. Avoid cheap no-name markers, and avoid permanent markers altogether for young kids.

Scissors. A good pair of scissors is an indispensable craft tool. Fabric scissors, pinking shears, and other specialty scissors (such as crazy scissors) are recommended for a few of the projects in this book. You'll also need a craft knife (with a screw-in, replaceable blade) or a utility knife (with a retractable blade) — both of which should be used by parents only.

Recyclables. From empty boxes to milk jugs to egg cartons, many activities in this book call for household recyclables. See page 38 for an extensive list of potential art supplies.

Tape. Scotch tape, double-stick tape, masking tape, and duct tape are all worth having in your supply closet. When tape is an outwardly visible part of the finished craft, you might opt for brightly colored electrical tape.

Tools. Desk tools, such as a hole punch (single hole is best), a ruler, and a stapler, will be necessary for some crafts. Kitchen supplies (cookie cutters, straws, toothpicks, rolling pins, forks) are useful for clay projects. A hammer, nails, and other carpentry tools will come in handy for the wooden crafts in this book.

Sewing supplies. For hand-sewn projects, make up a small sewing box for your child, including needles, thread of various colors, ribbon, buttons, fabric scraps, and felt (see the Perfect Sewing Box on page 195 for more ideas). A few of the projects in this book require a sewing machine.

Cleanup Tips

To make it easy for kids to get in the habit of cleaning up, try the following storage systems. Your kids will always know where to put their supplies at the end of a project.

✂ Try a fishing tackle box or toolbox for art materials.

✂ Fill a clear shoe bag with supplies and hang it on the back of your child's bedroom door.

✂ Label shoe boxes or clear plastic containers with drawings or words — markers, scissors, glue, paints and paintbrushes, and tape — and store on a low bookshelf within your child's reach.

✂ For more ideas, see A Child's Craft Corner on page 10.

14

Extras. You should examine each project's list of materials to see what you need, but here are a few things to keep an eye out for at craft supply shops: googly eyes, pipe cleaners, self-adhesive Velcro fasteners, glitter, paper fasteners, wooden dowels, Fome-Cor board, string, and twine.

Organizing Kids' Artwork

Most kids are prolific enough to fill a minivan with their artwork. So there's a good chance you have a fast-growing pile in your home of paintings, a cardboard tube castle, and a complete flour-and-salt zoo. Throwing it all away may break your heart (and your child's, too), but saving all of it could drive you out of house and home. The following tips will help you eliminate the clutter — and appreciate the crafts you treasure the most.

Save some and toss some. If a piece of artwork is simply stunning, save it. If it doesn't knock your socks off, take a deep breath and throw it out. (We're talking about at least a four-to-one ratio of chuck-to-save in the early years.) But beauty is not the only rea-son to save a piece of art. Consider saving anything that shows a developmental jump: the first scribbles, then shapes, the first sun, the first people and objects, and any self-portraits.

Stow the masterpieces. Professional artists store artwork in flat files (shallow chests of drawers) and in portfolios. Even secondhand flat files are expensive, so try a cardboard portfolio; for about $16, you can buy a 20- by 26-inch version that fits behind the couch or under the bed. Artists who work in three dimensions photograph their work and save photos in a book — not a bad idea for kids' sculptures.

Label each piece of art. Write in pencil at the bottom your child's name, age, and the subject, as told by the artist (*Shark Eating Monster* or *Paris in Spring*). If you want it to look professional, jot down the type of media.

Give some art away. If you run out of wall space, encourage your kids to think of their grandparents' houses (or anywhere else their art might be cherished) as museums for their work.

Displaying Kids' Art

Make a big to-do of your kids' artwork by putting it up around the house and rotating the displays periodically.

✂ The refrigerator door is a good first stop. Use as many heavy-duty magnets as you can find to make sure the stuff stays put.

✂ Inexpensive frames (either the glass clip kind or the inch-thick clear plastic boxes) are perfect for a rotating gallery of special drawings.

✂ Mat artwork on construction paper (which conveniently fades in the sun, letting you know when it's time to change the art).

✂ Hang artwork on a clothesline with clothespins (see page 21).

✂ Display small 3-D pieces and freestanding framed artwork on a shallow set of shelves. To keep frames from sliding off, you can nail a thin dowel along the edge of the shelf. You can use a regular bookshelf, but it helps if the shelves have adjustable heights so you can accommodate Popsicle stick sculptures or papier-mâché figures of any shape and size.

Setting Up

70944

Chapter Two

Let's Color!

ONE WINTER DAY when *FamilyFun* editor Deanna Cook was seven years old, her mother had an inspired idea. She took out paints, brushes, crayons, and markers and invited all six of her children to scribble on the walls in the front hallway. The kids thought she was joking. Paint on the walls? And not get in trouble? You bet — the room was going to be freshly wallpapered in a week. So the Cooks went to town, covering every inch of the walls with stick figures, animals, houses, and squiggles. They admired their homemade gallery for more than a week before the new wallpaper went up, and their handiwork disappeared. A few days later, Deanna's mother was shocked to find her youngest daughter, two-year-old Tobye, armed with a fistful of crayons, eagerly decorating the newly papered walls.

Like the Cook kids, children are natural scribblers. Just as crawling and toddling are the first stages of learning to walk, so scribbling is a prerequisite for learning to draw. What's more, fine motor skills, such as drawing, take a long time to develop, which means that kids need to be given a lot of unrushed and agreeable practice time with paint, markers, crayons, and other art supplies.

Contrary to what some parents remember from their childhood art sessions, there is no wrong or right way to do art. So what if your child chooses a black crayon for black paper or wants to mix blue and orange paint only to get a big brown blob? What really matters is that she has creative license to experiment. You don't have to go as far as letting your kid paint on the walls —

Watercolor Butterflies, page 20

newsprint or copy paper will suffice — as long you make her feel her artwork is worth looking at.

Stick to nonpermanent scribbler supplies.

Before you buy crayons, markers, paints, or other coloring supplies, read the back of the box and be sure they are washable and nontoxic. Instead of acrylic paints, which do stain, mix liquid tempera with 1 teaspoon of dishwashing liquid for easy cleanup. If a little color spills on your kids' clothes, spray with a stain remover and toss in the washing machine — and next time, be sure your child is draped in a smock (a big T-shirt, an old apron, or a garbage bag with holes cut out for head and arms).

Cover floors and furniture within paint-flinging range.

For paint projects, it's a good idea to cover your work area with a plastic tablecloth or trash bag; for crayon and other nonliquid art projects, newspaper works fine.

Hand out art supplies one at a time.

To keep from overwhelming your child, especially if he is under five years old, introduce coloring supplies one at a time (crayons, then markers, then paint, for example) and let him use each one for as long as he wants.

Work with your child.

The best way to help a child learn the joy of painting and drawing is to experience it yourself. If that brings up old fears about the right and wrong way to paint, just think of your sessions as doodling. Or, try working with your left hand (if you're right-handed) to get a little more freedom from worries about mistakes.

Take care of supplies.

You want them to last as long as possible, so when your child is done with a project, make sure markers and paint jars are capped, brushes are washed, and crayons are back in the box. For storage ideas, see A Child's Craft Corner, page 10.

Window Art, page 19

Paint

Marble Painting

Window Art

Don't like what you see outside? Then change it! Mix up a batch of this washable paint and let your kids bring some color to a gray day. Or, follow the example of *FamilyFun* reader Darlene Mihaloew of Springfield, Virginia, who waits for a sunny day to let her kids paint her glass deck doors from the outside — while she snaps photos of them from the living room.

Materials

    ½ tablespoon powdered tempera
       paint
    1 tablespoon clear dishwashing
       liquid
    Aluminum foil–lined muffin tin

Mix the powdered tempera with the dishwashing liquid until the mixture acquires the creamy consistency of house paint. (If you don't have powdered tempera, mix ½ cup liquid tempera with 1 teaspoon of dishwashing liquid.) Use the muffin tin to mix and preserve colors. Then, pick a window: picture windows are ideal for large scenes, while smaller panes can be filled either with a series of pictures that tells a story or with a single motif, such as a spring bouquet or a rainbow.

Line the window sash with masking tape, spread newspaper to safeguard the surrounding area, and your window artists can get under way. To remove dried paint or to make corrections while decorating, simply rub off the designs with a dry paper towel.

Marble Painting

It's easy to get on a creative roll with this project — after all, kids can hardly resist playing with marbles and generating masterpieces at the same time.

Materials

    Paper
    Paper plate
    Aluminum foil–lined muffin tin
    Tempera paints
    Marbles
    Spoon

Trim a sheet of paper to fit on a sturdy paper plate. Then, fill the muffin tin cups with different colors of paint. Have your child drop a marble into one cup and roll it around with the spoon. When the marble is coated with paint, transfer it by spoon to the plate. Use a gentle wrist action to swirl the marble around until the paint wears off. Or, try using two or three marbles simultaneously. To preserve the hues, use a different marble for each color. Lift the artwork from the paper plate to dry.

Spin Art

Emily Larson of Battle Lake, Minnesota, lets her kids use her old salad spinner to create paintings. The kids put a paper plate at the bottom of the spinner and squirt different colors of paint around the plate. Then, they cover the spinner, churn away, and hang their finished paintings up to dry.

Let's Color!

Squirt Painting

Watercolor Butterflies

This terrific idea came from *FamilyFun* contributor Jodi Picoult, who discovered it at her son Jake's preschool in Hanover, New Hampshire. After she saw his classroom ceiling alive with these butterflies, she and Jake made a slew of their own, which they clipped to curtains, hung from the kitchen chandelier, and even fastened to the telephone cord.

Materials

- Paper coffee filters (the round variety)
- Watercolors and paintbrushes
- Markers
- Glue and glitter (optional)
- Clothespins
- Colored paper

To color the filters, dab on watercolor paint with a brush or draw on designs with markers — or both. For a shimmery effect, add glitter-and-glue designs. Once the filter is dry, pinch it in the middle like a bow tie. Slide or clip the clothespin onto it and fan out each side of the filter to resemble a butterfly's wings. Cut two strips of construction paper, about the size of matchsticks, and glue them onto the clothespin for antennae.

Roll-on Paints

FamilyFun reader Joellen Pisarczyk of Cozad, Nebraska, found a creative way to reuse roll-on deodorant bottles. With a screwdriver, she pried off each ball. Then, she washed the bottles, filled them with slightly diluted tempera paint, and replaced the balls. Her three-year-old, Carrie, and six-year-old, Greta, had a blast making roller paintings at the table, and Joellen didn't have to worry about messy drips. After the fun, she replaced the caps, and the paint stayed fresh for next week's art session.

Squirt Painting

Kids get pumped up about this abstract painting technique: instead of applying careful brushstrokes, they get to squirt color onto a giant canvas. Liquid tempera works best for this project, but food coloring will do in a pinch.

Materials

- Old bedsheet or large piece of newspaper
- Clothesline and clothespins
- Squirt gun or empty plastic pump bottle (do not use bottles from toxic household cleaners)
- Tempera paint

First, use clothespins to hang your canvas from the clothesline. Then, fill the pump bottle three quarters full of water. Add just enough paint to color the water — too much will clog the spray nozzle. Tighten the cap and shake well. Have your child stand a few feet from the sheet, adjust the nozzle to shoot a thin stream, and squirt away. (If more than one child paints, have kids stand on the same side of the canvas.)

Clothesline Art
Gallery

Clothesline Art Gallery

To make a big to-do of your kids' artwork, string it up for all to see. Set up a clothesline and let your child clip on finished works, as well as projects still wet with paint or glue. Not only is it an easily movable gallery, but it's one that makes rotating in new artwork a cinch.

Bubble Prints

After reading about our bubble prints, *FamilyFun* reader Terry Wright of Scottsdale, Arizona, said that her kids, Bryan, age six, and Danielle, age four, had just as much fun blowing the colored bubbles as they did making the prints.

Materials

    2 tablespoons tempera paint
    1 tablespoon clear dishwashing
       liquid
    1 cup water
    Pie plate
    Straw

After covering your work surface with newspaper, measure all of the ingredients into an empty jar, cover tightly, and shake. Pour the mixture into a pie plate. Stick one end of a plastic drinking straw into the paint and blow through the other end (remind your child not to suck on the straw). When a large billow of bubbles forms, remove the straw and gently lay a sheet of white paper on top. As the bubbles break, they'll leave vivid impressions. Once the imprints dry, use markers to outline interesting shapes.

Let's Color!

Bubble Prints

Rain Painting

Rain Painting

This activity, from the If-You-Can't-Beat-'Em-Join-'Em Department, makes the most of rainy weather.

Materials

- Paper plate (Chinet or other uncoated plate)
- Food coloring
- White crayon (optional)

After sprinkling a few drops of food coloring on a paper plate, your child can don her rain gear and walk outdoors with the plate for about a minute. For a batik effect, try drawing a white crayon design on the plate before adding the food coloring.

MIX YOUR OWN

Shiny paint: Add white glue to liquid or powdered tempera paint.

Crystalline paint: Mix salt into liquid or powdered tempera paint.

Bubbly paint: Stir shampoo into liquid or powdered tempera paint.

Sweet-smelling paint: Add lemon extract to yellow tempera paint, peppermint extract to green paint, and vanilla extract to white paint.

Puffy 3-D paint: Mix together 2 tablespoons all-purpose flour, 2 tablespoons salt, and 2 tablespoons water. Add several drops of food coloring and stir until you get the desired shade. Pour the mixture into a plastic squeeze bottle. Your kids then can squirt designs onto paper, cardboard, or wood. As the paint dries, it will become puffy and textured.

Tub Art

Homemade Finger Paints

With a batch of this quick and easy paint (which keeps in airtight containers), you can turn your young artist loose on newsprint or in the bathtub at a moment's notice.

Materials

- 2 tablespoons sugar
- ⅓ cup cornstarch
- 2 cups cold water
- ¼ cup clear dishwashing liquid
- Food coloring (for vibrant colors, use food coloring paste)

Mix the sugar and cornstarch in a small pan, then slowly add the water. Cook over low heat, stirring until the mixture becomes a smooth, almost clear gel (about 5 minutes). When the mixture is cool, stir in the dishwashing liquid. Scoop equal amounts into containers and stir in the food coloring.

Tub Art: This paint contains dish soap, so it dissolves in water — which makes it perfect for bathtub finger painting. (Test to be sure bright paints won't leave a residue; most come clean with a powdered cleanser.)

Waxed Paper Painting

If you don't have time to mix up a batch of finger paint, try this tempera paint alternative, which is just right for little hands. Cover a tray with a sheet of waxed paper and have your child spoon tempera paint over it in different colors. Cover with another sheet of waxed paper. Your child can press down on the colors and watch them blend and move. If you wish, peel off the top layer to make a paper print of his design.

Let's Color!

QUICK DRAW

Drawing without looking at the paper may sound like a silly idea. And it is — when you try it, you'll definitely end up with the giggles. But it also helps teach kids how to study a subject before they start to draw. And even more important, it teaches artists not to agonize too much over their finished products.

To begin, family members take turns modeling, allowing 3 or 4 minutes for others to draw. Once the model is still, the artist places his pencil point near the top of the paper. Then, he looks at the model and begins drawing, recording every line he sees. He should slowly continue depicting the head, torso, arms, and legs, not concerning himself with whether lines are being drawn over one another. No matter how uncomfortable it may seem, the drawer may not peek at the paper! When finished, artist and model can look at the picture (often surprisingly expressive), then switch places.

Ready, Set, Draw!

The natural scribble instinct is hardly ever dormant in kids — but if yours need a little priming, here are three games to warm up their imaginations. Plus, they're a lifesaver any time you're stuck waiting in the doctor's office or at a restaurant (especially one with paper place mats).

Materials

Pens, pencils, or colored markers
Paper

Finish the Picture: This is a game well suited to preschoolers. To start, the first drawer closes her eyes and scribbles on a piece of paper; the next player must finish the picture by turning the shape into something recognizable.

Don't Finish the Picture: In this game (suited to older kids who delight in details), one player starts by drawing a stick figure. Others take turns adding elements to the drawing (hair, eyebrows, socks, shorts, funny shoes). The person who can't think of anything else to add must declare the picture finished.

Fold-up Aliens: Start with a piece of paper folded in three. The first child draws an alien's head on one third of the paper and refolds it so the head is hidden. The second child then draws the torso, refolds the paper, and gives it to the third, who draws the legs and feet, then unfolds the paper to discover a truly otherworldly creature.

Ready, Set, Draw!

Pencil Toppers

With this easy sculpting craft, your child can turn her pencils into the sharpest collection in school. Instead of clay, she can use kneadable erasers (available at art supply stores for about $1) to create a mistake-chasing task force.

Materials

- Kneadable eraser
- Pencil
- Butter knife
- Acrylic paint
- Paper clip
- Optional decorations: seed beads, pipe cleaner, pom-poms, white crayon tips
- Felt

Pencil Toppers

To make a head, use scissors (parents only) to cut the eraser in half lengthwise. Wrap one half around the end of a pencil and pinch together the sides and top. Use your fingers to mold the eraser into an oblong blob. Next, pull off a small piece of eraser from the unused half. Shape it into a nose and press it on to form a face. Use the same method to add ears, bushy eyebrows, or a duck's bill. With a pencil point or a pen cap, sculpt cheekbones and a chin. Carve a broad, openmouthed smile using the tip of a butter knife.

To style hair, roll a piece of eraser into a thin rope and cut it into short spikes or long locks. Press the hair ends onto the top of the head (or the chin for a beard) and tint with a coat of acrylic paint. Finally, accessorize with paper clip spectacles, seed-bead earrings, or pipe cleaner and pom-pom antennae. You can even make dragon fangs out of white crayon tips.

On paper, draw a headless stick figure with its arms and legs extended in a jumping jack position. The figure should measure approximately 4 inches from the neck to the heels and ¾ inch wide at the waist. Make the limbs about 1¾ inches long and ½ inch wide. Cut out the paper pattern and use a pencil or chalk to trace around it onto a piece of felt. Then, cut out the felt figure. Snip two ¼-inch X's through the felt figure's midsection. Push the tip of the pencil through both holes, as shown, and slide the figure up the pencil. Secure the felt in place below the head with a piece of tape applied to the back of the pencil.

Let's Color!

Shadow Silhouettes

They say it's impossible to catch your shadow — but if you can make it stay still long enough, your kids can trace it onto the wall to create a large-scale portrait.

Materials

Desk lamp
Blank wall
Chair
Crayons, markers, or colored
     pencils

Place the lamp on a table about 5 to 8 feet away from a blank wall. The subject sits, facing sideways, in a chair between the lamp and the wall. The artist turns on and aims the light so that the subject's shadow shows up on the wall, then tapes up a large sheet of paper so that the shadow is cast upon it. The shadow size can be decreased or increased by moving the subject nearer to or farther from the lamp. Now, the artist uses a crayon (or anything else that won't bleed through the paper) to trace the shadow. When the tracing is done, the artist continues decorating the profile with details such as hairstyle, jewelry, and clothing.

Tinted Photo

Tinted Photos

Coloring takes on a whole new dimension when your kids are trying to stay within the lines of a photocopy of their pets or best friends. Your artists can add neon purple stripes to a shirt, color their dog's ears hot pink, or draw a fort onto the top of a tree.

Materials

Family photos (for best results,
     choose ones with sharp contrast)
Photocopy machine
Crayons, markers, or colored
     pencils

To start, make copies of the photos you've chosen (experiment with the copy machine settings to get the clearest image). Then, let your kids hand-color the photo using anything from markers to crayons to colored pencils (even watercolors). There are no rules, and you should encourage the whimsical: how about coloring Uncle Steve, sleeping in a lawn chair with a three-headed alien lurking nearby?

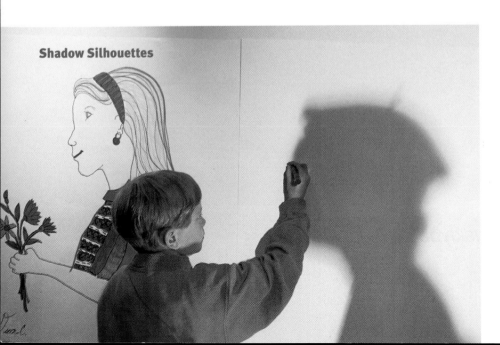

Shadow Silhouettes

The Magic Bean

Like Jack's famous beanstalk, this project always turns up surprises.

Materials

- Lima bean
- Paper
- Colored pencils or markers

Tape a lima bean to the bottom of a piece of paper. Have your child draw what she thinks will come out of the magic bean. Will it be a tree? A dinosaur? A rainbow? If you're all out of lima beans, try this variation: paste or draw a tail, tongue, or paw shape onto paper and ask your child to create an animal to go with it.

Moving Pictures

You may not realize it, but when you see a picture, your brain holds onto that image for nearly a tenth of a second after you've looked away. If a series of pictures is flashed in front of your eyes, your brain joins the pictures together, making them appear as one image in motion. A fun way for your child to test this phenomenon is to create her own animation.

Materials

- Scrap paper
- 2½-inch square of colored paper
- Drinking straw

First, practice sketching a simple two-part animation on scrap paper. In the first frame, for example, your child might draw a stick man with his arms held down by his sides. In the second frame, she should give him a new pose, perhaps raising his arms in the air and kicking out his legs.

Next, she should copy one of her sketches onto the 2½-inch square of paper (one sketch per side). Cut a pair of notches in the top of a drinking straw and slide in the bottom edge of the paper square. With the lower half of the straw held between both hands, she can roll the straw by sliding her fingers back and forth. Her drawings will seem to blend into one, and the stick man will appear to do a jumping jack. If not, try rolling the straw slower or faster.

Let's Color!

The Magic Bean

Moving Pictures

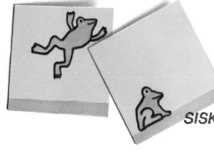

27

Faux Fishbowl

Foil Masks

FamilyFun contributor Jodi Picoult agrees with her kids that having one measly day a year for wearing costumes is not nearly enough. So, with these shiny masks, Kyle and Jake can celebrate Halloween any day of the week. Using permanent markers, the boys jazz up the shiny foil surface, making freckles, warts, and tattoos, so that they'll be sufficiently terrifying by the time Dad arrives home from work.

Materials

> 24- by 12-inch piece of heavy-duty
> aluminum foil
> Permanent markers

To make a mask, double up the foil into a 12-inch square. Press the foil onto your child's face, making sure to mold it over his cheekbones, nose, eye sockets, and lips. (It won't actually resemble your child that much, but the process is fun.) Pull the mask away, taking care not to bend it. With scissors, your child can cut strips of hair at the top; eye, nose, and mouth holes; and even eyelashes that can be curled on a pencil. Then, using permanent markers and pressing down gently, he can add in all kinds of colorful details.

MARKER MAGIC

Just when your kids are about to whine that there's nothing to do, put a tin of markers and white paper on the kitchen table and watch them gravitate toward it. Markers offer versatility and precision to artists who crave a line that isn't fuzzy and waxy. Here are several other marker projects:

✂ Draw a face with washable markers on a balloon.

✂ Decorate shoelaces with fabric markers.

✂ Sketch a fruit bowl with scented markers.

✂ Brighten up a window with dry erase markers (from an office supply store) and wipe away with a dry cloth.

Faux Fishbowl

For this tankful of tropical swimmers, you don't need aerators or fancy temperature controls — just a bunch of permanent markers and other household supplies. And if your kids overfeed them? Not to worry — unlike the real thing, these critters live forever.

Materials

> Clean Styrofoam meat tray
> Permanent markers
> Thread or fishing line
> Rocks and seashells
> Glass container, such as a fishbowl
>   or large mayonnaise jar
> Sand

On the Styrofoam tray, have your child draw and color in several fish with permanent markers. Cut the fish out with scissors, then punch a hole at the bottom center of each one. Run a long piece of thread or fishing line through each hole and tie each end to a rock or seashell.

Cover the bottom of a glass container with a few inches of sand, then place the rocks and shells on the sand. Add the weighted fish carefully, so that the threads don't get tangled. Slowly pour water into the container and watch the fish float.

Foil Mask

Marker Spirals

Marker Spirals

If you haven't yet put your phonograph out to pasture, here's a new use for it. Kids love choosing colors for this mess-free version of spin art — and you'll love the excuse to listen to all those old Beatles records.

Materials

　　Phonograph
　　Paper plate
　　Washable markers

Poke a hole in the center of the paper plate, then set it on the phonograph as you would a record and turn on the player. Have your kids hold the tip of one or more markers on the plate, moving them back and forth. Flip the plate and repeat on the other side. Then, starting at the outer edge of the plate, use scissors to cut around in a spiral, until you reach the plate's middle. String up one end of the strip and let it hang down in a curlicue.

Let's Color!

Make Your Mark

Sure, markers let you color and draw, but what about all the other amazing superpowers they have? Here's an illustrated guide to some of our favorite marker tips and techniques.

With fine-line washable markers, ink up a stamp to make a rainbow-hued print.

Scribble with a washable marker, then wet with a brush. When dry, add marker details.

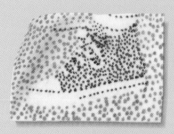

Lay tracing paper over a photo, then "dot" in the image with any kind of marker.

Make a design with washable markers, then spritz with water so the colors bleed.

With permanent markers, draw on a balloon, let dry, then inflate it to see the art grow.

Make a pet rock by adorning a small stone with a permanent marker creature.

Crayons

Crayon Rubbing

Pour all the crayons into a bucket of cool water, let them sit overnight, and squeeze off the papers. Although the papers keep the crayon from snapping easily, paperless crayons don't have to be peeled every five minutes.

A combination art project and treasure hunt, crayon rubbing can become a whole afternoon's worth of activity. The process makes you look anew at household objects — and realize how they can become gorgeous patterns.

Materials

Paper
Household objects: keys, coins, lace, sandpaper, onion bags, heavily veined leaves, paper clips, washer rings, corrugated cardboard, or combs
Crayons
String (optional)
Heavy-duty aluminum foil (optional)

Arrange a collection of objects underneath a piece of paper. Applying medium pressure, have your child rub a crayon over the paper (dark colors work best in early efforts) until the shapes and textures appear. By placing a few objects in patterns on a page, your child can design a wacky garden or a machine.

Textured Art: Draw a simple shape in black (try the outline of a city skyline or a big dinosaur) on a piece of paper, then have your child scour the house for textures to fill in the picture.

String Art: To make your own pattern, glue a length of string to a piece of cardboard in an interesting design. Let the glue dry, then use the string design for a single rubbing or a series.

Foil Rubbings: Fold a piece of heavy-duty aluminum foil into quarters and have your child draw on it with a pen so that the marks go deep into the top layer. Unfold it and use the back of the top layer for your rubbing.

FunFact

Crayons have been used by such art types as Paul Klee, Edgar Degas, Toulouse-Lautrec, and Pablo Picasso. Even modern-day celebrities get into coloring: Billy Crystal's favorite color is burnt sienna, Whoopi Goldberg likes magenta, and Mister Rogers is a fan of lemon yellow.

Textured Art

Rainbow Crayons

Wondering what to do with that mountain of stubby crayons in your kid's room? You can show your child how to create new crayons out of old ones — a recycling lesson and art project all in one. The crayons will actually draw different colors as they are used.

Materials

Old crayons
Empty tuna cans or a muffin tin
Aluminum foil

First, remove the paper wrappers from lots of brightly colored broken crayon pieces (see page 30 for the best way to remove wrappers from crayons). Then, fill each tuna can (or a muffin tin lined with aluminum foil) about halfway with contrasting crayon pieces, each about ½ inch in size. Bake the crayons in a preheated 300° oven for about 5 to 7 minutes. Watch them closely, because they melt quickly. Melt them just enough to blend the colors, but not so much that they completely liquefy and meld into one color.

Carefully remove the cans from the oven and let the crayons cool for about 30 minutes. When the rainbow crayons are completely cool, remove them. The new crayons should pop out easily when you tap the cans with a knife. If you used the muffin tin method, remove them from the tin and peel off the foil. The crayons should be more colorful on the foil side.

Solid Color Crayons: Use the same method as for rainbow crayons, but use only one color of crayons. This makes wonderful, easy-to-handle crayons suited for very small children.

Shaped Crayons: To make fish, stars, trees, and other simple shapes, follow the same directions but use cookie cutters for molds. Cover the bottom of a cookie cutter with a few layers of foil (let it bend up to cover part of the inside edges as well), making certain there are no holes in the foil. Fill the molds halfway with crayon pieces and use the same method to bake on a cookie sheet.

Crayon Hunt

For her son Mark's third birthday party, *FamilyFun* reader Alice Giarrusso of Amherst, New Hampshire, sent him and his eleven guests on a scavenger hunt. Since Mark was into art and drawing, they held a crayon hunt. Mom Alice bought several boxes of crayons and hid individual crayons around the yard. Mark and his guests went out armed with envelopes to collect as many as they could find. Because she had hidden so many, every child found quite a few. At the end of the hunt, all the kids received coloring books.

Color Me Mauvelous

The first box of Crayolas sold in 1903 for a nickel and contained only eight colors: black, blue, brown, green, orange, red, violet, and yellow. Today, with 112 hues to choose from, simply matching a color to its name is an art in itself. Give it a try with these.

1. timber wolf
2. wisteria
3. cornflower
4. tumbleweed
5. mauvelous
6. macaroni and cheese
7. thistle
8. bittersweet
9. cerulean
10. asparagus
11. periwinkle
12. razzmatazz
13. denim
14. dandelion
15. tropical rain forest

Answers: A-8, B-6, C-1, D-9, E-7, F-10, G-11, H-14, I-12, J-2, K-3, L-5, M-15, N-4, O-13

Let's Color!

Melted Crayon Paintings

Sun Catchers

FamilyFun contributor Lynne Bertrand calls this activity stained glass, but she says she's taking liberties. It's really just waxed-paper sandwiches, a classic art form for crayonists who tend to overuse their sharpener.

Materials

    Crayon shavings
    Waxed paper
    String, lace, or cutout letters
      (optional)
    Iron

To begin, have your child collect the crayon shavings from her crayon sharpener, or you can use a paring knife to create shavings for her (a cheese grater works on big crayons). Arrange and sandwich the shavings between two sheets of waxed paper. You can also make a collage of found objects inside the waxed-paper sandwich, placing string, lace, or cutout letters among the shavings. Iron the whole package on low (your job), just until the shavings melt, about 5 to 8 seconds. Cut the sun catchers into a circle, square, or any free-form shape and hang them in a sunny window.

Melted Crayon Paintings

Melted crayon is thick, aromatic stuff that cools and dries quickly on the brush. Painting with it produces great results, but the technique is a bit tricky. Large, sweeping brushstrokes don't work well; dabbing (in the tradition of Impressionism) works much better. Because the wax is hot, this project demands care and parental supervision.

Materials

    Crayons
    Electric or regular frying pan
    Aluminum foil–lined muffin tin
    Cotton swabs or old paintbrushes

To melt the crayons, fill a frying pan partway with water and set on low. Set a muffin tin in the warm water. Heat the crayons in the containers just until they melt, remove the pan from the burner or unplug it. Remind your child that the pan and the muffin tin are hot. Using cotton swabs or old paintbrushes (they might not be salvageable), your child can dab the melted crayon onto the page.

Sgraffito

A potter's term, *sgraffito* means scratching through one layer of color to get another. A crayon version of this simple etching technique is especially satisfying for young kids. Have your child start by covering a piece of paper with a rainbow of crayon colors. Then, apply black or dark finger paint over it and let your child fingerpaint his design, revealing the colors underneath.

Sun Catchers

Crayon Batik

Crayon Batik

Batik is a process commonly used in the design of cloth; here, it adds a neat texture to a crayon design on paper.

Materials

> Crayons
> Heavy piece of paper
> Paintbrush
> Watercolors, tempera paints, or ink
> Paper towel
> Iron

Have your child draw a thick crayon design on heavy paper, then crumple the paper into a ball and smooth it out again. Over the crumpled picture, she can paint a wash of watercolor, tempera paint, or ink. Dab the wash with a paper towel so it doesn't seep under the crayon. The wash will color wherever the crayon is not, including the cracks made by crumpling the page.

An adult can iron the artwork flat again by turning it over onto another sheet of paper (with a rag underneath that) and applying a warm iron for a few seconds. Be careful not to let it burn. Wipe the iron clean afterward and test it on a white rag before using it on clothes.

Birthday Boards

FamilyFun reader Ivy Delon Lee of Littleton, Colorado, came up with a great idea for her daughter Hanna's mermaid birthday party. Together, Ivy and Hanna used crayons to color a life-size (well, five-year-old-size) mermaid on a piece of Fome-Cor. Then, they cut out a circle for the face. At the party, Hanna's friends posed behind the board for a snapshot, which they later received with their thank-you notes. The project was such a hit that they repeated it for Ivy's brother's clown-themed birthday party a few months later.

Let's Color!

Chalk

Make Your Own Chalk

Rainy-day Sketches

When the rain keeps coming, resist the temptation to keep the kids indoors — an adventure (albeit wet) awaits them outside. Dress the kids in rain gear and send them out to try this art project, which is perfect for steady spring showers.

During a gentle rainfall, hand your kids some colored chalk and let them create an Impressionistic work of art. They can draw rainbows, family portraits, and nature scenes on the driveway, then watch the rain blur the edges (big, simple images produce the best results). To help the rain along, "paint" over the picture with a large, damp paintbrush.

QUICK SIDEWALK FUN

✂ **Trace around a friend's body, then add facial features, hats, wacky shoes, and outlandish costumes.**

✂ **Outline a huge sea serpent, dragon, or mythical beast and color it in.**

✂ **Copy a favorite comic strip onto sidewalk squares — or invent an original strip of your own.**

✂ **Draw a maze and see who can roll a marble through it fastest.**

Make Your Own Chalk

Sometimes, a bunch of giant chalk sticks is just what you need to turn the sidewalk into a summer canvas. With this simple recipe, making your own supply is easy. Here, we use toilet paper tubes as molds — but you can use any shape container (yogurt containers, butter molds, muffin tins) to make a collection of sidewalk art supplies.

Materials

> Toilet paper tubes
> Duct tape
> Waxed paper
> ¾ cup warm water
> About 1½ cups plaster of Paris
> 2 to 3 tablespoons powdered tempera paint

Begin by making a mold for the homemade chalk. Cover one end of the tissue tube with duct tape. Loosely roll up a piece of waxed paper and slip it into the tube. This lining will keep the plaster from sticking to the mold.

Pour the warm water into a disposable plastic container. Sprinkle in the plaster of Paris a little at a time, until the powder no longer dissolves (about twice as much plaster as water). Stir thoroughly with a spoon. Then, mix in the tempera paint. For pastel shades, combine white tempera with a primary hue. Rinse your spoon under an outdoor faucet to avoid clogging drains.

Place the mold sealed-end down on a level surface and pour in the wet plaster. Lightly tap the sides of the tube to release air bubbles in the plaster. Let the chalk harden for a couple of days. Then, remove the tape and slide the marking stick out of the mold.

Box of Chalk

Box of Chalk

This handy box is just the ticket for anyone who loves to doodle. After you finish your sketches on top of it, you can store art supplies in it.

Materials

- Covered box (stationery boxes or shoe boxes work well, but avoid using one with a glossy surface, since the paint may not stick to it)
- Can of chalkboard spray paint (available for about $6 in green and black at art supply stores)
- Chalk
- Felt

Place the box on newspaper in a well-ventilated area and spray-paint the top following the directions on the back of the can. Apply two or three light coats, allowing the paint to dry between coats (parents only). Let the box set overnight.

Before using the box, season its surface by rubbing the side of a piece of chalk (the type made from calcium carbonate, not clay) across the whole thing. Then, wipe off the chalk with a piece of felt or a dry sponge.

Beyond Hopscotch

Beyond Hopscotch

With a boxful of sidewalk chalk, you can turn a stretch of pavement into a colorful grid for this spiraling version of hopscotch called Escargot (that's French for *snail*).

Draw a large spiral (shaped like a snail's shell) on the ground. Make a circle in the center and label it Home. Divide the rest of the spiral into a dozen spaces. To start, the first player must hop on one foot, landing in each square, all the way to the Home circle where she can land on both feet before turning and hopping back out. If she completes the feat without stepping on a line, she can write her initials in the space of her choice. No other player can land there for the rest of the game.

The next person in line then tries hopping to and from the center, skipping over the initialed space. If he succeeds, he earns a square. Play continues until no one is able to reach Home. Whoever earns the most spaces wins.

Let's Color!

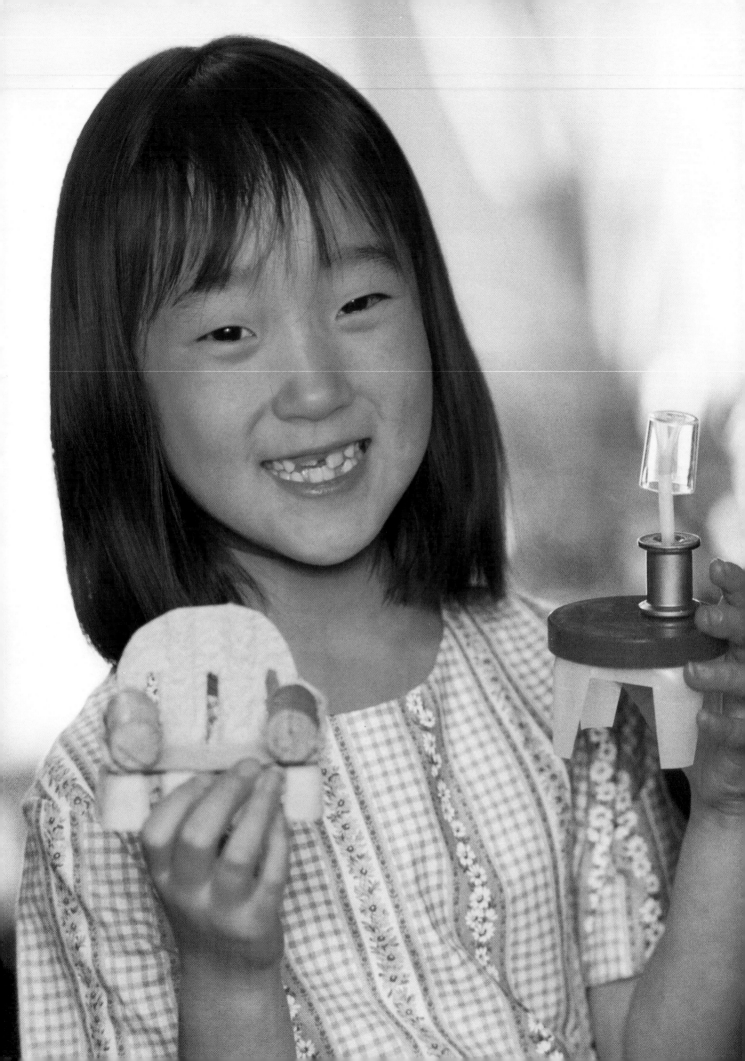

Chapter Three

Likable Recyclables

To PARENTS, an empty cardboard box has two possible fates: fill it with stuff and shove it in the attic — or recycle it. But to kids, it belongs in the same category as mud and dirt and sand: it is one of the raw materials of play. Along with jelly jars, milk jugs, egg cartons, and pretty much anything else you might toss in the recycling bin, a cardboard box is a blank slate for a kid's imagination. With a scrap of felt and a layer of cotton batting, it is ready for a sleepy baby doll. With ample application of markers and paint, it's a moon-bound rocket. Additionally, in the process of transforming trash into treasure, kids reveal a bit about themselves — who they'd like to be, what they'd like to do, things they'd like to know.

Craft projects that use household recyclables have always been favorites with *FamilyFun* readers, mainly because the materials can be found right under the kitchen sink — and they're free. Which means, of course, that it doesn't cost you a cent to go wild. You and your kids can follow our directions to the letter, alter them to suit your whimsy, or use them as a springboard to a brand-new vision of fun. Whatever you do, you really can't go wrong. After all, your mistakes are completely recyclable.

Start a junk box. You don't need to comb through your kitchen garbage to extract every ounce of recyclable waste, but you do need to keep an eye out for interesting trash — and salvage it for a "junk box." Into the box (perhaps a large cardboard one or a sealable plastic bin) goes anything with art potential — see the list on page 38 for good green candidates.

Egg Carton Critters, page 45

Give your recyclables a good scrub. Before launching into any of the crafts in this chapter, make sure the containers

Just about anything belongs in a junk box, but here are a few of our favorite toss-ins.

• Cardboard and plastic containers, all sizes

• Plastic soda bottles and milk jugs

• Cardboard scraps

• Popsicle sticks

• Glass jars (save those of interesting shapes and colors as well as baby food jars)

• Thread spools

• Matchboxes

• Catalogs, magazines, newspaper, brown paper, wrapping paper, and envelopes

• Aluminum tins and foil

• Styrofoam

• Bottle caps

• Broken toy pieces

• Packing materials

• Wallpaper and fabric scraps

• Stickers and stamps

• Yarn, ribbon, string, bows, buttons, and beads

are clean (a few drops of leftover milk can spoil an afternoon project). If you're using glass jars or milk jugs, fill your kitchen sink with soapy water and let your kids "do the dishes." They'll love playing in the water and peeling off the labels. One *FamilyFun* reader uses this trick to get her kids involved in the recycling process — the clean jars go straight into her recycling bin.

Let the kids invent their own toys from the trash. Offer your kids a refrigerator box, empty milk carton, or egg carton and see what happens. They can enhance it with any household junk they please, as long as they give you a report of their creation when it's complete. You may discover some serious pretending going on.

Be a green consumer. Think twice before you buy products made from materials you can't recycle (and yes, we count using them for an art project as one way to recycle). Once you get the hang of it, you may find yourself buying a special brand of crackers so your kids can use the box for the dollhouse on page 46 or purchasing a special color of egg carton for the silly disguises on page 44.

Recycle the end results. After your kids have enjoyed their toys from the trash, don't throw them away. Separate out the recyclables — plastic milk jugs, tin cans, and so on — and toss them in the recycling bin. Not everything will be recyclable in your community, so find out what qualifies at your local recycling center.

Cans & Bottles

Coffee Can Stilts

Kids are forever wishing they could be bigger and taller. One way they can reach new heights is with these home-made stilts. Coffee cans and 28-ounce fruit cans work best for this activity.

Materials

2 large, matching tin cans
  (opened at one end only)
Hammer
Ruler
Nail
Phillips head
  screwdriver
About 10 feet of
  ⅜-inch cotton rope

First, lay each can on its side on a hard work surface. Use a hammer to flatten any jagged edges along the inner rim (parents only). If you're using coffee cans, replace the plastic covers.

On the side of one of the cans, make a mark an inch from one end (either the open or closed end; either can be the bottom of the stilt). Make a similar mark on the opposite side of the can. Do the same with the second can. Use the hammer and the nail to punch holes through the cans where marked. With the screwdriver, widen the holes to about ½ inch. Try to tap down any rough edges with the hammer.

Cut two pieces of rope that measure three times the length from your child's knee to the floor. Attach a rope to each can by threading the ends through the holes from the outside. Tie overhand knots in the rope ends. Then, pull the rope so the knots rest against the insides of the can.

When using her stilts, your child should wear rubber-soled shoes to avoid slipping off. At first, she may need help stepping up onto the cans and balancing. Once she's comfortable, she can grip the ropes as she would two bucket handles, straighten her legs, and start walking tall.

FunFact

In Padova, Italy, a scale model of the Basilica di Sant'Antonio di Padova was built from 3,245,000 empty cans. It took 20,000 hours to construct.

Coffee Can Stilts

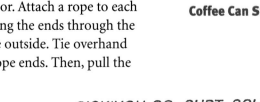

Tin Can Lanterns

Tin Can Lantern

In Colonial times these lanterns were a popular way for children to carry around candles safely. This project takes some planning, but the result is well worth it — whether you parade your lamps outside or use them to give a spooky feel to a nighttime picnic.

Materials

    Large tin can, label removed
    Markers
    Towel
    Hammer
    Nails of different sizes
    Small screw-in hook
    20-inch wooden dowel
    Coat hanger or thin wire for
        hanging loop
    Votive candle
    Dried spaghetti noodle for lighting
        the candle

On the outside of the can, have your child draw a pattern for the lantern holes. Fill the can with water and freeze it for two days. (The ice keeps the sides from collapsing when you hammer them.) When the water in the can is frozen solid, place the can on its side on top of a towel and use the nail tips to hammer in holes according to the design. Make two holes near the top, on opposite sides, for stringing a handle.

Remove any chunks of ice from inside the can (a parent's job, since the hammered-in holes have sharp edges). Help your child screw the hook into one end of the wood dowel, then string the length of wire through the hook. Wind the ends of the wire through the hanging holes on the can until they are secure. Use a bit of melted wax to affix the votive candle to the bottom of the can. The dried spaghetti noodle is a handy way to light the lantern; it burns steadily and lessens the likelihood of scorching your fingers.

Holiday Lights

After reading about tin can lanterns in *Family Fun*, Patty Meldrum of Grafton, Ohio, decided to try them out with her son's Cub Scout den. She reports that "it made for an interesting meeting, with eight second-grade boys pounding frozen tin cans in my basement." The lanterns were such a hit that the Scout troop took them Christmas caroling at the town parade. (Santa and Scrooge, who arrived on a fire truck, were duly impressed.)

40

Croquet Mallets

Rather than purchasing an expensive croquet set, help your kids make mallets for the classic backyard game.

Materials

- 2 1-liter plastic bottles
- Craft knife
- ¾-inch wooden dowel for a handle
- Hot glue gun
- Colored tape

Cut off each bottle bottom starting 5½ inches from its base with the craft knife (parents only). Make a few 3-inch vertical cuts in the sides of one bottom and fit its open end into the second bottle end. Next, cut a ¾-inch hole in two sides of the joined bottles. Fit the dowel through the holes so the end is flush with the side of the bottle. Glue your dowel in place with a glue gun (parents only) and wrap the handle with colored tape.

Piggy Bank

Pigs are good for all sorts of storage. Here are two you can create, inspired by "McCall's Creates" booklet 14215, using empty plastic bottles: a piggy bank for a kid's savings and a swinish pencil holder.

Materials

- 4 thread spools
- Pink paint
- Plastic soda bottle and cap
- Hot glue gun (Krazy Glue will work, too)
- Pink felt
- 2 matching buttons
- Craft knife
- Pink pipe cleaner

To assemble the pig, begin by having your child paint the thread spools pink. Once they're dry, he can glue them to the bottle, positioning them as shown below for legs. Make the ears next, cutting a pair of 3-inch-wide triangles out of the felt. Fold the base of each triangle in half and glue the lower edges together. Use paper clips to secure them while drying. Trim the felt into ear shapes and glue them to the bottle. Glue on the button eyes. Use the craft knife (parents only) to poke a small hole in the bottle for the pipe cleaner tail. Cut a slot in the top through which your child can feed coins to the pig.

Piggy Pencil Holder: Follow the instructions for the Piggy Bank, but instead of a slot for coins, use the craft knife (or a wood-burning tool, if you have one) to make holes in its back for pencils.

FunFact

Believe it or not, the pig has been a popular bank shape for almost three hundred years. It dates back to the Middle Ages, when a dense, orange clay known as pygg was used throughout western Europe in the making of pots and jars, which frugal people used to save their money.

Piggy Bank

Piggy Pencil Holder

Likable Recyclables

Milk Jugs

Dollhouse Dinners

When *FamilyFun* reader Robin Taplitsky made a milk jug house with her daughter, three-year-old Bayley came up with her own idea for decorating. She cut out magazine pictures of food and glued them to the miniature tables — creating a ready-made dinner for her dolls.

Milk Jug Garage

Milk isn't the only thing that packages well by the gallon. With a little help, your child can turn an empty plastic jug into a portable hot-rod garage or dollhouse, one of the many recycling crafts featured in *EcoArt!* (Williamson Publishing).

Materials

    Plastic gallon milk jug
    Craft knife
    Construction paper
    Black marker
    Toothpick
    Cardboard
    Thread spool

First, cut a 3½-inch-square garage door opening in one of the container's flat sides with a craft knife (parents only). Glue construction paper roof shingles around the top of the jug. Next, add a business sign, made of construction paper and hung on a toothpick. Poke the toothpick into the jug just above the garage door.

To make a floor, set the jug on a piece of cardboard and trace around the base. Trim the edges so it will slide easily through the doorway. Decorate by gluing on construction paper tiles.

Glue on a construction paper fuel pump and air hose by poking a hole in the side of the jug and tying on a piece of string. A thread-spool car lift finishes off the interior.

Milk Jug Dollhouse: For this variation on the Milk Jug Garage, cut a

Milk Jug Garage

Milk Jug Dollhouse

3½-inch-square door opening in one of the container's flat sides with a craft knife (a parent's job). Cut out windows, if desired. Glue construction paper roof shingles around the top of the jug. For a chimney, use a black marker to draw a few rows of bricks on a strip of red construction paper. Wrap the paper around the jug spout and glue it in place. Stuff a puff of cotton "smoke" into the spout. Then, add paper window boxes on the dollhouse.

To make a floor that fits inside the jug, set the jug on a piece of cardboard and trace around the base. Trim the edges of the floor so it will slide easily through the doorway. Decorate the floor by gluing on paper rugs.

Dollhouse Furniture:

• Mold a sofa out of modeling clay and add pom-pom throw pillows.

• Use an alphabet block for an end table.

• To make a table lamp, start with a round wooden bead. Bend up the lower end of a pipe cleaner and push it into the bead. Shape the upper end into a frame for a shade. Wrap a strip of paper around the frame and glue.

• For a houseplant, fill a thimble with short snips of a green pipe cleaner.

Likable Recyclables

Whale of a Water Scoop

As dismal as water seems to kids when it's streaking down the windows, it's a blast to pour, splash, and play with indoors. Some days, when *FamilyFun* contributor Jodi Picoult's kitchen sink gets a little cramped, she moves to larger seas — the bathtub. Her two boys, Kyle and Jake, like to sneak up on their rubber duckies with this great whale scoop (it also makes washing one's hair much more fun). For added adventure, they dot the seas with a few shaving cream icebergs.

Materials

   Plastic gallon milk jug
   Permanent marker

Turn the gallon jug onto its side so that the handle is at the top. With the marker, draw a mouth shape on the base of the jug and extending partway up the sides, as shown. Cut along the lines with scissors, creating a widemouthed scoop (a parent's job). Using the marker, outline the edge of the mouth and add eyes and a blowhole.

Blast Off

During the week, *Family Fun* reader Annette Hayes of Dalton, Georgia, watches two little boys in addition to her son. One afternoon, they all invented this costume idea: they cut up plastic gallon milk jugs and decorated them with crayons to make NASA space helmets. The children turned over a table, draped it with a blanket, and they were off to the moon for the afternoon.

Whale of a Water Scoop

Egg Cartons

Nosy Disguises

Nosy Disguises

Does your child need a quick disguise for the school play? Start scrambling eggs — and use the empty carton to create stylish animal snouts and ears.

Materials

> Cardboard egg carton
> Hole punch
> Stapler
> Sewing elastic
> Light-gauge craft wire
> Headband
> Acrylic paints and paintbrushes
> Colored markers

For a basic pattern, cut out an individual egg cup, make breathing holes in the bottom, and staple the ends of sewing elastic (cut to fit around your child's head) to the sides. Cut ears out of the carton top (the corners or the flat part, depending on the shape you want), punch holes in the bases, and use wire to attach them to a headband.

White Rabbit: Paint the nose white and glue on a pink pom-pom. Draw on a mouth with a marker. Poke holes in both sides of the nose, then feed white pipe cleaner whiskers through the holes (push the centers of the pipe cleaners into the bottom of the egg cup to make room for your child's nose). Paint the backs of the ears white and the insides pink.

Tiger Cat: Paint the nose orange (or black for Halloween) and add whiskers. In place of the pom-pom, glue on a small paper triangle. Make the ears short and pointed.

Little Piggy: Onto a pink snout, draw large nostrils. Cut broad pig ears from the flat portion of the egg carton lid. Fold the base of one ear so that it flops forward.

Hound Dog: Paint a nose brown, black, or white with black spots. Glue a paper triangle to the front and use a marker to draw on a mouth. Add ears.

TRASHY COSTUMES

Let your kids get a last laugh out of old, worn-out clothes by recycling them into outlandish costumes. They might dress up an old pair of sneakers with pom-poms and paint, add plastic dinosaurs and sequins to a floppy summer hat, or make giant buttons for one of Dad's old shirts by decorating colorful milk jug caps. When they've got a boxful of duds all fixed up, let them invite friends over for a "trashy fashion" show.

Egg Carton Critters

When *FamilyFun* editors brought the materials for these egg carton critters into a local fifth grade classroom, the kids made a slew of the six-legged bugs with many clever adaptations. We swear your kids won't stop after making one.

Materials

- Cardboard egg carton
- Tempera paints and paintbrushes
- Glue
- 12 pairs googly eyes
- Hole punch
- 12 pipe cleaners, assorted colors and thicknesses

Cut the twelve cups out of the egg carton bottom and trim them. Paint the outside green or another bug color and let them dry. Glue on the eyes and punch a hole for the mouth, positioning the hole at the edge. Add three leg holes on each side with the hole punch. Cut all the pipe cleaners into 4-inch sections for the legs and antennae. Poke two holes above the eyes for the antennae (you will need to use a push-pin or pencil or snip with scissors). For the legs, insert one pipe cleaner piece through one side hole and out the other side. Bend it up inside the shell and into shape for the legs and feet. To make the antennae, push the pipe cleaner through one hole and out the other, bending it into shape. Now let the critters crawl.

A Bug House

To house a colony of egg carton critters, open an egg carton and press the five center dividers down flat to make room for the bugs. Make grass out of paper and glue it onto the carton, bending the blades upright. The house is now ready for your litter of critters.

Buggy Buggy

Christine Silveira of Plainfield, Connecticut, found that a box full of sprightly egg carton creatures really sparked the imaginations of her two kids, two-year-old Nicole and three-year-old Jimmy. After having a ball making the critters, the kids have played "buggy buggy" (as Jimmy dubbed the game) time and time again. The game has no particular rules — rather, each time the kids play, the little critters have different names and different things to do.

Egg Carton Critters

Likable Recyclables

Simple Dollhouse Furnishings

Sofa: Cut one end from a Styrofoam meat tray. On the bottom, glue two cups from a cardboard egg carton (see model at right). Turn upright and drape on a cloth cover.

Easy chair: Attach paper clip legs to an egg carton cup.

Curtains: Fold down the top ½ inch of a fabric square and glue the edge of the flap down. Insert a straw or toothpick and hang with paperclips.

Lamp: Use a spool or bottle cap base to support a toothpick or straw; use a bottle cap for a shade.

Pictures: Glue postage stamps to the walls.

Kitchen counter: Cover one end of a cracker box with a square of aluminum foil and draw on burners. Cut an oven door.

Sink: Glue the bottom of a plastic cup to a fitted opening in the countertop. For faucets, glue on the tops of flexible drinking straws.

Kitchen table: Invert a plastic cup and draw four legs on the sides. Cut away the sections between the legs.

Kitchen chairs: Glue short sections from a drinking straw to the bottom of a milk jug cap. Use a section of a cardboard tube for a chair back.

Plates: Set out a few colored buttons.

Frying pan: Attach a paper clip handle to a bottle cap.

Living Room

Dollhouse-in-a-Box

Part of the fun of having a dollhouse is arranging the furniture just the way you like it — and then rearranging it the next day. Here's a recyclable version that makes use of everything but the kitchen sink.

Materials

Lightbulb cartons
Egg cartons, assorted recyclables, and household odds and ends
Glue

To make the basic room, cut open the outer sleeve of a lightbulb carton at one corner. Fold the sleeve in half lengthwise, cut out windows, and then set the sleeve on edge to form an L-shaped room divider.

Give a kitchen a tile floor by gluing paper squares onto a cardboard base. For instant living room or bedroom carpeting, lay down a colored paper napkin or a piece of felt. Furnish the house with the ideas at left.

Kitchen

46

Cardboard Tubes & Paper Bags

Cardboard Castle

With tall spires, stone walls, and a wooden drawbridge, this castle has the makings for an afternoon of adventure. The project is adapted from *Crafts from Recyclables* (Bell Books).

Materials

- Assorted cardboard tubes
- Gold and other poster paints
- Small sponge square
- Craft knife
- Black marker
- Construction paper
- Popsicle sticks
- Metallic cording or paper clips

Color the toilet tissue and paper towel rolls with a coat of gold poster paint. Once they are dry, you can create the appearance of cut stone by applying a contrasting color with a small sponge square. Using a craft knife (parents only), cut windows in the tube towers or just draw them on with a black marker. Cut notches around the tops of several turrets.

When assembling the castle, start from the center. Glue together two or three taller tubes for the main towers. Then, stack smaller rolls around them, interlocking the towers with tabs cut in the tube bottoms (as shown). Create the castle's front wall using a 4-inch square of construction paper. Draw on an ornate door frame and sandwich the wall between the front two towers.

For roofing, cut a circle out of construction paper. Make a single snip into the center and form a cone by overlapping and gluing together the cut edges. Glue the roofs in place on top of the towers. For a drawbridge, glue Popsicle stick planks side by side onto a piece of cardboard. Attach the drawbridge to the castle wall with metallic cording or paper clip chains.

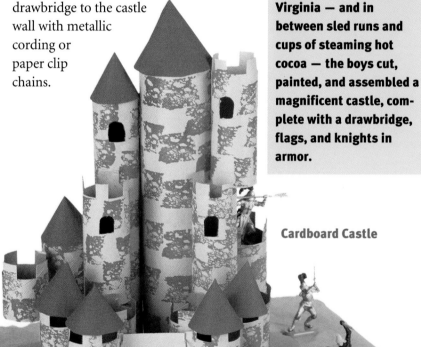

Cardboard Castle

Likable Recyclables

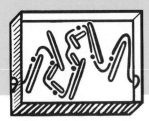

Into the Labyrinth

This handheld version of the popular wooden game tests a player's skill at working a marble through a craft stick maze. Build the maze by gluing sticks on edge to a shoe box lid, as shown. Cut pitfall holes and Start and Finish doors.

Marble Maze

All it takes is a little ingenuity and some Rube Goldberg styling to create this runway made just for marbles. Half miniature golf game, half physics experiment, this project is delightfully flexible. Your kids can construct a simple runway one day, then add other twists and turns as they collect more cardboard tubes.

Materials

Assorted cardboard tubes

Tape (masking tape is fine, but colored electrical tape will give the chute a cheerful look)

Marbles — the bigger the better

Scissors

Stacks of books, cereal boxes, toys, blocks, wastebaskets, and other objects for supports

Offer your kids a bunch of paper tubes — as varied a selection as you can find. Long wrapping-paper tubes are the most efficient for covering distance, paper towel tubes are good for the shorter runs, and toilet tissue tubes make great corner pieces. Then let the kids tape the tubes together to form a runway. You may need to cut some tubes into shorter lengths for corner sections before taping them together.

Help the kids set up a platform for the start of their run. A stool or the back of a chair or sofa works well. Then, arrange several stacks of books, toys, and other objects for supports, so the marble run will slope down toward the floor.

Marble Rolling Tips:

• If you slip one tube inside another, be sure the larger tube is on the downward side of the run.

• Make sure the end of the run is at floor level. Flying marbles can be dangerous.

• A combination of closed tunnels and open sections (where kids can see the marbles moving) makes everything a lot more interesting. To make an open section, simply cut a tube in half, lengthwise, or cut a narrow window in its top.

• Larger marbles tend to roll better than smaller ones. Small rubber balls can travel well, too.

Marble Maze

Paper Bag, U.S.A.

Once you introduce your children to paper bag architecture, you'll find yourself setting aside a store of lunch bags earmarked for enthusiastic city planners. This is a wonderful activity for a group of kids — each child can make a building, then add it to the growing bag town.

Materials
- Paper lunch bags
- Crayons or markers
- Colored paper
- Newspaper
- Cotton balls

For each building, your child will need two lunch bags. Have her draw or color a building on one of the bags that is positioned either horizontally or vertically. She may want to color bricks or clapboards, then sketch in doors and windows, complete with shutters. A window box filled with flowers or a vine growing up one side of the building is a nice finishing touch.

Next, stuff the second bag with crumpled newspaper and slip the decorated bag on top.

Help your builder cut out signs and awnings from colored paper, then glue them onto the buildings. Fashion roofs out of paper rectangles and top them with paper chimneys; use cotton balls for smoke. Doors can be made by folding construction paper into a small card, decorating the front, and gluing the back to the bag. Help your child set up the city on the floor or on a table, add a few little cars and dolls — and you've got your own boomtown.

FunFact
Before Charles Stilwell invented the grocery bag as we know it today, these paper bags were hand-glued and V-shaped.

Paper Bag Hometown

Lisa Burmester and her kids, Joshua and Amy, were so inspired by *FamilyFun*'s "Paper Bag, U.S.A." project that they decided to build a paper bag replica of their hometown of Roscommon, Michigan. In three evenings of steady work, the young architects constructed Roscommon's school, gas station, doughnut shop, and firehouse — not to mention their Gramma's house and the Burmesters' own home.

Paper Bag, U.S.A.

Likable Recyclables

49

Fabric

Pocket Purses

With a few easy snips and stitches, your children can turn an old pair of hip-huggers into over-the-shoulder purses.

Materials

> Old pair of blue jeans
> Fabric scissors
> Needle and thread
> Ribbon, an old belt, or braided rope about 1 yard long
> Decorations (iron-on transfers, fabric paint, patches, embroidery thread)
> Velcro, buttons, or snaps

Begin by cutting out a back pocket of an old (but not threadbare) pair of jeans, being careful to cut outside the seams so the pocket stays intact.

If your child is old enough to use a needle and thread, have her sew a long piece of ribbon, an old belt, or braided rope to the sides of the pocket to make a shoulder strap. This should be about a yard in length, but you'll want to adjust it to suit her height. You can also make a handbag by using a smaller, thicker piece of ribbon for a handle.

Next, let the outside of the purse become a canvas for ornaments. Decorate with iron-on transfers, fabric paint, beads, patches, appliqués, or whatever you can dig up in your junk drawers. More ambitious kids might even like to embroider their initials or other designs on the denim for an authentic seventies look.

To hold the purse shut, sew strips of Velcro, buttons, or snaps to the inside of the pocket. Finished purses will add a retro edge to any wardrobe, and your child can bump, hustle, and keep on truckin' through summer.

Pocket Purses

Book Jackets

It's never easy for a kid to relinquish a favorite old shirt to the rag bag. One way you can soften the blow is to help her turn the treasured gear into the latest in back-to-school fashion — denim, flannel, and buffalo plaid book jackets.

Materials

    Measuring tape
    Old shirt, jacket, or piece of fabric
    Fabric scissors
    Double-sided, iron-on seam binding
    Thread and needle
    Buttons and patches

First, you'll need to calculate the book jacket dimensions. Determine the width by measuring from the right edge of the book's closed cover, around its spine and across the back, and then adding 2 to 3 inches for each jacket flap.

The height of the book jacket will depend on the type of material you're using. Fabric that won't fray (like flannel or T-shirt cotton) can be trimmed to the same height as the book. Denim and other materials prone to fraying should be cut with an

Likable Recyclables

inch allowance, top and bottom. This lets you hem the edges by folding them over a strip of seam binding and pressing them with a hot iron.

Have your child spread the cloth jacket right-side down on a flat surface and center the book on top of it. Fold the right flap around the book's back cover. Stitch the corners of the flap to the upper and lower edges of the jacket (as shown below). Fold the left flap around the front cover, pulling the jacket taut for a snug fit before stitching the corners.

Your child can accessorize the jacket by adding colorful buttons, embroidered patches, or a pocket she can fill with pens, erasers, and other school supplies.

A Keeping Quilt

In Patricia Polacco's story-book *The Keeping Quilt*, a family of immigrants sews a special quilt from the clothing of their relatives in Russia and uses it to teach new generations of children the story of their ancestry. When they read the story, *FamilyFun* contributor Janet Goldstein and her three children were inspired to create their own "keeping quilt." Along with the kids' first baseball jerseys and favorite, worn-out dresses, they patched together shirts and fabric scraps donated by aunts, uncles, cousins, and grandparents. Piecing and sewing the quilt provided hours of fun family time — and now that it's done, it's a storehouse of Goldstein family lore.

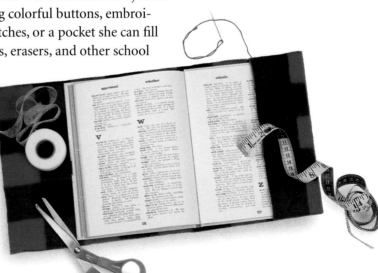

Cardboard Boxes

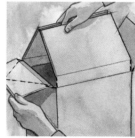

Little Red Barn

Since age five, *FamilyFun* reader Jade Littlefield has been collecting Breyer Horses, plastic figurines that come in nearly every breed and color. Her horses had been living in a wicker basket — until Jade made them a new stable. After all, every precious possession needs a home, even if it is just a cardboard box.

Materials

    Utility knife
    15- by 18- by 21-inch corrugated
      cardboard box
    Ruler and pencil
    Packing tape

    Extra cardboard
    Small paint roller
    Acrylic paints and paintbrushes
    8- by 8- by 13-inch box
    Paper fasteners

Cut a 4-inch slit down each corner of the larger box. Fold the two 18-inch sides in toward each other so that they form a peak (to make them fold easily, score the folds). Holding the peak in place (figure 1), raise the other two flaps to meet the peak. Trace the peak shape on each side flap, then cut away the excess. To make the ridgepole, cut out a 1½- by 21-inch strip of cardboard.

Cut a small notch in the top center of each side flap. Set one end of the ridge-

Little Red Barn

pole in each notch, then fold up the roof so it meets the ridgepole. Tape all the roof edges in place.

To make the left Dutch door (figure 2), mark off a 6- by 10-inch rectangle (position it about ½ inch from the bottom and top of the front panel and 1 inch from its left edge). Cut along the top, right edge, and bottom of the rectangle and also cut the door in half. Repeat, reversing the directions, for the right door, and make two more doors on the opposite side. Score down the hinged edges so that the doors open easily. Cut a 2- by 3-inch, four-pane window about ½ inch down from the roof peak on each side of the barn.

For the stalls, cut a 4½- by 18-inch and a 4½- by 14-inch piece of cardboard. Make a 2-inch notch in the center of each strip, then interlock them to form a cross. Slip the cross shape inside the barn.

Use the roller to paint the barn red and the roof gray; when dry, use the brush to paint on the white trim.

To make the tack room, fold in the peak of the small box. Measure and cut the side flaps as for the barn. Tape in place — minus a ridgepole this time. Cut a front door and windows. To attach the tack room to the barn, poke four matching holes through one side wall of the tack room and one side wall of the barn. Slip a paper fastener through each hole and bend into place.

Easy Storage Boxes

Looking for an inexpensive way to round up your kids' books and CDs? Here's one, courtesy of your empty laundry detergent box, that needs only a few touches to beautifully organize a bookshelf or desk.

Materials

> Empty laundry detergent box
> Colored paper
> Glue
> Felt

Cut off the top half of the box and recycle it. Then, cut the bottom portion of the box in half vertically to create two open-face cases with rounded edges. Use a pencil to trace around the sides and back of each case onto a piece of colored paper. Cut out the paper tracings and glue them onto the outside of the cases. Then, cut out felt pieces to cover the undersides of the cases and glue them on. Now, your kids can decorate the cases to suit their tastes with stickers, colored tape, glitter glue, or original drawings.

Easy Storage Boxes

A Recycled Castle

Everyone knows that cardboard box playhouses are a blast to make, but few discover that playhouse-building can be downright educational. Ask the eleven-year-old twins of *FamilyFun* readers Maureen O'Meara and Bill Hursh. The twins got a good dose of history when their baby-sitter Andy Turner helped them build a cardboard castle with appliance boxes from their local recycling center in Bethlehem, Pennsylvania. While they were building, Andy talked about the history of castles — so that when the kids showed Mom and Dad their palace, they made up an amazing story of famous figures, including King Arthur and Galileo, who had once lived in it.

Likable Recyclables

Airplane-in-a-Box

Recycle your cardboard boxes into this winning costume, which was inspired by the book *Build It With Boxes* by Joan Irvine (Morrow Junior Books). Once you've made the costume, hand the pilot a pair of swimming goggles and a winter hat with earflaps, and he'll be ready for takeoff in your backyard or at a local park.

Materials

    Large cardboard box
    Scissors or utility knife
    Metallic spray paint
    Cardboard scraps
    Aluminum foil
    Long paper fastener
    Plastic wrap
    Masking tape

Start with a large box that is big enough to cover half your child's body. Cut off the bottom flaps of the box with scissors or a utility knife (a job for parents). Cut out rectangular wing flaps on the sides, making sure that they are a little longer than your child's arms and directly across from each other. When cutting, leave the tops of the wings attached to the box at the shoulder line.

For the head hole, cut out a rectangle on the top of the box that's big enough

for your child's head but not too close to the edges of the box. You should make the opening for the head on the smaller side to prevent the costume from slipping off your child's shoulders.

Paint the entire box with the spray paint (regular tempera works fine, too). For the propeller, cut two strips out of cardboard and cover them with aluminum foil.

Fasten the strips to the front of the plane with a long paper fastener and give the propeller a trial spin.

For the windshield, cut a frame out of cardboard. Tape a piece of plastic wrap inside the frame to make it look like glass and attach it to the box with masking tape. Finish the plane by adding a cardboard tail fin to the back.

Airplane-in-a-Box

Chicken-in-a-Box:

Use the same construction as for the airplane

Chicken-in-a-Box

but leave off the paint, propeller, and windshield. Help your child cut feathers out of yellow construction paper. Using masking tape, attach one row of feathers to the bottom of the box, then overlap it with a second row; continue until the box is completely covered. Fashion a tail out of a piece of cardboard and layer it with feathers as well. Make a mask by taping a construction paper beak and feather to a store-bought mask.

Box Office

Kids on the go will appreciate the portability of this lightweight cardboard desk, not to mention all the nooks and crannies for storing stuff.

Materials

Large cardboard box
Utility knife
Pencil
Cereal, cookie, and pasta boxes
Colored tape
Glue
Clear Con-Tact paper

With scissors, cut the flaps off the large cardboard box. Turn the box bottom up. Then, make an opening for your child's legs by drawing an arch on one of the longer sides and cutting it out using a utility knife (parents only). Using the cutout as a pattern, cut an identical shape from the opposite side of the box. Discard both pieces.

Next, cut the tops from all of the food boxes. Attach the deeper boxes to the sides of the desk with short pieces of tape. Then, wrap longer pieces of tape all the way around the desk and side pockets to firmly secure them.

For pencil holders and other desktop compartments, arrange smaller cartons and canisters along the back edge of the box and secure them by gluing the bottoms to the top of the desk. Lastly, make the working surface spillproof by covering it with clear Con-Tact paper.

Homework Helpers

It's not easy to make a stack of homework look inviting, but you can start by encouraging your child to jazz up his collection of school-work equipment. Here are a few craft ideas to try.

Pencil Toppers, page 25

Book Jackets, page 51

Easy Storage Boxes, page 53

Piggy Pencil Holder, page 41

Homemade books, page 75

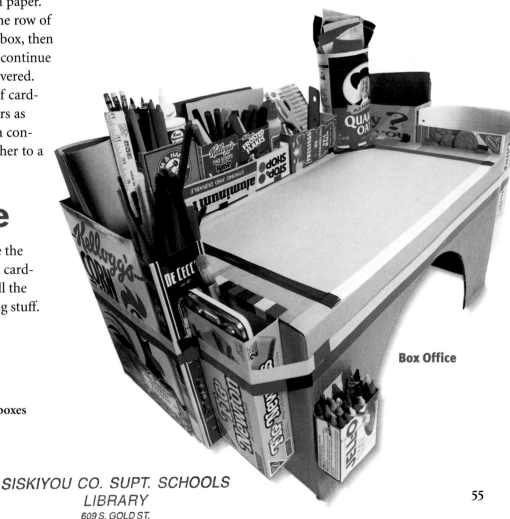

Box Office

Likable Recyclables

A Winter Wonderland

When your family comes down with cabin fever, build a replica of your cabin and add it to this Lilliputian landscape to make a twinkling decoration for the winter holidays.

Materials

- Pint-size cardboard milk cartons and assorted cracker boxes
- Craft knife
- Construction paper
- Glue
- Colored markers
- Large sheet of poster board
- Masking tape
- Mini Christmas lights (optional)
- Nonflammable batting (available at craft stores)

Using the craft knife (adults only), remove the bottoms from the cartons and boxes. Then, make siding for each building by tracing around the sides onto a sheet of construction paper. With scissors, cut out the individual pieces and glue them onto the carton. For the roof, cut a paper rectangle from a contrasting color. Fold the roof over the top of the carton, as shown, and glue it in place.

Next, draw on windows, doors, and corner boards with the colored markers. Then, cut out the window openings with the craft knife. Finally, decorate the doors by gluing on tiny wreaths cut out of colored paper.

Arrange the finished buildings side by side on top of the poster board and lay the unplugged string of lights behind them. Fit a few bulbs into each building through the bottom and tape

A Winter Wonderland

the wires to the inside so that the bulbs are in the center of the carton. Then, if necessary, use tape to secure the bottom edges of the buildings to the poster board.

For snow, spread the batting around the buildings, being sure to cover the electrical wire running between them. Then, your kids can add small figures, paper trees, and toy cars. You can even use a small mirror for a skating rink.

Back to Schoolhouse

When older brothers and sisters head off to school, younger siblings need not feel left behind. They can attend a special class of their own — in a miniature schoolhouse made out of boxes, an egg carton, and thread spools.

Materials

    Empty cereal box, tea box,
        and cardboard egg carton
    Craft knife
    Glue
    Paper
    Drinking straw
    Pipe cleaners
    7 thread spools
    Felt
    Permanent markers

To make the schoolroom, use a craft knife (adults only) to cut a large flap in the front of the cereal box. Pull the flap down to serve as the classroom floor. Next, cut a small tea box in half diagonally and glue one of the halves onto the top of the classroom for a peaked roof.

Top off the roof by drawing a miniature flag on a piece of paper. Cut out the flag and glue it to the side of a drinking straw.

Likable Recyclables

Cut a small *X* in the side of the roof and push the bottom of the flagpole through it.

To make desks, remove the front row of cups from the egg carton and recycle them. Then, cut out the remaining six cups individually, leaving a portion of the egg carton cover attached to each one for a desktop (see photo). Glue the desks to the schoolhouse floor.

Now it's time to round up some pupils and a teacher. To make each figure, push the ends of a pipe cleaner through the holes in the top and bottom of a thread spool and then bend the tips (this forms the torso, legs, and feet). For arms, sandwich the thread spool between two short pipe cleaners. Then twist together the ends of the pipe cleaners. Glue on felt clothes and hair. Finally, use permanent markers to draw on faces.

Back to Schoolhouse

Chapter Four

Paper Play

WHEN WE asked craft expert Susan Milord to contribute a paper project to *FamilyFun*, she offered up the beautiful paper boxes on page 74 — and along with them, a surprising story. Apparently, as soon as she had taught her son, Angus, how to fold the paper squares, he began to fill the house with them. He made little boxes to hold tiny treasures and larger ones to store everything from school supplies to letters from his grandparents. Once Angus got on a roll, he couldn't stop. Of course, Susan had seen this before. It's what happens, she reminded us, when a child meets just the right kind of craft project. No matter how simple it is, he'll take it to the hilt and turn it into something extravagant.

Paper is one of the most basic craft mate-rials there is. Around the house, it has a host of mundane uses (like grocery lists, cat toys, and homework). But as a craft mate-rial, it's irresistible. Kids can fold, tear, or cut it into shapes. In a pinch, it can become a toy, such as a paper airplane, a wildlife menagerie, or a dress-up costume. It comes in vibrant colors and all different weights and sizes. Best of all, you can even make it yourself.

In this chapter, we'll show you and your kids a few of the grander uses for a piece of paper. It won't take your child long to get the hang of the origami pinwheels on page 72 or the homemade envelopes on page 70. Perhaps she'll want to try her hand at Angus's famous boxes. But you'd better be prepared — if your child discovers a favorite project, as Angus did, you should have a good stock of sup-plies on hand.

Keep a paper bin. Scraps of white paper — as well as magazines, envelopes, bags, newspapers, gum wrappers, and junk mail

Rain Forest Vines, page 64

Paper Players

Aside from the papers you ordinarily have around the house (such as newspaper, tissue paper, and copy paper), here are others you may want to have on hand.

Construction paper comes in many colors; a generous supply will satisfy any kid's passion for cutting and pasting. Its downside: it fades quickly.

Butcher paper (also called craft paper) is lightweight brown paper available in rolls at art and craft stores. It's suited to large-scale projects, such as body tracings, and murals.

Card stock is about twice as thick as regular paper. It comes in many colors and is available at art stores or copy shops. It's great for — yep — cards.

Drawing paper is sturdy white paper available in large sketch pads. It's more expensive than computer paper, so save it for special projects.

Newsprint is lightweight, inexpensive paper available at art supply stores in large pads perfect for scribbling.

Poster board is heavy, colored paper. It comes in 22- by 28-inch sheets and can be found at craft and stationery stores.

Instant Dresses, page 78

— all can find new life in crafts. Tuck a scrap box by your recycling bin, so you're always reminded to save anything that might work for a project.

Use a portfolio for storage. To keep large or especially nice pieces of paper flat, you can store them in a paper artist's portfolio. These are available at art supply stores for about $7 to $13, and they fit well under a bed.

Buy in bulk. Butcher paper and newsprint, in particular, are worth buying in bulk. Also, stock up on colored tissue paper, wrapping paper, ribbons, and greeting cards when they go on sale after the holiday season. Wallpaper scraps for decorative proj- ects can be salvaged from unwanted sample books at home improvement stores.

Cut carefully. Scissors are the tool of choice for most paper projects. However, if there's a need for a paper cutter or craft knife, that's a job for parents only. Kids should be cautioned not to use those tools unsupervised.

Glue it all together. Paper has a way of buckling and bending when it interacts with glue, especially regular white glue. While white glue, a glue stick, or rubber cement suffices for most projects, Sobo glue (from an art store) works better for delicate projects that use thin paper, such as books or collages.

Try making paper. Making paper at home is a science lesson and art project in one. Learn on page 68 how to turn old sheets of paper into pulp and create new paper.

Take a trip to the art supply store. For a special treat, let your children purchase a few sheets of specialty paper at an art store. Colored paper comes in vibrant hues and is usually "lightfast," which means it won't fade. In addition, the store may stock stamp-printed papers, fragile Japanese papers, and recycled papers with woven-in fibers, dried flower petals, or glitter. These varieties aren't cheap, but they do make crafts look terrific.

Colored Paper

Pop-up Neighborhood

This neighborhood rivals Mister Rogers's hometown for entertainment — and it folds right up to fit under a bed or dresser.

Materials

24- by 18-inch piece of green poster board
Heavyweight colored paper
Glue

Fold up the top of the poster board 6 inches from the edge to form a backdrop. For sky, cut out an 18- by 3-inch strip of blue paper. Scallop one long edge to create a hilly horizon. Glue the sky to the top of the poster board flap, so that the edges of the paper and the board are flush. Cut out a sun, clouds, and trees (pinking shears create a leafy look) and stick them to the backdrop. Next, glue on a winding paper road that runs from the lower edge of the poster board to the edge of the backdrop. To create the illusion that the road continues, it should get progressively narrower.

For houses, cut out paper rectangles — large ones for the foreground and smaller ones for the background. Glue on paper windows, roofs, shutters, and chimneys. Fold back the completed houses ½ inch from their lower edges and glue the bottom edges to the poster board. Use the same method to add Stop signs, shrubs, and picket fences. Then, your child can populate the neighborhood with little toy people and pets.

Pop-up Neighborhood

Paper Play

Fold-up Animals

With a collection of these exotic beasts, your kids can host a living room safari. Set out pillows for boulders and a plush towel for grassland — and let the wildlife roam.

Materials

> Heavyweight colored paper
> Glue

Crocodile: This is the easiest animal to make. Fold a single sheet of paper in half. With the crease serving as its backbone and the top of its head, sketch a rounded body, legs, and a lower jaw. Cut out the shape. Create teeth by using pinking shears to trim along the mouth opening.

Hippopotamus: To make this water dweller (*hippopotamus* means river horse), use the same method as for the crocodile, except make short, straight cuts for teeth. Glue on small rounded ears and a tail.

Lion: This mighty beast needs a mane and a tufted tail. For a shaggy effect, use a butter knife to score an outline of the mane, then tear out the shape. Cut into the center of the mane and slip it around the lion's neck. Glue a torn-out tip onto the tail

Elephant: For floppy ears that reach the tops of his legs, sketch a large angel-wings shape. Make a snip near the back of the elephant's head and slip the ears into the groove.

Giraffe and Baboon: For long-necked animals such as these, start by drawing an outline of the legs and belly, but not the head, neck, and tail. Next, unfold the paper and spread it flat. Draw the rest of the animal's body above the crease. Cut around the head, neck, and tail. Then, refold the paper and cut out the remaining parts.

A Menagerie of Crafts

If your child is an animal-lover, be sure to check out these other projects:

Fold-up Animals

Curlicue Critters

These cheerful habitats, made from rolled strips of paper, are a project for an older child to curl up with on a quiet afternoon. Once she's shaped a few animals, she can use them to design a greeting card or turn them into a decorative pin to wear on a favorite jacket.

Materials

Several ⅛-inch-wide strips of
    construction paper
Round wooden toothpicks
Glue

Moisten an end of one strip of construction paper and press it against the middle of a round wooden toothpick. Hold an end of the toothpick in one hand and, using your thumb and index finger, roll the paper around the toothpick to form a loose coil. Slide the paper off the toothpick. Secure the free end using clear-drying white glue applied with the tip of a second toothpick.

Once you've made a coil, you can turn it into a teardrop by pinching one side. Squeeze the opposite side, too, and you get an oval.

Or, space the creases closer together to form a semicircle. Glue these shapes together and you can create the animals described here or make up your own.

Caterpillar: Coil seven 4-inch strips and glue them side by side to form the insect's body. Add a round head made from a 6-inch strip and fold a ½-inch strip into V-shaped antennae.

Rabbit: Use a 12-inch strip, a 4-inch strip, and a 3-inch strip to roll circles for the bunny's body, head, and tail. Make oval ears out of 3-inch strips and loop a ¾-inch strip to form a long rabbit's foot.

Duck: With a 12-inch strip, make a teardrop to use for the bird's body. Use a 4-inch strip to make a round head and a V-shaped snip for a bill.

Turtle: For the turtle's shell, shape a semicircle out of a 12-inch strip. Use 3-inch strips to make two smaller semicircles for feet. Glue them flat side up to the bottom of the shell. With another 3-inch strip, make a teardrop head. Add a short curled tail.

GO FISH

For a quick game, let your kids cut out paper fish from construction paper — while they're at it, they can also cut out a deep blue sea. Poke paper clips through the mouths of the paper fish. Then tie a magnet to a string on a pole and send your kids fishing on the floor.

Curlicue Critters

Paper Play

Wind Sock

This sprightly wind sock can catch the breeze outside your house any day — or you can save it for a special day, as *FamilyFun* reader Judi Ensler did. With these directions, she made a bright pink clown-face wind sock to decorate the porch for her daughter Lindsey's second birthday party.

Materials

6- by 18-inch strip of construction paper
Markers, paint, crayons, glitter, or sequins
White glue
9 26-inch-long crepe paper streamers
Stapler
30-inch piece of string

Have your child begin by decorating the strip of construction paper with markers, paint, crayons, glitter, or sequins. She can make stars, flowers, or birthday candles or give the wind sock a face by gluing on paper cutouts of eyes, ears, a nose, and a mouth.

Next, glue the paper streamer strips to the back of the bottom edge of the construction paper. Then, staple the ends of the paper to form a tube. Finally, knot the string at each end and staple the knots to the tube sides to make a handle. Hang the wind sock on a porch or patio where it will be protected from strong winds and watch it ride the gentle breezes.

Wind Sock

Rain Forest Vines

When *FamilyFun* contributor Jodi Picoult noticed that a spell of damp weather was making her house feel like a rain forest, she ran with the idea and made these vines. Her kids were transfixed by this activity, and the fruits of their labors stayed wound around their hallway railings for months.

Materials

Construction paper
White glue
Twine or yarn
Glitter, markers, and scraps of felt

First, cut out lots of matching pairs of construction paper leaves (cut and trace a leaf template, if you wish). While you're at it, make matching pairs of paper flowers. On a long table or on the floor, set out all the pairs in a long line.

Flip over half of the flowers and leaves so that their "wrong" side is facing up, then spread glue on each one. Cut a length of twine or yarn and drape it over the middle of each glued flower or leaf. Press down each matching flower or leaf on top of its glued mate (in short, you're making a yarn sandwich), until you have a connected line of double-sided flowers and leaves. When dry, your kids can decorate the vine with glitter, markers, and felt or add construction paper details, such as petals and curlicue vine tendrils.

Rain Forest Vines

Once your kids have mastered the paper collage, encourage them to try making collages out of any of the materials from the list below. Using a piece of heavy cardboard as a backing, have your children glue items together (the word *collage* means "to glue" in French). You may want to provide a theme to work with, such as a shape collage, which would focus on squares, circles, and other geometric figures cut out of fabric, felt, construction paper, or wallpaper. Another theme that younger children especially enjoy is a color collage, constructed with yarn, cloth pieces, and magazine pictures of the same color.

Here are some materials to keep on hand for collages:

- Torn notebook covers
- Yarn
- Fabric scraps
- Strips of foil
- Wallpaper
- Dried foods, such as rice, seeds, and beans
- Pieces of sponge
- Tiny pebbles or leaves
- Broken eggshells
- Bottle caps
- Broken toy parts
- Leaves
- Labels and wrappers

Matisse Cutouts

When Henri Matisse developed arthritis and could no longer paint, he began creating paper collages, known as cutouts. In this project, which is best for kids ages six and up, kids use scissors to cut paper shapes and arrange them into dynamic designs.

Materials

Colored paper

White or black paper

Black or dark blue construction paper

Glue

Before your child begins creating her design, look together for a book from your library that shows Matisse's collages. Notice how he used geometric shapes and organic ones (those found in nature) in his compositions. Geometric shapes, such as triangles, circles, and squares, are symmetrical. This is not the case with many organic shapes, which include squiggles and blobs.

Set out the colored paper and a pair of scissors and let your child begin cutting out shapes (younger kids may need help with the scissor work). You don't need to give her much direction in this activity, but if you like, you might encourage her to vary sizes and colors. Resist the urge to "tidy up" your child's cutouts. Her stars may not be perfectly symmetrical, but they will look beautiful when joined with the other shapes in the final collage.

Once she has amassed a collection of shapes, she can arrange them on a sheet of white or black paper. When she has settled on an arrangement, she can glue the cutouts in place. If the collage was done on white paper, mount the work onto black or dark blue construction paper to create a striking contrast or mount it against a dominant color within the collage.

Tissue Paper

Tissue Paper Painting

Tissue Paper Painting

Even small kids can master this effective technique for "painting" a white sheet of paper. The results make neat greeting cards — simply write on top of your designs with a black pen.

Start by cutting shapes out of colored tissue paper. Any shape will do — although solid, blocky shapes are the easiest to handle in the painting process.

Set out a bowl of water and a piece of heavyweight white drawing paper. Dunk your tissue paper shapes one at a time into the water. Pull the shape gently along the rim of the bowl to squeeze out excess water, then place it directly on the white paper (try not to slide it). Keep placing pieces down until you're done, then set the piece aside to dry. When dry, the tissue paper should lift off easily to reveal your design.

Paper Blossoms

These paper flowers are beautiful, quick to make, and, unlike the real things, guaranteed to last.

Materials

    Colored tissue paper
    Crayons
    Pipe cleaners

For each flower, cut eight 3½-inch squares out of the tissue paper. Using the side of a crayon, color along two opposite edges of each square. Place one of the squares on a flat surface with the uncolored edges at the top and bottom. Starting at the top, fold the square as you would a paper fan. The pleats should be about ½ inch wide. Fold the remaining squares using the same method.

For a stem, bend a pipe cleaner 1½ inches from an end to form a hook. Stack the pleated squares (without unfolding them). Place the stack inside the hook and twist the hook end around the stem. Now, to open up the flower to full bloom, twist the petals a half turn near the stem.

Paper Blossoms

Stained-glass Hangings

These designs look luminous when hung in a bright window. The larger and bolder your design, the easier it will be for small hands to cut and glue. Besides the car shown above, you might try making a butterfly, house, flower, sun, or peacock.

Materials

    Black construction paper or card
       stock
    Pencil
    Glue or glue stick
    Colored tissue paper
    Thin cord or thread

Have your child fold a piece of black paper in half and draw a simple shape, such as a car, on it. After cutting out the design, she will have two identical car shapes. On one car shape, cut out sections for the windows, wheels, and doors. Placing the cutout shape on top of the other, carefully trace and cut out matching holes on the second car shape. On one of the car shapes, glue pieces of colored tissue paper over the holes. After the glue dries, glue the two car shapes together so the tissue paper shows through the holes. Tape a loop of thread to the top as a hanger.

66

Flower Lei

Your child can say "aloha" any time of the year by dressing in homemade tissue paper leis — and you can complete the outfit with the paper grass skirt, below.

Materials

- 16 pieces of uncooked ziti
- Tempera paints and paintbrushes
- Colored tissue (or crepe) paper
- 3-foot piece of string or yarn
- Large sewing needle

Have your child color the uncooked ziti with the paints. Let dry. Next, cut out bunches of three-petaled flower shapes from the tissue paper. Loosely tie a knot in one end of the string. Thread the other end through the eye of the needle. Sew through the centers of a dozen or so flowers. String on a piece of painted ziti. Continue sewing on flowers and pasta, stopping 3 inches from the end of the string. Undo the knot and tie together the string ends with an overhand knot.

Flower Lei

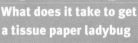

Jitter Bug

What does it take to get a tissue paper ladybug to dance? A lemon. Don't believe us? Try this: cut an 8-inch square out of red tissue paper. Use a black marker to draw a ladybug fáce and antennae centered above the lower edge of the paper. Decorate the rest of the square with spots. Then, twist all four corners of the paper to form a dome. Place a fresh lemon on a smooth, hard surface and set the dome on top of it, so that the fruit is hidden. Gently push the lemon, and the ladybug will bob and wobble.

A Paper Grass Skirt

To complete a Hawaiian outfit, make a swishy grass skirt for your child. Cut two sheets of brown wrapping paper 6 inches wider than your child's waist and as long as you want the skirt to be. Staple one piece on top of the other about $1/2$ inch from the waist edge. For a waistband, use a long, 4-inch-wide paper strip. Glue the lower half of the waistband to the stapled edge of the skirt front. Fold over the waistband top and glue it to the inside of the skirt. (For a decorative waistband, you can twist together two paper strips and glue them on.) Use scissors to fringe the skirt from the hemline to just below the waistband. Finally, stick one part of a Velcro fastener to the front of one waistband end and the matching part to the back of the opposite end of the waistband. Wrap the skirt around your child's waist and fasten.

A Paper Grass Skirt

67

70944

Cards & Envelopes

Homemade Paper

Making paper is a wonderful way to teach children about recycling. Once you have constructed a basic frame and mixed some paper pulp, your kids can turn household paper trash into cards, picture frames, and works of art.

Materials

- Frames (see below)
- Window screening
- Paper scraps
- Blender
- Large dishpan
- Sponge
- Piece of cloth or paper bags

A basic papermaking frame, called a mold and deckle, consists of two frames and a piece of screen. You can use two picture frames of the same size, artist canvas stretchers (available at art supply stores), or frames made out of 2-by-1s. For the mold, which will catch the paper pulp, nail or staple a piece of window screen onto one of the frames. To keep the sheet of paper properly shaped, the other frame, the deckle, is simply held on top of the mold.

1. Gather some old homework paper, scraps of gift wrap, or half-finished art projects (avoid glossy paper). Tear the sheets into confetti and soak them in warm water in the blender for about an hour; for every cup of paper, add about 1 cup of water. Blend your "pulp shake" until it is mushy. Add extra water if necessary, keeping in mind that the smoother the pulp, the more uniform the paper.

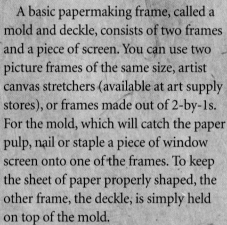

2. Place your mold (screen side up), with the deckle on top, in a large dishpan and fill the pan with water. Pour in the pulp and, gripping the deckle onto the mold, shake the frame to distribute the pulp evenly as it filters onto the screen. After a minute or so, the pulp will settle into a thin film.

3. Lift the mold and deckle from the dishpan and let the water drip off the paper. Take the deckle off the mold. Using a sponge, press out as much water as possible. (If the pulp sticks to the sponge, it's too wet.)

4. Carefully flip the mold over onto a piece of cloth or paper bags. Let the paper dry flat or iron it between two dish towels. If a sheet does not work out, return it to the blender and repeat the process.

Creative Additions: For textured paper, add glitter, dried flowers, sawdust, or threads to the mold before you press out the water. Or, place ferns or leaves on the paper once it comes off the screen and roll it with a rolling pin. To make paper shapes, use cookie cutters instead of the deckle. For colored paper, add food coloring to the blender or sprinkle on the finished damp sheet.

Artful Stationery

Nothing so charms far-flung relatives as a letter on homespun stationery — especially if it sports one-of-a-kind artwork made by the apples of their eyes. To create a stash of your own, you need paper, a simple envelope pattern, and access to a copy machine.

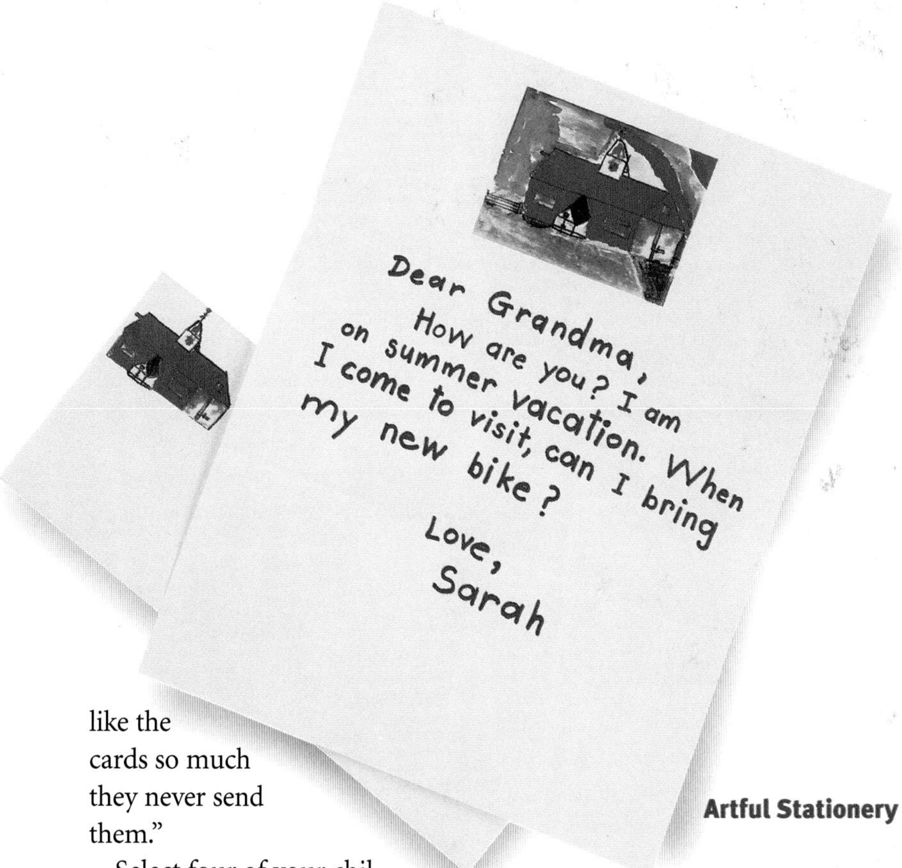

Materials

Store-bought envelope
Children's artwork
Writing paper
Pencil
Glue

Carefully open up the envelope and trace its shape onto a piece of paper. Shrink a piece of your child's artwork on a copier, cut it out, glue it onto the blank envelope pattern. Copy it again and cut it out to create the envelope. Use the same technique for making the writing paper. Black and white copies are cheap (about 6 cents a copy) and yield great results (plus, kids can color them in before sending them out). Color copies run $2 to $3 each, but you can fit lots of small cards on one big piece of paper.

Postcard Gift Pack:
When she was an art teacher in Hudson, Iowa, *FamilyFun* reader Debra Roach turned her students' drawings into postcards, which they gave away as gifts. The results were a hit; the principal used them for his personal stationery, and the town even included some in its tourism packet. "The only drawback," Debra reports, "is that people like the cards so much they never send them."

Select four of your children's favorite designs (simple black and white drawings will reduce and copy best). Then, take the artwork to a photocopy shop and reduce each design to 4¼ by 5½ inches. For copying purposes, paste the four postcards onto a standard 8½- by 11-inch sheet of paper. Ask the store staff to photocopy the designs onto card stock and to cut the cards. Black and white is the least expensive (100 cards cost about $12), but you can also try two-color cards (about $25 for 100 cards).

Postcard packets can be grouped by artist, by theme, or by assorted designs. Insert a slip of paper with a gift message, then finish off with a bow, as shown here.

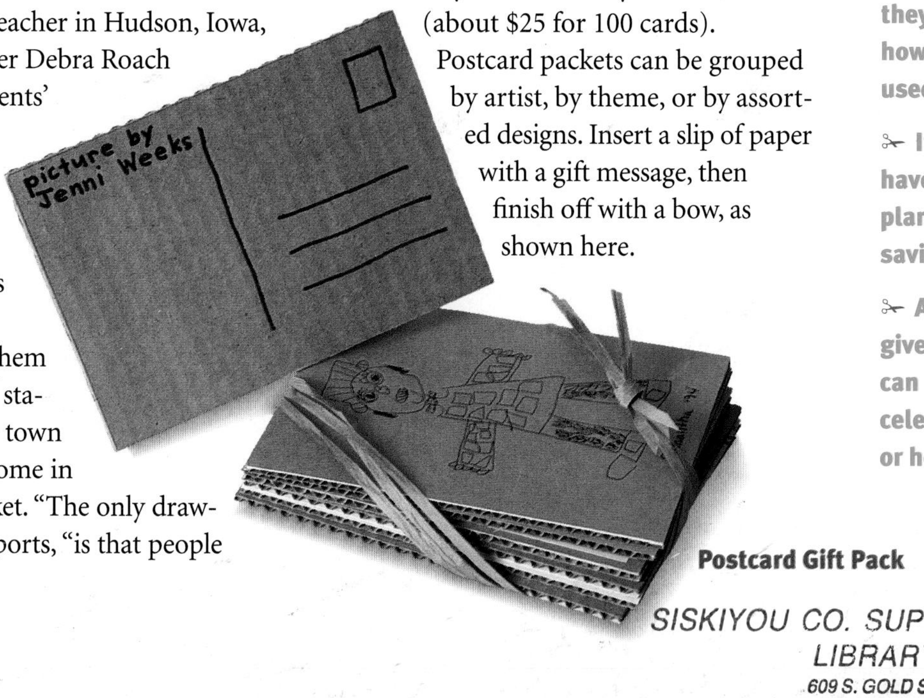

Artful Stationery

Picture by Jenni Weeks

Postcard Gift Pack

NOTEWORTHY NOTES

Kids often are stumped about what to write in thank-you notes. Here are some suggestions to start them off:

✂ Have them tell the gift-giver how they felt when they opened the gift.

✂ Let them explain how they plan to use the gift (or how it already has been used).

✂ If they receive money, have them write what they plan to buy or what they are saving the money for.

✂ After thanking the gift-givers, your children can describe how they celebrated their birthday or holiday.

Paper Play

69

Rubber Stamps

Rubber Stamps

Any child old enough to palm a stamp is old enough to make his own stationery. But for older kids, half the fun of stamping is in making the stamp itself. This one, crafted from erasers or packing foam, lasts much longer than its potato-based cousin.

Materials

Pencil

Scrap paper

Dense foam or art gum eraser (available at art supply stores)

Craft knife

Construction paper

Ink pad

Have your child start by drawing a simple design on paper. Next, copy the design onto the flat side of a piece of dense foam or an art gum eraser. Help her carefully cut around the design with a craft knife, making deep, smooth incisions. Turn the eraser or foam to one side and cut so that the new incision intersects the cuts made from the top. Continue cutting until the surrounding rubber or foam falls away from the design. The finished design should be raised above the base.

Stamps Made from Artwork

Food Stamps

Most kids are familiar with the trusty potato stamp. But have you tried turnip stamps? Or zucchini stamps? Or rutabaga stamps? Any hard, solid vegetable can be carved into a stamp — just follow the directions for the rubber stamp on this page. Most fruits are not carvable, but they still make neat designs; just ink and print half a lemon or a strawberry and see what happens.

Stamps Made from Artwork:

Any drawing composed of simple, strong lines can be made into a rubber stamp. First, shrink it to stamp size on a copy machine to get a preview of what it will look like. If you like, type or handwrite the name of the artist onto the drawing before handing it over to the stamp shop (if there's no stamp shop nearby, try your local stationery store or copy shop). The cat and bird above cost about $13 each.

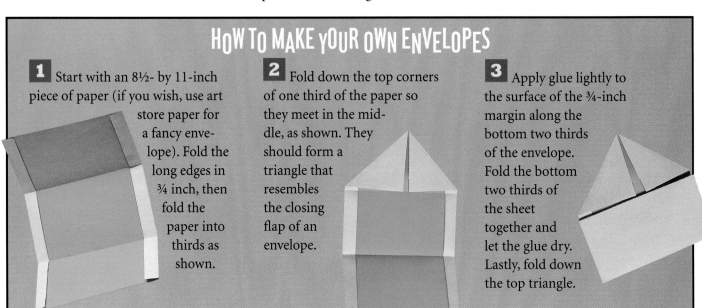

HOW TO MAKE YOUR OWN ENVELOPES

1 Start with an 8½- by 11-inch piece of paper (if you wish, use art store paper for a fancy envelope). Fold the long edges in ¾ inch, then fold the paper into thirds as shown.

2 Fold down the top corners of one third of the paper so they meet in the middle, as shown. They should form a triangle that resembles the closing flap of an envelope.

3 Apply glue lightly to the surface of the ¾-inch margin along the bottom two thirds of the envelope. Fold the bottom two thirds of the sheet together and let the glue dry. Lastly, fold down the top triangle.

Famous Families

Here's a project for kids who dream of fame and fortune — or who just enjoy a good laugh. By pasting the heads of family members (don't forget the family dog) onto a group shot of a sports team, music group, sitcom family, or crew of astronauts, you can create a greeting card that is guaranteed a prime spot on its receiver's refrigerator.

Materials

Family snapshots
Magazine or postcard cutouts of a
   group photo
Glue
Colored card stock

Start by selecting a family snapshot in which everyone's head is about the same size (you may have to mix and match from a pile of snapshots). Then, send your kids on a hunt for a magazine or post-card shot of a famous group of people. Tell them to look for a shot that has about the same size heads (or slightly smaller) as the heads in your snapshots. When you've got the right one, cut out the heads from the family snapshots and glue them onto the image you found. If the heads are not quite the right size — and you're feeling picky — you can color-copy the photos to enlarge or reduce them.

To mass-produce your card, copy it in black and white or color on card stock. For extra laughs, add dialogue bubbles to the photos.

Paper Chain: Here's another greeting card project that uses up outtakes that didn't qualify for the photo album. Have your kids make a people paper chain with as many links as there are members of your family. On each link, let a family member paste on a cutout head shot of himself. Then, he can decorate the body to his liking and write a personal greeting on the back. Fold up the paper chain, tuck it into an envelope, and send.

BIRTHDAY MUGS

To send homemade birthday greetings to faraway relatives, *FamilyFun* reader Nancy Barnett of Manheim, Pennsylvania, took pictures of her kids holding a "Happy Birthday" sign they had colored. She then mounted the developed photos onto cards and let her kids write a personal note inside.

Famous Families

CARDS (RIGHT) © 1997 APPLE CORPS LIMITED; (LEFT) © 1997 LUCASFILM, LTD.

Paper Play

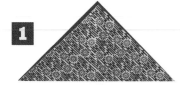

Origami

Paper Pinwheels

In Japan, origami is not only a traditional craft, but also a tool used to teach young children the arts of patience, accuracy, and concentration. With these commendable qualities and origami paper, your kids can turn your backyard into a twirling garden of pinwheels.

Materials

- 4 sheets of origami paper
- Glue (a glue stick works well)
- Pushpin
- Thin wooden dowel or pencil

1. Place one sheet of paper on a table, with the plain side up, and position it in a diamond shape. Fold the bottom point up so it is even with the top point and make a light crease. (The less you flatten your creases and the less glue you use later on, the more freely your pinwheel will turn.) Fold the left corner across to the right corner, make a light crease, and unfold.

2. Fold one layer of the top point down to the fold and secure with a spot of glue. Take three more squares of paper and repeat steps 1 and 2; you will need four of these units for each pinwheel.

3. Position one unit so the unfolded plain corner points toward you. Slip the printed point of a second unit into the first unit as shown, aligning the fold with the center crease. Secure it with a spot of glue.

4. Tuck the printed point of a third unit into the second unit, aligning the fold with the center crease. Glue it in place.

5. Hold the fourth unit so the unfolded plain corner points to the left and tuck the downward point into the third unit (make sure that the plain corner slides behind the first unit).

6. Secure the last corner with a dab of glue. To complete, use a pushpin to attach the paper wheel to a wooden dowel or to the eraser of a pencil.

Rainbow Flier

Rainbow Flier

Like the real thing, this rainbow flier from *Hands Around the World* (Williamson Publishing) can brighten a rainy day. Have your kids stockpile a handful of them, then hold a throwing contest when the sun comes out — they soar just like Frisbees.

Materials

8 3½-inch squares of origami paper
Glue

1. To make a flier, fold one square in half so that the crease is at the top (see diagram below).
2. Then, fold down the upper left corner to form a triangular pocket.
3. Fold up the lower right corner. This will create a parallelogram. Repeat the process with the other squares.

To assemble the flier, fit the open triangle of one parallelogram into the triangular pocket of the next, working clockwise to complete a circle. Dab glue between the pieces to secure them. Once dry, the ring is ready to fly.

Gum Wrapper Chain

The classic gum chain, a playground favorite, is really a version of origami — with teeny-weeny pieces of paper. A word of warning, though: once your children figure out the simple technique, they will be working their choppers day in and day out to generate the raw materials for a record-breaking chain.

Materials

Lots and lots of gum wrappers
(from long sticks of gum)

To start, tear a gum wrapper in half the long way. Fold the long sides of one strip in so they line up in the center, then fold it in half on the line. Now, you should have a long skinny piece. Fold the ends in so they meet in the center and fold the strip in half where they meet.

Make a second link and slide it into the first as shown (the two ends of one link slip into the folds of the two ends of another). Presto! You're on your way.

The world's record for the longest gum chain is 7,400 feet.

PERFECT FOLDING PAPER

Origami paper, which often is printed on one side and plain on the other, is available in craft supplies stores, but kids also can cut their own squares from writing paper, wrapping paper, Sunday comics, scraps of wallpaper, or any other thin paper. Typically, origami squares are 6 by 6 inches.

Gum Wrapper Chain

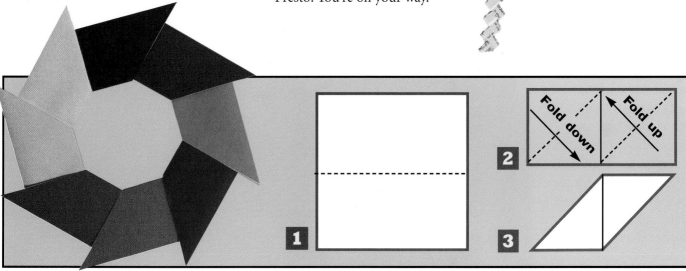

73

LIBRARY
609 S. GOLD ST.
YREKA, CA 96097

20944

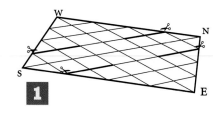

1

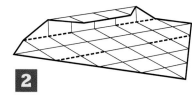

2

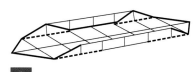

3

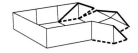

4

Paper Boxes

With this simple technique, your kids can turn out a cache of colorful boxes to decorate and fill with treasures. Our sample measures 4 inches across and 2 inches deep, but your child can vary the dimensions by changing the size of the two paper squares she starts with.

Materials

Heavyweight drawing paper, cut into one 10⅝-inch square and one 11-inch square

Crayons, markers, stickers, or paints

To make the bottom, fold the smaller paper square in half diagonally, first one way and then the other, creasing the folds well before unfolding them. Next, fold in all four corners so they meet in the center; crease them well and unfold.

Fold one of the corners so that it meets the farthest crease line opposite that corner, crease, and unfold it; repeat with the three other corners. Finally, fold each corner to its closest crease line. Unfold all the corners to reveal an overall pattern of creased squares.

1. Make two cuts in the paper at one corner, two squares deep and two squares apart. Make identical cuts on the opposite corner.

2 and 3. Orient the paper with the cuts facing north and south. Fold in the east and west corners along the crease lines two times, finally bringing the two sides up vertically.

4. Bend the pointed ends of the east and west sides toward one another, crossing them. Bring the tongue-shaped portion of the paper (the one facing south) up and over the crossed ends, folding it down over the ends and tucking it so that it stays put. Do the same with the north end of the paper. This completes the bottom of the box.

To make the lid, fold the larger sheet of paper the same way you did the bottom of the box. Before you cut and assemble the lid, decorate the paper using crayons, markers, stickers, or paints.

Paper Boxes

Homemade Books

Accordion Book

Even if your kids can't read or write yet, they can help create a versatile accordion-style book and dictate their tales to a parent or older sibling to record. Folded books are fun to make and to read — they can be spread out for a panoramic effect or closed up and read by turning the pages as you would with an ordinary book. When they are flipped over, there is room for a second story.

Materials

    9 8½- by 14-inch sheets of colored
       paper
    Ruler
    Double-sided tape or glue
    Cardboard
    Ribbon or string

Accordion Book

1. Fold nine 8½- by 14-inch sheets of colored paper in half so they each are 7 by 8½ inches, then unfold. Overlap the right half of the first piece with the left half of the next piece and so on. Attach the overlapping pages with double-sided tape or glue.

2. Fold up the pages accordion style. Attach the front and back pages to pieces of cardboard that are just a bit bigger than your pages.

3. As a finishing touch, attach a piece of ribbon or string to the front and back covers for tying the book closed.

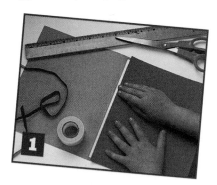

Mini Matchbook

This tiny book is just the right size for a story. Crease a 1¼- by 12-inch-wide strip of construction paper, accordion style, into 1¼-inch sections. For the front and back covers, cut two 1½-inch cardboard squares and glue to the front and back pages. Stretch a rubber band around the book to hold it closed on the shelf.

Paper Play

Hand-sewn Blank Book

BOOKS UNDER COVER

Fancy coverings for school notebooks make a backpack of homework seem more inviting. Here are a few ideas to start with.

✂ **Use bold wrapping paper, with shiny, floral, or polka-dot designs.**

✂ **Cover a piece of your child's art or a favorite greeting card with clear Con-Tact paper and trim it to fit.**

✂ **Cut covers out of the Sunday comics. Or use the black and white daily strips and have your kids hand-color them first.**

✂ **Recycle a favorite old shirt into a fabric cover (see page 51 for specific instructions).**

Hand-sewn Blank Book

This adaptation of the traditional Japanese sewn binding can be used to create books of any size. The punched holes make it easy for even young kids to have the satisfaction of assembly.

Materials

> White or colored paper
> Card stock or construction paper
> Pencil
> Ruler
> Craft knife
> Hole punch
> Yarn or embroidery thread
> Blunt tapestry needle

1. Determine the finished size of your book and, using the ruler and craft knife, help your child cut sheets double the final size from the paper and the card stock. (If you want the final book to be 4 by 6 inches, for example, start with sheets that measure 8 by 6 inches.) Fold all the sheets in half vertically, sandwiching the pages between the front and back covers. Mark a row of evenly spaced dots about ½ inch in from the folded spine. As shown, punch holes in all the sheets where marked. Cut a piece of yarn or embroidery thread that is about four times the length of the book.

2. Thread the needle and, starting at the top of the book (leave a loose end of a few inches), sew it together with a running stitch: up through the first hole, down through the second, up through the third, down through the fourth, and so on.

3. After sewing down through the last hole, loop the yarn around the bottom of the book as shown and insert the needle in that hole again. Pull the thread tight, then insert the needle in that hole once more, this time looping the yarn around the spine of the book. Work your way back up the spine, sewing through each hole two times — once to complete the running stitch and the second time to loop the yarn around the spine. Tie the two loose ends together at the top with a small bow.

Gently score a vertical line (do not cut all the way through!) on the front cover near the lacing to make the book easier to open. Your child can decorate the cover any way she likes.

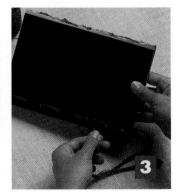

Creative Bookmarks

Kids who are hooked on chapter books can mark their reading progress with personalized bookmarks, which are easy to make, sturdy, and even may speed up the page turning.

Materials

  Construction paper or poster board
  Pinking shears or crazy scissors
  Clear Con-Tact paper (optional)
  Hole punch
  Ribbon

For each bookmark, begin with a piece of construction paper or poster board 6 inches long and 2 inches wide. Let your kids decorate it however they like (see suggestions below). For a glossy finish, cover the bookmark with clear Con-Tact paper. If you're using pinking shears (or one of Fiskars's line of crazy scissors) to make jagged edges, cover the bookmark before you trim it to size. Lastly, punch a hole in the top and tie on a festive ribbon.

Stickers Galore: Kids can show off their sticker collections on their bookmarks. Put one large seal on the bottom of the paper or line several smaller ones in a row.

Rubber Stamps: Print colorful figures or shapes onto the paper. If you track down alphabet stamps, your kids can print their names or the book's title. For a homemade rubber stamp, see page 70.

Magazine Collage: Cut out bright pictures from magazines or travel brochures. Overlap the images and lightly glue them onto the bookmark.

Geometric Designs: Cut a strip of graph paper to the same size as the bookmark and glue them together. Working from the center out, use fine-tip markers or colored pencils to create geometric designs in the squares. Try diagonal stripes, symmetrical patterns, or random designs.

Photo Collage: Gather snapshots of family members, friends, or pets. Cut out figures and lightly glue them onto the paper. Then, jazz up the images with funny bubble captions.

Glitter: Sprinkle the bookmark with glitter, then cover it with a piece of clear Con-Tact paper. Trim the paper, leaving a ¼-inch border.

Keepsake Scrapbook

To practice and enjoy writing, drawing, and photography over school vacation, help your kids create a summer scrapbook. Begin with a large blank or lined book, a glue stick or white glue, and photo corners or clear tape. Divide the pages into categories — ticket stubs, photos, nature finds, family stories, jokes, dreams, or a tally of ice-cream cone flavors and sports scores. Enter the headings on different pages throughout the scrapbook. If it's kept in an accessible place, your child's journal will become a summer catchall, organized around the principle that anything goes.

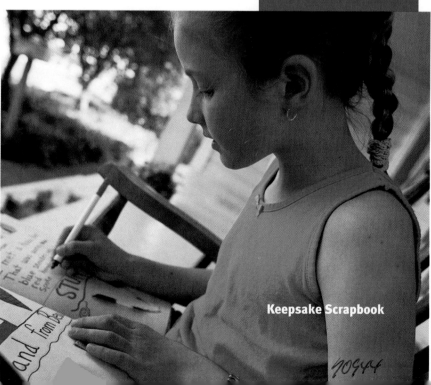

Keepsake Scrapbook

Newspaper & Butcher Paper

**Instant
Dresses**

Instant Dresses

Not only are these disposable dress designs a snap to make, but they also cost little more than the price of paper and tape.

Materials
- Sheet of newspaper
- Butcher paper
- Tape
- Paint or colored tape
- Sponges

First, make a basic shift-style dress pattern. Spread open the newspaper sheet and refold it in half horizontally. Turn the sheet so the fold is on the right, then cut a U-shaped armhole in the upper left corner. Spread the sheet open again and cut out a U- or V-shaped neckline in the center of the top edge. (This will form shoulder straps between the armholes.) Hold up the pattern in front of your child and trim the paper where necessary for a better fit.

Next, trace around the pattern onto two pieces of heavyweight butcher paper. Extend the length to suit your child's height. Cut out both pieces and tape together the shoulder and side seams. Decorate the dress with sponge-painted designs, colored-tape stripes, and paper buttons.

Woven Baskets

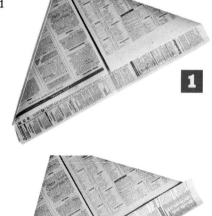

Woven Baskets

Native Americans of many tribes used baskets to store seed, gather crops, and sift meal. Their materials ranged from grass and reeds to tree bark — but kids can easily imitate their resourcefulness by making baskets of newspaper "reeds."

Materials

Newspaper
Glue stick
Tempera
   paints and
   paintbrushes

Make a reed out of a 13½- by 22-inch sheet of newspaper. Starting with a long edge, tightly roll the sheet into a tube. Flatten the tube and use a glue stick to secure the open edge. Assemble seven more reeds. Lay four of the reeds side by side on a flat surface and weave in the remaining four, as shown. Slide the strips together to make the bottom of the basket. Fold the ends of the reeds up to form the side spokes.

Now, cut newspaper sheets into four 11- by 27-inch rectangles. Using the same method as before, roll four more reeds. Tape the end of a reed to the base of a spoke. Weave the reed in and out of the spokes, around the basket. Tuck the end behind a spoke. Weave in the other reeds, one above the other. Fold the tops of the spokes into the basket and tuck them behind a reed. Use tempera paints to coat the finished basket inside and out.

Paper Hats

This classic chapeau is an instant costume, especially with the addition of a few swashes of paint and some sewing box odds and ends.

Materials

Newspaper
Pom-poms, tassels, or other
   decorations

1. Keeping the newspaper folded as it would be if you were reading a front page, turn the long, unfolded edge toward you. Fold down the top two corners so they meet. This will leave a double-layered strip of paper at the bottom, as shown.

2. Fold the top strip in half lengthwise, so that its edge meets the folded-down triangles. Then fold it up again, so that it rests on top of the folded-down triangles.

3. Turn the paper over. Fold in the two sides so they meet in the middle. Once again, there should be a strip left at the bottom. Fold this strip up along the bottom edge of the hat.

4. Tuck in the top edge of the fold you just made to create the hatband.

5. Fold the triangular tip of the hat down so its point tucks into the hatband and give it some flair.

Cabin Fever

Sometimes, all it takes to lift a kid's spirits is a change of scenery. With this paper log construction technique from *Kids Create!* (Williamson Publishing), your child can build a frontier cabin without ever leaving home.

Materials

> 3- by 2-inch strips of butcher or
>   construction paper
> Pencil
> Ruler
> 3½-inch cardboard square
>   (for house base)
> Glue
> 3½- by 5-inch paper rectangle
>   (for the roof)
> 5-inch paper square
>   (for the chimney)

Make logs out of the strips of craft paper by wrapping each one around the pencil, taping down the open edge, and sliding the cylinder off the pencil. Make twenty-four 3-inch logs: seventeen to use as is and seven to trim into shorter lengths as called for.

Assemble the cabin on top of the cardboard square. Glue 3-inch logs along three edges of the square, staggering the log ends, as shown. On the fourth side, create a front door opening by gluing a 1-inch log and a ¾-inch log to either corner. Glue on two more rows of logs, alternating the shorter lengths on the sides of the door. Add another two rows of 3-inch logs all around. For the last four rows, build onto the front and back only, using progressively shorter logs. Taper the ends to create an A-shaped roofline.

For a roof, fold the paper rectangle in half and glue it in place atop the cabin. To make a chimney, loosely roll up the 5-inch paper square and glue down the open edge. Then, glue the cylinder to the rear of the cabin.

Cabin Fever

Newspaper Palm Tree

Part craft project, part magic trick, this activity lets your kids twist a few sheets of newspaper into an impressively tall paper palm tree. Each tree takes only a few minutes to turn out, so by the time dinner's ready, they can turn your recycling pile into a shady grove.

Materials

>   Newspaper
>   Ruler
>   Rubber bands or masking tape

To begin, your child should open up a sheet of newspaper in front of her, as though she were about to read it. Starting at the bottom edge, roll up the sheet just 2 or 3 inches short of the top edge.

Placing the bottom edge of a second piece of newspaper over the 2- to 3-inch section of the first sheet, roll together the two sheets, again stopping about 2 or 3 inches from the top edge. Repeat this step four more times. Roll the last sheet of newspaper all the way up so that it becomes a long skinny tube.

Holding the tube carefully, your child should make five 4-inch cuts into one end of it (this will become the top of the tree). At this point, she will need an assistant to help her make the tree

Newspaper Palm Tree

grow. As she holds onto the base of the tree, another person should put his thumbs inside the top of the tree and gradually pull the inside layers out. The tree will grow longer and longer, and the paper slits will extend down the trunk of the tree like feathery leaves. Keep pulling the tree apart until it reaches its full height of about 6 feet. To keep the tree in one piece, wrap a few rubber bands or strips of masking tape around its base.

A Tree Grows in Michigan

When *FamilyFun* reader Barb Beach of Grand Haven, Michigan, had to come up with an idea for her Girl Scout troop's International Festival project, she was happy to find instructions for newspaper palm trees in the magazine. She said, "The trees were easy and fun to make, and they were perfect for our display about Nigeria. The girls even spray-painted the trunks and added construction paper leaves."

Paper Play

Chapter Five

Squish & Sculpt

IF THERE'S ONE craft a kid can't resist, it's sculpture. Why? Because kids are born to squish, roll, tear, and stick stuff together. Think about it: little kids regularly pile blocks into towers, heap stuffed animals into fluffy, bedside totem poles, and create standing sculpture with whatever dinner food you provide. By the time they get their hands on real art materials, such as clay, wax, papier-mâché, soap, and plaster, they're masters at messing around in three dimensions.

In this chapter, you'll find a host of projects for moldable art materials, along with recipes for homemade clays, doughs, and even goo. Aside from being less expensive than store-bought varieties, these concoctions are often easier to manipulate, especially for preschoolers. The ingredients, mostly common kitchen staples, take minutes to mix up, which means a near-

instant project for your children and one less trip to the art store for you. If you don't want to bother making the materials from scratch, by all means, purchase a batch of Play-Doh or modeling clay and cut straight to the project. But keep this in mind: although you may end up with a cleaner kitchen, you'll miss out on a lively part of the process.

Set up shop in the kitchen. Most of these craft projects are wonderfully messy and best kept to the kitchen, where cleanup is just a walk to the sink and the garbage can is a toss away.

Let your child measure ingredients. Combining ingredients is half the fun (not to mention a good math lesson), but remind your kids to measure carefully. After you've put all the ingredients in one recipe together, feel free to make changes, but do so gradually. For instance, if a clay feels too crumbly, add water by the spoonful. Also, keep in mind that not all brands

Basic Play Clay, page 85

No-cook Dough, page 85

83

of tempera paint or glue have the same consistency, so experiment with yours until you get the right texture. And be sure to pencil in any changes in this book.

Remind toddlers that these projects are nonedible. To a toddler, a big blue ball of clay may look tempting enough to eat. Although most of the art materials in this chapter are nontoxic (if you're unsure which materials are toxic, check the glossary on page 246), remind your youngest artists that sculpting materials are not meant to be nibbled on.

Let the project be free-form. The appeal of a squishable craft is its sensory quality — the texture and even the smell. Don't focus too much on making specific things or you'll end up performing while your kids watch. Instead, let them simply explore the feel of the clay.

Never pour leftover clays, plaster, or other mixtures down the drain. Any child with a penchant for kitchen concoctions should learn how to dispose of art materials without clogging drainpipes. Instead of pouring them down the sink, put them in a plastic bag, seal it securely, and drop it in the trash. Or, wait until it has hardened into a piece of artwork, then toss the creation (after you've admired it).

Wipe up quickly. It's easier to sponge a surface when it is still wet than when sculpting material has hardened onto it. Also, many of the materials listed in this chapter can leave stains, so clean your work area as you go — or, work on plastic trays, waxed paper, or a plastic tablecloth.

Basic Play Clay

Clays & Doughs

Basic Play Clay

Welcome to the world of homemade clays. This popular clay recipe can be used over and over and lasts for weeks. A child just learning to model will appreciate how soft and cooperative it feels in her hands, especially when it's warm.

Materials

    1 cup all-purpose flour
    1 cup water
    ½ cup salt
    1 teaspoon vegetable oil
    ½ teaspoon cream of tartar
    Food coloring (for vibrant colors,
        use cake decorating paste)

Mix the flour, water, salt, oil, and cream of tartar in a saucepan. Cook over medium heat until it holds together (keep mixing or it will stick to the bottom of the pan). When the clay is cool enough to touch, knead it on a floured surface, divide it into smaller balls, and add a different shade of food coloring to each ball. Store in an airtight container.

Basic Play Clay

No-cook Dough

For the independent young child who wants to do it "all by myself," this humble dough is the natural choice. There's no cooking on a hot stove, and the more your child squishes, tugs, and pounds, the more pliable this stuff becomes. The dough's sturdiness makes it a winner for kids who want to cut it into shapes with cookie cutters.

Materials

    1 cup all-purpose flour
    ⅜ cup salt
    ⅜ cup hot water
    Food coloring (for vibrant colors,
        use cake decorating paste)

Have your child combine the flour and salt in a medium-size bowl, then pour in the hot water and stir well. Knead on a lightly floured surface for at least 5 minutes, working in a few drops of food coloring. The dough will keep for up to 1 week when refrigerated in plastic bags or containers.

No-cook Dough

Working with Homemade Clays

✂ **If the dough gets dry, revitalize it with a few drops of water; if it's too sticky, knead in more flour, bread, or cornstarch (whatever the dry material is in your recipe).**

✂ **As you work, cover any extra clay with a damp cloth or plastic wrap to keep it from drying.**

✂ **To join two pieces of clay, dab a drop of water on the surfaces to be joined, then press together. If the pieces come apart when dry, reattach them with white glue.**

Squish & Sculpt

SISKIYOU CO. SUPT. SCHOOLS
LIBRARY
609 S. GOLD ST.
YREKA, CA 96097

70944

White Bread Dough

PAINTING CLAY
For best results, apply one layer of white paint as a primer, let dry, then apply colored paints.

White Bread Dough

This recipe, made with white bread and glue, has a fine, elastic texture that won't crack, even during intricate modeling projects like earrings, beads, or tiny figurines. It dries out quickly, so it's best to make only as much as your child will use in one sitting.

Materials

    1 to 2 slices white bread, crusts
        removed
    1 tablespoon white glue
    Acrylic paints and paintbrushes
    Gloss (equal parts glue and water)

Rip one slice of bread into tiny pieces and drop into a bowl. Add the glue and mix with a fork until all the bread is moist. The mix should be pliable and sticky. If it's too wet to roll, mix in more bread. Knead the dough until it becomes elastic and satiny. After your sculptures air-dry (1 to 3 days), paint with acrylics and brush on several coats of gloss.

Cinnamon Hearts

When *FamilyFun* reader Margi Acker-man of Hazleton, Pennsylvania, made these fragrant ornaments with her son's sixth grade class, it was a hit. "We couldn't keep up," says Margi, who ran back and forth with batches of the nonedible dough for kids to roll and shape. The craft is also a tradition at home; it's easy enough for Margi's five-year-old to do on her own, and it yields gifts that last all year.

Materials

    1 cup applesauce
    1½ cups (or 6 ounces) cinnamon
    ⅓ cup white glue
    Large cutting board
    Rolling pin
    Heart-shaped cookie cutters
    Plastic straw
    Ribbon

Mix the applesauce, cinnamon, and glue to form a ball. Refrigerate for at least 30 minutes. Sprinkle cinnamon on the cutting board and roll out the dough to a ¼-inch thickness (don't make it too thin). Cut with heart-shaped cookie cutters. Using the straw, punch a hole at the top center of each heart (if you're planning to create garlands, make two holes). Let dry on a cooling rack for about 2 days. When the color has changed from deep brown to light brown, loop ribbon through the single holes to make ornaments or string ribbon through the double holes to fashion a garland.

Cinnamon Hearts

Sawdust Clay Dog

Sawdust Clay

We had our doubts about this clay made out of sawdust when we saw it in *Kids Create!* by Laurie Carlson (Williamson Publishing), but no longer. Easily shaped when wet, after a day or two the clay dries as hard as particle-board (which it resembles) and can then be sanded and painted. If you can't sweep enough sawdust off the basement floor, head to a lumberyard or hardware store where sawdust can be found by the bucketful — and usually for free.

Materials

> Large bowl or bucket
> 2 parts clean sawdust (no chunks of wood; watch out for nails and splinters)
> 1 part all-purpose flour
> Water
> Wooden spoon or paint stirrer

In a large bowl or bucket, mix together the sawdust and flour, then stir in water until the mixture has a stiff but squishy consistency. Knead the clay to blend thoroughly. If it's too crumbly, add more flour. The clay can be shaped into figurines, bowls, or other vessels, or it can be rolled flat and cut with cookie cutters into holiday ornaments or window hangings (make a hole with a straw). To speed up the drying process, set your pieces out in the sun.

Sawdust Clay

Tools of the Trade

The most useful tools for shaping clay may be found right under your kitchen counter. Try using the following, for starters.

• Narrow wooden block or ruler for shaping flat sides

• Rolling pin for flattening dough

• Pencil for rolling out small pieces of dough or for making dotted textures or lines

• Cookie cutter or open-ended can to cut out flat shapes

• Drinking straw, toothpick, or nail to poke hanging holes

• Garlic press for crazy hair or grass

• Fork, toothbrush, or comb for rough textures

• Coins, buttons, shells, pasta noodles for interesting designs

Squish & Sculpt

1

2

Oven-baked Craft Dough

One way to get a rise out of your child is to mix up a batch of craft dough he can turn into a family of stand-up dolls and pets. Once the figures are baked, he can outfit his collection by painting on features, clothes, and accessories.

Materials

    3 cups all-purpose flour
    1 cup salt
    1 cup water
    Food coloring or glitter (optional)
    Acrylic paints and paintbrushes

    To make the dough, combine the flour, salt, and water in a mixing bowl. Knead the dough until it is smooth and rubbery.

    1. For each doll, first form a head by rolling a piece of dough between your palms (it should be roughly the size of a Ping-Pong ball). Make a second slightly larger ball for the torso. Or, if you want to dress the figure in a skirt, shape a triangular trunk. Press the head onto the torso, applying a few drops of water to make the dough sticky, if necessary.

    2. Next, shape and attach cylindrical arms and legs. Pinch the lower ends of the legs to form feet. Attach ears and a nose and use a toothpick to etch facial features. Bake the figures on a foil-lined cookie sheet for 1 hour in a 275° oven. Remove from the oven and set aside until cool enough to handle.

    Now your child can fashion footwear for his dolls by flattening pieces of dough into thin circles and wrapping them around the feet. (Remember, the bottoms of the shoes will need to be flat for the figure to stand up on its own.) Use the same method to craft a wig for the doll's head.

    Bake the figures for an additional hour. Let them cool before painting (acrylics work best). Unbaked dough will keep in the refrigerator for about a week.

Oven-baked Craft Dough

Papier-mâché

Papier-mâché Paste

We've sampled lots of papier-mâché recipes and found that this one creates a smooth, light paste that's easy to work with.

Materials

    ½ cup all-purpose flour
    2 cups cold water
    2 cups boiling water
    3 tablespoons sugar

In a bowl, combine the flour and cold water. Add to the saucepan of boiling water and bring to a boil. Remove from heat and stir in the sugar. Let it cool; it will thicken as it cools. Once it does, it is ready to use.

Puppet Pals

Kids can decorate these papier-mâché puppets to look like their twins — or they can make up a whole new cast of characters for an impromptu play.

Materials

    1 balloon
    Newspaper strips
    Papier-mâché paste
    2-foot-long wooden dowel
    Masking tape
    Acrylic paints and paintbrushes
    Construction paper
    Glue

To start, blow up the balloon and knot the end. Dip newspaper strips into the papier-mâché paste and cover the balloon, leaving a small opening around the knot. Let dry for about 12 hours. Apply two or three more layers.

For a nose, use your fingers to mold a few paste-coated strips. Gently press the wet shape onto the face. Once the nose dries, pop the balloon with a pin at the knot and remove it. Slide the dowel through the bottom opening until the inserted end rests against the top of the head. Tape over the opening. Anchor the dowel with another layer of papier-mâché.

Now, your child can paint on a face, covering the head with a skin-tone base before adding features. For hair, cut strips of construction paper. Use the straight edge of scissors (adults only) to curl the ends. Then, glue the paper locks onto the head.

Papier-mâché Tips

✄ **Give yourself enough time. One coat of papier-mâché can take up to 2 days to dry.**

✄ **Work outside — fresh air helps the pieces dry faster.**

✄ **Clean up as you go, while the paste is wet.**

✄ **Make only the amount of paste you need; even in the refrigerator, paste spoils quickly.**

✄ **When painting the finished piece, use thick paint, such as tempera or acrylic, to cover up newsprint.**

✄ **For a glossy finish, brush with a mixture of equal parts white glue and water or use spray-on varnish.**

Puppet Pals

Balloon Piñata

A piñata distills many of the most exciting elements of childhood into a single package. Consider: It conceals hidden treasures that are sweet and plentiful. It hangs just out of reach, creating mystery (compounded by the blindfold!) and delicious anticipation. And to receive a piñata's bounty, some lucky kid gets to break everyday rules and smash the thing open. Our hot air balloon is both simple for first-time *piñateros* to make and, as a nice, fat target, also easy for kids to break. Leave a week for construction, so you don't feel rushed — and so you have time to enjoy your creation before it's demolished.

Materials

> 14-inch balloon, inflated
> Papier-mâché paste (see recipe on page 89)
> 1 two-page spread each of regular newspaper, colored comics, and plain newsprint
> String
> 32-ounce plastic yogurt container, cut in half horizontally
> Hole punch
> 5 sheets of colored tissue paper, cut into 3½-inch squares
> Glue stick
> 4 pounds of wrapped candies

1. For stability, place the balloon in a 10-inch bowl. Fold the spread of newspaper in half and then in half again. Tear it into 1½-inch-wide strips (the torn, rough edges help make a smooth overall surface). Drag a strip of newspaper through the paste, wipe off excess with your fingers, and place it at an angle on the balloon. Place a second strip so that it slightly overlaps the first. Continue until the balloon has been covered except for a 2-inch square at the top, through which the candy will

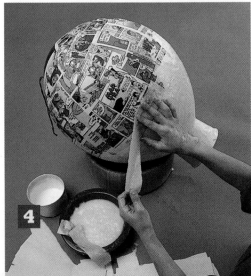

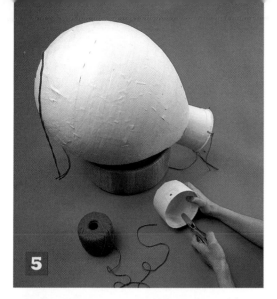

5

6

7

go. Allow 24 hours to dry. Cover left-over paste with plastic so it doesn't dry out (if it does, add warm water).

2. For the piñata's hanger, wrap the midpoint of a length of string around the bottom of the balloon, pulling the ends up to the top; tape it to the balloon in a few places. Knot together the ends of the string 6 inches above the top. For the neck of the hot air balloon, tape the top half of the yogurt container to the bottom of the balloon.

3. Cover the balloon, including the string and the neck, with a layer of comic strips at a different angle from the first layer. (The different colored strips help you distinguish one layer from the next.) Cover the bottom half of the yogurt container, which will become the hot air balloon basket. Allow the balloon and basket to dry.

4. Cover the balloon, neck, and basket with strips of plain newsprint going in a third direction. Smooth over any rough edges as you work. Allow the balloon to dry thoroughly.

5. Punch four holes into the neck of the hot air balloon and four into the basket. Attach string to the neck to later suspend the basket about 3½ inches from the base of the balloon.

6. Dot the corners of a tissue square with a glue stick and place it just to the side of the 2-inch square on the top of the balloon. Follow with other squares in the same color, working diagonally to the bottom of the balloon. Start at the top with a new color, fitting the squares into a houndstooth pattern. Cover the entire balloon.

7. Attach the basket to the balloon. Puncture the uncovered balloon at the top and remove all of the balloon fragments. Make sure the inside of the piñata is completely dry before you fill it, so the candy won't stick to the sides. Fill it about halfway, cover the opening with some tissue squares, and it's ready to hang.

PIÑATA VARIATIONS

The instructions for our piñata balloon are easily adapted to suit any party theme. For a Halloween party, try a monster head, a ghost, or a pumpkin. For a dinosaur birthday party, make a giant, colorful dinosaur egg. For an undersea party, try an octopus or a jellyfish with crepe paper tentacles.

FunFact

The origins of piñata-breaking have nothing to do with celebrating single-digit birthdays. Their original significance was religious. A popular pastime during Lent, the breaking of piñatas represented the rewards inherent in destroying evil.

Faux Fruits

Not all papier-mâché recipes require cooking; for this project, all you need is a simple white glue solution. This idea was contributed to *FamilyFun* by Marianne Cashman of Binghamton, New York, who likes to brighten up her kitchen with a bowl of fruits and vegetables. Because fresh fruits disappear quickly and store-bought silk ones are pricey, Marianne and her daughters have taken to crafting papier-mâché versions to keep the bowl stocked. Experimenting with different produce is their favorite part, but Marianne recommends using hard fruits and vegetables. "The peppers come out nicely," she says, "but lettuce gets soggy."

FunFact
The earliest surviving objects made from papier-mâché are two Chinese helmets created during the second century. They were painted with many coats of lacquer in order to strengthen them for battle.

Materials
- Assorted fruits and vegetables
- Nonstick cooking spray
- White paper towels
- White glue solution (mix 1 cup glue with 3 cups water)
- Waxed paper
- Serrated knife
- Masking tape
- Acrylic paints and paintbrushes
- Sealer

Wash and dry the fruits and vegetables, then spray with nonstick cooking spray. Cut strips of paper towel 1 to 2 inches wide. Dip a strip into the glue solution, pull between your fingers, then wrap it around the fruit. Cover with several layers. (If layers become too wet, apply a layer of dry strips.) Let dry on waxed paper for 2 days.

When the pieces are dry, use a serrated knife to slice each in half lengthwise. Remove the insides, including the skins or rinds. Prepare more glue solution and reassemble each piece by taping the halves together, then covering with layers of glue-moistened strips to conceal the seam. Let dry for 1 day.

To make stems and leaves, cut shapes from paper towels that have been soaked in glue solution and dried. Glue in place, then paint the fruit with two coats. In a ventilated area, spray on glossy sealer (parents only). For a slightly different effect, you can wrap on glue-moistened strips of colored tissue paper instead of painting.

Faux Fruits

3-D Photo Frame

This lasting papier-mâché project lets your child customize a frame for a favorite photo or piece of art. The directions are for a frame with a 5- by 7-inch opening, but you can adapt them for other photo sizes.

Materials

- Metal ruler
- Pencil
- Corrugated cardboard
- Craft knife
- Paintbrush
- White glue solution (⅓ cup white glue and ⅓ cup water)
- 4-inch polystyrene dome
- Newspaper
- 2 adhesive wire-loop picture hangers
- Wire rack
- Sandpaper
- Colored latex enamel paints
- Sealer (optional)
- Heavyweight paper
- Masking tape

First, choose a three-dimensional design for the frame — a soccer ball, a globe, or a flower (simple shapes are easiest to sculpt from the polystyrene). Next, decide what size photo you'd like to frame. Use the ruler and pencil to measure and mark the photo dimensions in the center of the piece of corrugated cardboard. Then, draw the outline of the frame around the window. (Try a 5-inch top border and 2½-inch side and bottom borders.)

Using a craft knife and ruler, cut out the frame, then paint the front and back of the cardboard with the glue solution. This helps stiffen the cardboard and reduce warping. Let the frame dry for several hours. Next, position and glue the polystyrene dome on the dry frame and let it dry.

Tear several sheets of newspaper into inch-wide strips 4 to 6 inches long. Show your child how to paste these strips to the cardboard by first brushing the glue solution on the cardboard's surface, next laying on a newspaper strip, and then smoothing the strip with his fingers. Apply three layers of overlapping strips to the front and back of the frame, being certain to completely cover the polystyrene and all the raw edges. Position the two hangers on the back of the frame 3 to 4 inches from the top edge and secure with glued paper strips. Lay the frame on a wire rack and let it dry for several days, turning it occasionally to ensure even drying.

Have your child lightly sand any rough edges and bumps with the sandpaper before covering the frame with a base coat of paint. Once the paint is dry, he can embellish the design with additional colors. For a protective finish, you can spray sealer (in a well-ventilated area; parents only) on the front and back of the frame. Lastly, place a piece of heavyweight paper a little larger than the frame's opening on the back of the frame; tape it in place, leaving the top edge open for inserting photos or artwork.

3-D Photo Frame

FRAME IT
For more picture frames, turn to page 194

Soap

Soap Block Prints

This technique lets you have some good, clean fun with printmaking. We road-tested several brands of soap before coming up with one soft enough to carve and solid enough to hold a pattern. Kids can easily use the soap blocks to make one-of-a-kind stationery or bookmarks. And the best part is that when you finish, cleaning up is right at your fingertips.

Materials

Bar of glycerin soap (don't substitute), such as Neutrogena
Old-fashioned vegetable peeler, with a carving tip (wrap masking tape around the sides to cover sharp edges) or a toothpick
Acrylic paint
Small paint roller or paintbrush
Paper

Help your kids carve a design in the bar of soap using the vegetable peeler or toothpick. Remind them to dig deep — at least ¼ inch down. When the design is complete, they can blow off the little shavings of soap that cling to the surface and make sure all parts of the design have been carved deeply. Help them roll or brush a small amount of paint onto the surface of the soap block, just enough to coat it.

Place a sheet of paper over the soap and press down firmly on top of the block, being careful not to shift the paper once it has been settled. Peel the paper off; you will have a print of the carved design. If you're making several prints, you'll probably have to reapply paint each time. Periodically use a toothpick to clean the excess paint out of the carved furrows.

Soap Block Prints

Soapy Snowmen

With this frost-free recipe, your kids can sculpt snow folk without leaving the comfort of your family room.

Materials

- 2 cups Ivory Snow
- ½ cup water
- Toothpicks
- Twigs, cloves, shirt buttons, a strip of felt, seed beads, cardboard egg cups, and pipe cleaners

To mix up a batch of faux snow, pour the Ivory Snow in a bowl with the water and whip with an electric beater until the mixture is doughy.

Shape the damp soap into three balls. Stack them by gently pushing a toothpick halfway into the center of the bottom ball. Then, push the middle ball down onto the toothpick until the two balls touch. Do the same for the snowman's head.

Now, add twig arms, clove eyes, shirt buttons, and a felt scarf. To make a smiling mouth, press on a row of seed beads. For a mini carrot nose, color the tip of a short twig with orange paint. For a hat, use an egg cup from a cardboard carton. Or craft a pair of earmuffs out of a pipe cleaner.

As the soap dries (this can take a few hours), it will lose its grayish tinge and turn bright white.

Big Bubbles

Goo

Several *FamilyFun* readers wrote us that they made up packets of our delightful goo for birthday party favors, which we thought was a terrific idea.

Materials

- 8 ounces white or carpenter's glue
- Food coloring (optional)
- 1 cup water
- 20 Mule Team borax

Combine glue, food coloring, and ¾ cup water in a bowl. In a separate bowl, combine 1 tablespoon borax and ¼ cup water. Add the borax mixture to the glue mixture, stirring until a blob forms. Remove the blob. Add another batch of the borax-and-water mixture to the glue mixture. Repeat the process until the glue mixture is all gone. Knead the blobs together and store in an airtight container.

Soapy Snowmen

Squish & Sculpt

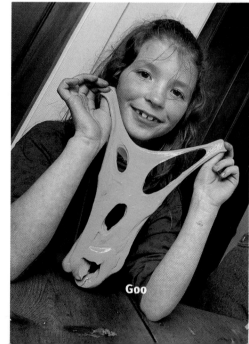

Goo

Plaster of Paris

Miniature Mosaics

Miniature Mosaics

Mosaics are made by pressing small pieces of glass, stone, pottery, or other objects into wet cement or plaster, which then hardens into a permanent work of art. Since time is of the essence, make your plaster mixture a little more watery than directed so you have a few more moments to assemble your design before the plaster dries.

Materials

Shallow plastic container, such as a margarine tub
Pencil and paper
Mosaic tiles (available at craft stores) or colored beads, buttons, marbles, stones, or dry beans
Plaster of Paris
Water
Large plastic bucket
Paint stirrer or long-handled spoon

First, your child should turn her plastic container upside down and trace its circumference onto a piece of paper. Then, she can arrange her mosaic pieces onto the traced area in the design she wants. The simpler the design, the easier it will be to transfer it to the drying plaster. When she is pleased with the arrangement, she can carefully set it aside.

Help your child stir the plaster of Paris and water together in a large bucket, following the directions on the box of plaster. Fill up the plastic container halfway with the prepared plaster. This is a crucial measurement: pouring less than half can produce a mosaic that is too weak to be removed from the container; pouring more than half can result in a mosaic whose design is overwhelmed by too much plaster.

Test the consistency of the drying plaster by lightly touching it every 2 minutes. When the plaster feels like soft clay, your child can begin arranging her design. Starting at the center of the container, she should gently press the first piece into the plaster, then continue until the mosaic design is complete (encourage her to work quickly, as the plaster dries rapidly).

Let the plaster dry for at least 1 hour before trying to remove it from the mold. Help your child gently pull the sides of the container away from the plaster. (If you notice cracking, the plaster has not dried and needs a little longer to set.) Using the balls of your fingers, carefully loosen the mosaic by pushing up on the bottom of the container. Place a soft rag on top of the mosaic to provide cushioning, then gently flip it upside down.

Beach Footprints

On beach vacations, sand seems to end up everywhere, especially between the toes. A simple plaster-casting project lets your child capture that sandy bare-foot feeling — and a record of his feet.

Materials

Plaster of Paris
Small bucket
Water (seawater works fine)
4-inch lengths of string or wire (for hangers, if desired)

Choose a site to cast your molds — the moist, hard-packed sand near (but not too near!) the water's edge works best. Have your child firmly press both feet into the sand. The prints should be about 1½ to 2 inches deep. If your child can't press down hard enough, he can use his fingers to dig down into the print, following its shape. Mix up the plaster of Paris according to the directions on the package, so that it has a thick, creamy consistency. Pour the plaster gently into the prints.

If you want to make hangers, tie a knot about a half inch in from each end of your pieces of wire. As the plaster begins to harden, push the knotted ends into the plaster and let dry. After 10 to 15 minutes, gently dig the foot-prints out of the molds and brush away any excess sand. Set sole-side up in the sun for a while to let harden.

> ### MORE FUN IN THE SUN
> For more beachside plaster crafts, check out the Sea Creatures on page 121 and Animal Tracks on page 128.

Plaster of Paris 101

Plaster of Paris can be found at hardware, craft, and hobby stores (a 4-pound box should cost between two and three dollars). For best results, avoid stirring more than the directions suggest. Also, if you use a mold, make sure it is clean and coat the inside with a thin coat of petroleum jelly to prevent the piece from sticking. Once the plaster has been poured, tap once to release any air bubbles. Allow pieces to dry completely before removing, and use a shellac before painting.

Beach Footprints

Squish & Sculpt

Wax

Wax

Hand-dipped Sparkle Candles

Hand-dipping candles is an almost hypnotic process — and one that's wonderfully old-fashioned, like something out of *Little House on the Prairie*. The slow building of layers takes time, though, so save this project for a free afternoon. This is one craft you want to savor, not rush through.

Materials

    2 to 3 pounds paraffin wax, in chunks
    Wax melting supplies (see sidebar
        at left)
    Wicking, ruler, and scissors
    2 dipping sticks per child (chopsticks
        or 6-inch lengths of dowel)
    Permanent marker
    Tall container of water
    Drying rack
    Pot holders
    Cotton cloth
    Aluminum foil or paper
    Assorted sequins and beads

Follow the directions at left for melting wax (an adults-only job). While you tend the wax, enlist your kids to clear the dipping area and cover it — and the floor — with newspaper. Have the children measure two 9-inch lengths of wicking and tie the pieces to their dipping sticks. Mark each stick with each child's initials. Set up the hot plate, water bath, and drying rack with plenty of space between, and establish a path of traffic flow. When the wax is melted, carry the can to the table using pot holders and place it on the hot plate, set on low heat. Stand or seat

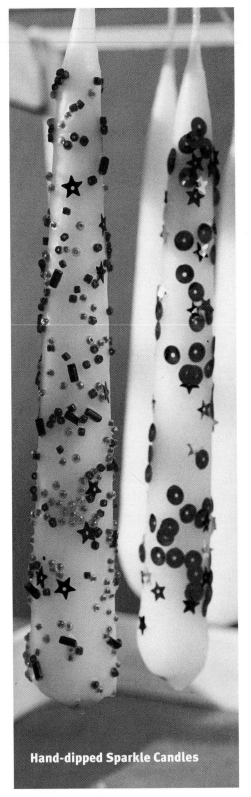

Hand-dipped Sparkle Candles

yourself next to the wax station for close supervision.

1. Invite the kids, one at a time, to prepare their wicks. First, they should dip a wick into the wax, let it cool momentarily, then pull it taut to straighten. Next, they can dip it in

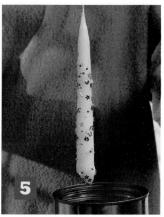

water and run the clean cotton cloth down the wick to dry it. Leaving this wick on the rack, they can repeat the process with a second wick.

2. After the wicks are coated, the kids can begin dipping in earnest. Alternating between candles, they should dip and raise their wicks in a smooth, continuous motion. Remind them not to stop mid-dip: if the wick stays in the wax too long, the candle melts away. After each wax dip, the kids should move aside to dip their candles in the water and dry them with the cloth. This cools and straightens the candles. It takes about twenty-five wax dips to form a candle ½ inch in diameter.

3. In between rounds of dipping, let the wicks air-dry on the rack.

4. Once the candles are ½ to 1 inch in diameter, set out a piece of paper or aluminum foil and sprinkle on sequins and beads. Dip the candles and quickly roll them in the decorations.

5. To seal in the beads, dip each candle quickly in and out of the wax. Allow the candles to air-dry or dip them in water and dry them. The kids can repeat these steps a few times to get good overall coverage of the sequins and beads but should not apply more than two or three layers, or the candles will be lumpy.

LIGHT UP THE NIGHT

For other luminaria craft projects, check out the Tin Can Lanterns on page 40, the Ice Lanterns on page 122, the carved pumpkins on pages 224 and 225. and the Turnip Top Flashlights on page 230.

BIRTHDAY CANDLES

FamilyFun reader Cathy Moore of Kennesaw, Georgia, reports that her two daughters had a ball making these hand-dipped sparkle candles. Nine-year-old Sarah managed the whole project by herself — and even came up with a way to make it easier for her four-year-old sister, Rachel. The girls grabbed a box of birthday cake candles, dipped them one by one into the melted paraffin, and then rolled them in the sequins. Now they can't wait to light them in honor of the next birthday in the house!

Squish & Sculpt

Sand Candle

CANDLE SUPPLIES

Paraffin wax is available at almost all grocery stores. The other materials for the projects on these pages are available at most candle-making stores or from one of these mail-order sources.

General Wax & Candle Company sells sheets of honeycomb beeswax, wax dyes, and wicking; call 800-WAX-STORE for a catalog.

Yankee Candle Company (800-243-1776) sells paraffin, wax dyes, and wicking.

The HearthSong Catalog (800-382-6778) offers white ball candles, beeswax kits, and decorating wax.

If your kids truck home enough sand after a day at the shore to build another beach, here's a great use for it. A word of caution: your help with this project is crucial for safety.

Materials

> Large heat-proof mixing bowl
> Sand, enough to nearly fill the bowl
> Coffee can of melted paraffin (see page 98 for melting directions)
> Wicking
> Thin wooden dowel or stick

Fill the bowl three quarters full with slightly damp sand and ask your child to dig a mold the size of his fist. Using your hands, bend one side of the empty coffee can rim to form a spout. Fill the can halfway with paraffin and melt; when the wax has melted, turn off the heat. Cut the wicking to 6 to 8 inches longer than your mold is deep. Rest the dowel across the bowl's top and tie one end of the wick around it. Press the other end into the bottom of the mold. Now, pour the wax (parents only) into the mold until it reaches about 1 inch from the top. When the candle is cool, remove it from the mold, brush off excess sand, and trim the wick.

Flower Candles

With this easy technique, kids can turn a plain, store-bought candle into a delicate table decoration.

Materials

> Store-bought pillar candle
> Pressed flowers, leaves, and petals (must be thoroughly dry)
> Glue stick
> Pliers
> Coffee can half full of melted, uncolored paraffin (see page 98 for melting directions)

Your child can decorate the sides of the candle by rubbing a glue stick on the wax and then carefully pressing on the flowers, leaves, and petals with her fingertips.

To seal in the design, grip the wick firmly with the pliers and dip the whole candle once or twice into the can of melted wax (go slowly and be careful that the wax doesn't spill over).

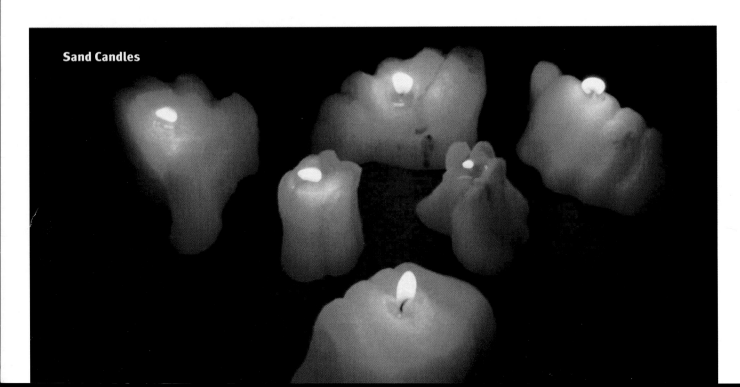

Sand Candles

color over a long length of another and roll them into a tight spiral log ½ inch in diameter and 1½ inches long. When you've made about eight logs, use the knife to cut each one into as many slices as you can. Firmly press the wax slices all around the outside of the candle, starting at the base and working up. Continue placing the slices as closely together as possible until the whole candle is covered.

Spiral Candles

Spiral Candles

When *FamilyFun* contributor Maggie Megaw's daughter Anna took one of these to school, all her friends wanted to learn how to make them. Happily, the project requires little instruction and, like the rolled candles on page 102, no dipping. Young kids can do everything but slice the spirals. Older kids can take the candle from start to finish.

Materials

Decorating wax strips (see page 100 for candle-making supplies)

Craft knife or unserrated butter knife

Plain ball or short pillar candle

Have your child choose a few favorite combinations of decorating wax. Cut each strip into two pieces that are 2¾ inches long and one piece 2 inches long. Lay a short length of one

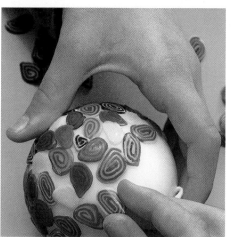

FunFact

A candle 80 feet high and 8½ feet in diameter was exhibited at the 1897 Stockholm Exhibition.

Beeswax Totem Pole

This totem pole is an absorbing project for older kids, who have the patience and dexterity to work with detailed designs.

Materials

> Sheet of any color honeycomb beeswax
> 9-inch length of wicking
> Decorating beeswax

Help your child cut a 5⅓- by 8-inch piece of beeswax. Lay the wicking along the 8-inch edge of the wax and roll it into a straight ¾-inch cylinder (below left and center). To adorn the pole, cut strips of decorating beeswax for the faces and bodies of the animals and embellish them with beady eyes, beaks, lips, teeth, wings, paws, or claws (below right). (It's easiest to work down from the top.) To differentiate between one creature and another, knead contrasting colors of wax into thin snakes and lay them around the candle between two sections, or use them to outline the features in the faces.

Beeswax Totem Pole

Rocket Ship

Perfect for a dinner table launchpad, this spacecraft gets its tapered shape from a diagonally rolled beeswax base.

Materials

> Ruler and craft knife
> 8- by 8-inch sheet of white honeycomb beeswax
> Wicking
> Blue and red honeycomb beeswax
> Yellow decorating or honeycomb beeswax

Help your child measure and cut a 3-inch-wide strip off one end of the beeswax sheet. Cut the remaining rectangle in half, corner to corner. Set one triangle aside and turn the other so that the 8-inch end is facing your child.

Have him cut a piece of wicking about 9 inches long and lay it along the end closest to him, starting ½ inch in from the right angle. Crimping the edge of the wax carefully over the wick, he should roll it up one section at a time. Once he has gotten the candle started, he can spread out his fingers along the length of the candle and roll it the rest of the way. If the candle rolls up a bit off center, stand it on a flat surface and gently press down.

Once the base is finished, use the ruler and knife to cut wax strips about 2¼ inches wide in blue, white, and red.

Wrap the blue strip around the base of the candle, cutting away any excess so that the ends just meet. Line up the end of the red strip with the ends of the first and wrap it around the candle so you create one continuous outer surface. Cut off any excess length and repeat for the third band.

Rocket Ship

Help your child cut a piece of blue beeswax and wrap it around the tip of the rocket to form the nose cone.

From a piece of cardboard, work together to design a template for the tailfins and cut out six of them in red beeswax. Pair them up and press their edges together, then press the fins gently but firmly onto the body of the rocket, spacing them evenly around the fuselage. Finally, help your child cut out the letters *U*, *S*, and *A* (or the letters of her name) from a strip of yellow decorating wax or knead yellow beeswax and form them by hand.

Beeswax Castle

This easy design makes the best use of the honeycomb pattern, cleverly mimicking a real castle's stone walls.

Materials

- 2 sheets of any color honeycomb beeswax
- 4 4-inch pieces of wicking
- Toothpicks
- Decorating beeswax

Help your child cut four 3- by 16-inch pieces of wax to make the towers. Position each piece with the short end toward her, lay the wick along the edge, and roll the wax into a straight cylinder. Cut four more strips of wax, each 1 inch wide. Wrap one strip around each tower, making a sleeve about ½ inch thick. Then, slide the sleeve off the tower, place it on a flat surface, and cut out the crenellations. Slide the sleeve back onto the tower. For walls, cut out four 2½- by 3½-inch pieces. Cut crenellations along one long side of each piece and attach to the towers. Decorate with windows and doors in contrasting colors and medieval-style banners made from wax and toothpicks.

Working with Beeswax

The primary material for these candles — honeycomb sheets of beeswax — is a wonder. It comes in an array of bright colors and can be rolled, cut, pressed together (the pieces stick together without any glue), kneaded, and shaped in many ways. And because there's no melting of hot wax, these projects are suitable even for very young children (with an adult to help cut and position the pieces).

Beeswax Castle

Squish & Sculpt

Chapter Six

Back to Nature

O NE THING we learn early on as parents is that if you're planning to take your kids on a hike through the woods, along a beach, or even across a meadow, you'll need to allot plenty of time. It's not that our children can't keep up with us, but rather that they lag behind on purpose — to watch a ladybug climb to the top of a blade of grass, to marvel at the intricacy of a spiderweb glistening in the dew, or to pocket an unusual stone (if they can resist skipping it across a stream). For kids, the natural world is instantly and totally fascinating, even rivaling a store-bought toy or the latest video game.

That's what this chapter is all about. It's filled with ideas that let your kids take their favorite outdoor experiences a step further, by turning natural finds into lasting treasures. For example, they can build a toy raft out of sticks (page 107), fashion a crown out of daisies (page 116), or sculpt a giant rabbit out of snow (page 122). And that's just for starters. With a little imagination and seasons full of opportunities, the possibilities are endless.

Craft with the seasons in mind. Once you have read this chapter, pick out a few seasonal projects your family would like to try. Go on an autumn leaf hunt and make leaf-print greeting cards. Plant a house of sunflowers in your garden in the spring, or build a backyard bird feeder on a winter day.

Think with your senses. When choosing a project, take your clues from the natural world. If you love the smell of pine needles or eucalyptus leaves, mix your

Homemade Potpourri, page 115

Shell Painting, page 120

own potpourri. If a certain rock looks like a bullfrog or a turtle, make a painted doorstop.

Work outside whenever practical. Make the environment part of your kids' crafting experience. Set up the supplies you'll need on a backyard picnic table, under a shady tree, or even on the beach, if it makes sense.

Seize the opportunity to learn. While nature crafts are a blast in and of themselves, don't stop there. Are you planning to look for animal tracks and cast them in plaster? Pick up a guidebook at the library so you'll be able to read up on the creatures that left their distinctive mark.

You don't need a backyard to try nature crafts. Just because you live in the city doesn't mean the crafts are off-limits. Take your family on an outing to a park or beach to collect pinecones, leaves, or shells for your craft projects.

Show respect for wildlife and their habitats. Above all, follow the lead of true conservationists and make it a family policy to have as little impact on the natural world as possible. If you need sticks for a particular project, search the ground for fallen branches instead of cutting them from trees. If you discover a salamander under a rock, remind your kids that it belongs in the wild.

Stone-aged Art, page 110

Sticks & Stones

Wooden Raft

Huck Finn knew how to ride out the dog days of summer: drifting down-river on a homemade raft. Your kids can follow suit (on a much smaller scale) by building a miniature craft out of sticks to launch in a stream or a wading pool.

Materials

Dry sticks
Hedge clippers
Glue
Fishing line
Small piece of cloth
String

For the raft base, use the clippers to cut two foot-long lengths from the thickest stick (a parent's job). Lay them on a flat working surface, 6 inches apart and parallel to one another.

Cut the remaining sticks into 10-inch lengths to use for flooring (you'll need about two dozen). Lay the flooring across the base, one stick at a time. Start in the center and work your way toward the sides, gluing the pieces in place as you go.

To make sure the raft holds (the wood will swell when it's wet), lash the flooring ends to the base with fishing line. Tie a piece of line to an end of one of the base sticks. Then, weave the line over and between the flooring boards and around the base, working your way to the other end. Tie off the line. Use the same method to lash the opposite side of the raft.

For a sail, cut a triangle (8 inches tall and 7 inches across the base) from the piece of cloth. Apply glue along the

Wooden Raft

8-inch edge of the sail, then wrap the glued portion around a slender stick. Wedge the lower end of the stick between the flooring and use string to tie the top of the mast to both sides of the raft base.

Finally, tie a long piece of string to the back of the raft for launching the craft and then pulling it back to shore.

Pine Needle Nannies

Stick Figures

Children have a knack for imagining entire worlds in the crook of a tree or a patch of meadow grass. This autumn craft lets them bring those musings to life by turning acorns and sticks into a village of woodsy elves.

Materials

> Unshelled acorns
> Fine-tipped marker
> Craft knife
> Twigs
> Leaves
> Glue
> Meadow grass and other nature finds

Babes in the Woods:
Draw eyes and a mouth on the bottom of an unshelled acorn — the pointed tip of the shell will serve as a nose. Next, use a craft knife (a parent's job) to bore a small neck hole into the side of the shell at the base of the cap. For a body, fit the end of a short, forked twig into the neck opening. Then, glue on a leaf shawl or cape. Or, wrap a colorful leaf dress around the twig body and belt it with a blade of grass.

Pine Needle Nannies:
Make acorn heads following the method given above. For the nannies' wispy bodies, just fit the stemmed end of a clump of pine needles into each neck opening

and use a drop of glue to secure it, if necessary.

Mr. & Mrs. A. Corn:
For each figure, make a body by gluing together the ends of two forked twigs — one fork should resemble outstretched arms; the other should look like legs. Attach acorn heads, as previously described. For Mrs. Corn's grass skirt, tie the top of a bunch of pine needles around her trunk with a piece of grass. To make Mr. Corn's pants, glue a smaller bunch of needles around each leg. Then, glue a leaf sweater around his arms and trunk. Finally, glue on a pair of pumpkin seed shoes.

Pinecone Pony:
To make the pony's body, glue the ends of four straight twig legs to a medium-size pinecone. For a head and neck, glue a small pinecone to the end of a pine needle–covered twig and trim the needles to create a spiky mane. Then, glue the base of the neck to the body. Lastly, glue a thick bunch of pine needles to the back of the body for a flowing tail.

Straw Man:
Cut twenty 5-inch lengths of dry meadow grass with scissors. Tie them together in a bunch, an inch from the top, with another piece of grass or string to create a head and body. Divide the body to form legs and bind each one with grass a half inch from the bottom. For arms, slip a single 4-inch shaft of grass through the center of the body. Finally, use a fine-tipped marker to draw on a face.

Straw Man

Babes in the Woods

Pinecone Pony

Mr. A. Corn

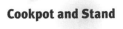

Cookpot and Stand

Mrs. A. Corn

Cook Pot and Stand: First, make the stand — you'll need two forked twigs and a single straight stick. Using a pair of gardening clippers, trim both twigs to create matching V shapes, as shown. Set the Vs upside down on the ground, then tie the ends of the straight stick to the tops of the twigs with twine or string. For the cook pot, cut a short piece of twine and glue its midsection to the inside of an inverted acorn top. Once the glue dries, loop the twine ends around the middle of the stand and tie them together.

Paper Tepee

This takeoff on a Native American dwelling, made from wooden poles and paper (instead of hide), makes an exciting playhouse. Set it up in a corner of your yard or, if you don't have the space outdoors, try building it indoors.

Materials

8 6-foot bamboo poles (available at garden stores) or 16 4-foot-long wooden dowels (with ½-inch diameters)

Twine

Masking tape

2 paper drop cloths (available at hardware or paint stores)

Poster paint

Back to Nature

Paper Tepee

Pile the poles on the ground with the ends lined up. (If you're substituting wooden dowels, use two to create a 6-foot pole by overlapping the ends and then taping them together.) About a foot down from the tops, loosely tie the ends of the poles together with twine. Stand the bundle on the ground and spread the untied ends into a large circle. Tape the drop cloths to the framework (you may want to cut them in half first for easier handling). Be sure to leave a large opening for an entrance.

Next, your kids can use poster paints to decorate the tepee walls with pictures and symbols. The floor can be covered with leaves or, if you have one, an old rug for extra comfort.

Under the Tepee Top

When *FamilyFun* reader Judy Bacarisse Evans from Houston suggested that her daughter's Daisy Troop recreate our paper tepee for their Thanksgiving feast, her coleaders were skeptical — it would have to be big enough to hold ten active five-year-olds. Judy's husband was able to locate eight 10-foot metal poles and helped wrap the paper around the frame. Then, the girls painted the exterior using twigs and pine needles for authentic-looking decorations. The tepee was a rousing success — and roomy enough to fit everyone in for a feast of beef jerky and corn bread.

Paper Cave Paintings

You don't need a stone wall to mimic the expressive and elegant technique of cave painting. Here's a project that lets your child create "ancient" art on brown paper.

To begin, help your child prepare the surface of a brown paper bag so that it has a rough and worn appearance like a cave wall. Crinkle the paper and then spray it with water in the sink (don't soak it). Let it dry completely (you can use a hair dryer to speed the drying time).

Using a pencil, your child can then sketch the animals, figures, or symbols of his choice on the paper. Next, he should go over the pencil marks with black marker, making the lines bold. Then, he can color in details, such as eyes, ears, horns, tails, or antlers.

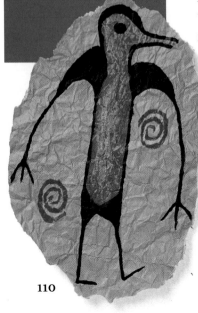

Stone-aged Art

More than 15,000 years ago, some of the world's earliest artists recorded history by drawing charging buffalo, leaping deer, and wild horses on cave walls. They used burned wood, soil, and leaves to create strong, black outlines and muted colors. Your kids can tell their own stories cave painting style by using paints and berry ink to draw stick figures or local landmarks on stone. Later, they can use their stone-aged art to decorate a garden or patio walkway.

Materials

    Flat, porous rocks, such as
        sandstone or flagstone (available
        at garden stores)
    Acrylic paints and paintbrushes
    Natural berry ink (see
        recipe below)
    Sandpaper or steel wool

First, help your kids clean the rocks with water and a brush. Then, they can use the paintbrushes to add designs. Or, for fun, they can try using pussy willows or feathers to apply the paint. Remember, the simpler and more primitive the designs, the easier they are to create. When they've finished painting, the kids can then enhance the images by outlining them with natural berry ink.

To give the finished art an aged look, just place the rocks outdoors and let the sun, wind, and rain work their magic. You can speed the process along by scrubbing the stone with sandpaper or steel wool. The porous rock sucks in some of the paint, so there's no danger of erasing your images entirely.

Natural Berry Ink: Mash 1 cup of blueberries or blackberries in a large bowl. Then, place them in a saucepan with ½ cup of water, 1 teaspoon of vinegar, and 1 teaspoon of salt. Bring to a boil. Reduce heat and simmer for 5 to 10 minutes. Let cool. Pour the mixture through a strainer, catching the ink in a clean glass bowl or jar.

Rock Group

With some paint and a little imagination, your child can turn a pocketful of stones into a family of rock stars or an entourage of stony-faced creatures.

Materials

- Assorted pebbles and stones
- Glue
- Acrylic paints and paintbrushes

First, wipe off any sand or dirt and then study each stone to see what its shape or composition suggests. A rough, chunky rock may resemble a crouching cat, a toad, or an owl. Tiny, smooth pebbles can make great ladybugs or bumblebees. A flat, round stone can be used for a snail shell or a face; long, thin ones make natural arms, legs, and tails.

To make an animal, start with a larger stone as a base for the body. Then, use glue to attach smaller stones for eyes, ears, wings, antennae, and feet. For stone people, glue arms, legs, and heads to rock bodies or leave the limbs unattached for future mixing and matching.

Use acrylics to highlight the facial features and paint on hair. Dress the figures any way you want — in stripes or checks, ties or dresses, tutus or Stetsons.

Rock Group

Back to Nature

Plants & Mushrooms

Leaf Critters

PRESERVING LEAVES

Here's a trick that will let your kids preserve their favorite fall leaves to use as colorful bookmarks or to arrange in a glass jar for a vibrant winter bouquet. In a saucepan, combine two parts water and one part glycerin (available in small bottles at most pharmacies) and bring the mixture to a boil (a parent's job).

Meanwhile, your kids can prepare their leaves by gently brushing away any dirt. Next, pour the heated solution into a plastic container. Carefully place the leaves in the solution, using a pencil to completely submerge them. Keep the container in a cool, dark place until the leaves change color slightly. Then, remove the leaves and wipe off the excess solution with a paper towel.

Leaf Critters

This strutting rooster and swimming frog are just two of the playful creatures featured in *Look What I Did With A Leaf!* (Walker and Company), a beautifully illustrated children's book that identifies different types of leaves and how they grow.

Materials

Leaves
Paper towels and newspaper
Cardboard
Rubber cement
Clear Con-Tact paper

First, gather leaves of various colors, shapes, and sizes. Soak them in warm water and blot them dry with paper towels. Place the leaves between two pieces of newspaper and cover with telephone books to press. After a week, the leaves will be ready. Set up a work space with cardboard, rubber cement, and the pressed leaves. Begin sorting your leaves and designing your animal (a sawtooth leaf for a rooster's tail or a tiny leaf for a mouse's eyes?). Cement the leaves to cardboard and dry for a day, then cover with Con-Tact paper.

Autumn Card Deck

With this variation on Old Maid, your kids won't have to go outdoors to shuffle through the leaves. It's played with a deck made from bright fall leaves.

Materials

Leaves (10 matching
    pairs and a
    single odd one)
Paper towels
Glue
21 index cards

First you'll need to press the leaves by laying them between paper towels and stacking books on top. After a few days, remove the leaves and glue each one onto an index card. Let the glue dry.

To play the game, you'll need four kids. Pass out all the cards and have the players hold their cards in their hands (blank side out). In turn, each child picks a card from the person on his left and lays down any matching pair. Continue until all the pairs are matched. The child left holding the odd leaf wins.

Autumn Card Deck

Leaf-print Cards

Going on a leaf hunt is part of the appeal of making these cards, which are great to send to relatives during the holidays.

Materials

> Writing paper (white or off-white, preferably)
> Autumn leaves
> Poster paints and paintbrushes

First, make a blank card by folding a sheet of paper in half widthwise. Next, place a leaf vein-side up on top of a newspaper-covered surface and have your child dab paint onto it. Carefully picking up the leaf, she should place it paint-side down on the front of the card and press on it with her hand to make a print. (You may need to make a few test prints to figure out the right amount of paint.) Repeat with other leaves, let dry, then add your holiday greeting.

Leaf Rubbing: To make quick and pretty cards without using paint, try this leaf-rubbing technique. Pick your leaves while they're still on the tree. (The dried-out variety will crumble if the artist gets too enthusiastic.) Place a leaf, vein-side up, inside a blank card. Then, with the colored pencils of her choice, your child should gently rub over the leaf, so that the shape becomes visible on the cover of the card.

Designer Mushrooms

Mushrooms may be great on pizza and burgers, but place a few on a piece of paper and they're truly amazing. After a while, they will release spores from their caps to create distinctive patterns.

Leaf-print Cards

White button mushrooms work well for this project.

Materials

> Fresh, whole mushrooms (edible varieties from the grocery store only)
> Paring knife
> Construction paper
> Drinking glass or glass bowl
> Nonaerosol hair spray (optional)

Carefully remove the stems from the mushrooms. Expose the gills by using a knife (a parent's job) to trim back the lower edges of the caps. Place the mushrooms on a sheet of paper and cover each one with an inverted glass. Let stand overnight. Then, gently lift first the glasses, then the mushrooms, to reveal the spore prints. To preserve the designs, coat them with nonaerosol hair spray.

Designer Mushrooms

Flowers

Sunflower House

Sunflower House

You don't need a hammer and nails, or even wood, to build this pretty little house — just sunflower seeds for planting the walls and a little TLC to help them grow.

Materials

Gardening tools
Mammoth sunflower seeds
Teddy Bear or Dwarf sunflower
    seeds

The best time to start planting will of course depend on your location, but generally any time after the last frost should be okay. Choose a sunny spot where the soil is dry and drains well — sunflowers can take the heat but will suffer from overwatering. Keep in mind that the taller sunflower varieties will also need moderately rich soil, although the shorter ones will grow in poor soil conditions.

Before planting, loosen the soil with the gardening tools. Then, sow the seeds (according to the package directions) in a horseshoe shape, alternating Mammoth sunflower seeds (for height) and Teddy Bear or Dwarf sunflower seeds (to fill in the walls).

While waiting for the seeds to sprout (it takes 2 to 3 weeks in warm temperatures), your child can spruce up the grounds around her house site — laying a stepping-stone walk-way to its door or making a welcome sign.

Flower Pounding

At a craft fair two years ago, *FamilyFun* reader Fredda Parish Lake of Doylestown, Pennsylvania, saw a woman make prints by hammering on a leaf between two pieces of fabric. Fascinated, Fredda wondered if you could make prints with flowers. She went home and tried with husband Larry and daughters Laura and Julia (ages eleven and seven) as willing partners. They found that pansies didn't work, and that blue lobelia printed well; red impatiens were too bright, but pink ones left a delicate color. "You just need to play with it," Fredda says. The girls have since used the technique to make stationery, a table runner, and quilt pieces. One of Laura's designs even won her first place at the Middletown Grange Fair.

Materials

- Paper bags
- Unbleached muslin cloth
- Fresh leaves and flowers
- Hammer
- Butter knife
- Paper

Cover a smooth, hard surface with paper bags and spread out the fabric. Arrange a leaf and flower design on one half of the fabric, then fold the other half over the design. Using a hammer, pound on top of the leaves or flowers, being sure to go all the way to the edges. When the color has bled through the fabric, open it up and scrape off the plant residue with the butter knife. You'll have a mirror image of the leaves and flowers. The fabric pieces make great pillow fronts or quilt

Flower Pounding

squares, though they will fade after repeated washings (use cold water).

For an alternative to the mirror image method, simply place the flowers on the fabric, cover with a sheet of waxed paper, and pound away. You can also use the same method to pound leaves and flowers onto paper to make floral stationery or gift tags.

HOMEMADE POTPOURRI

Throughout history, fragrant flowers and herbs have been mixed together to freshen the air and add a little spice to life. Here's how your kids can custom-mix a colorful blend of potpourri to use in their rooms or to give as a gift.

When a bouquet starts to fade, remove the petals and spread them out to dry. Later, place them in a bowl or basket. For extra color and texture, blend in natural objects, such as bark, pine needles, seashells, or eucalyptus leaves. Or liven up the mixture by adding cinnamon sticks and citrus peels, dried rosemary or basil, or even a quick spray of your favorite cologne.

Back to Nature

Daisy Crown

to another. In case you didn't catch the directions back when you were a flower child, here they are.

Materials
Bunch of daisies (or dandelions)
Craft knife

Pick a slew of daisies or dandelions with stems at least a few inches long. Each child will need about twenty-five, which includes extras for error. Use the craft knife (a parent's job) or a fingernail, if you're making a dandelion crown, to make a small slit in the flower stems, 2 inches below each blossom.

Next, show your child how to slip one flower's stem through the slit in a second stem and pull it until you get to the blossom. Continue to add daisies in this manner until you've made a chain the right length for your child's head.

To turn the chain into a crown, twist the last stem around the first. Then, if the stems are long, intertwine them to make the crown more secure.

FunFact
The world's longest daisy chain was made on May 27, 1985, in Great Britain and measured 6,980 feet and 7 inches.

Daisy Crown

Funny how you can pack your summer full of exotic activities, and then your kids will remember this one: sitting with you on the edge of a field, weaving together daisy chains. Making a floral crown is one of those woodland skills traditionally passed along from one kid

Coloring Carnations

Your kids can learn about capillary action with a trick that gives a new tint to white carnations. When purchasing the white carnations at a neighborhood florist or supermarket, avoid the "elegant" variety; they do not work as well.

To start, help your child trim the ends of his carnations at an angle, cutting the stems 6 inches from the flower. Place each carnation in its own glass or vase and fill the glasses with 2 inches of water. Add a few teaspoons of food coloring to each one (your child can mix the colors to arrive at his favorite tints). In about 24 hours, the edges of the petals will be flecked with color. Within 2 days or so, the color will have spread to give a faded tint to the whole flower. The longer you leave the stems in the water, the brighter the color will be.

Flower Press

Flower Press

Pressed flowers make wonderful keepsakes from a summer hike or memorable vacation spot — and they can be used for an assortment of crafts, like sprucing up some plain stationery. Just arrange them on a sheet and then cover them with pieces of clear Con-Tact paper.

The easiest way to press flowers and leaves is to lay them between the pages of a heavy book (telephone books are ideal). But, if your family plans to collect flowers on a trip, or if you choose blossoms that wither rapidly, a flower press will come in handy.

Materials

　　Cardboard (2 rectangular pieces
　　　that are the same size)
　　Craft knife
　　2 36-inch lengths of ribbon
　　Paper or newsprint (cut an inch
　　　smaller than the cardboard)

Dried Flowers

Using the craft knife (parents only), cut four slits the width of the ribbon in the corners of each piece of cardboard. The slits should be parallel to the longer sides and 1 inch in from the edges. Stack the cardboard pieces. Thread the ribbon as shown. (The press should be able to open like a book.) Place several sheets of the paper between the cardboard pieces to absorb moisture from the flowers.

When laying the flowers in the press, be careful to arrange the blossoms and stems between the paper sheets so that the plants are not touching. It's also a good idea to place flowers of the same thickness between the same sheets of paper in order to apply equal pressure.

Once the blossoms are in place, pull the ribbons tightly and tie the ends together. To increase the pressure, place several heavy books on top of the press and leave it for about a week, or until the flowers dry. If the paper becomes damp or corroded, you should replace it every few days.

Dried Flowers

Your family can enjoy summer blossoms year-round by turning their favorite picks into everlasting bouquets. Choose ones that are just about to open completely. Cut them in the morning, after the dew has dried but before the flowers droop in the midday heat. Divide them into small bunches and twist a rubber band around the stems (larger bundles prevent air from circulating). Then, hang the bunches upside down, keeping them spaced at least 6 inches apart.

For the best results colorwise, let them dry thoroughly in a dimly lit area, such as an attic or pantry. They will not cure properly in basements or other damp places. Your everlastings should be ready to arrange within 2 weeks.

Back to Nature

70844

Sand & Shells

An Octopus Built of Sand

Sculptor Dale Zarrella, who lives on Maui with his eight-year-old daughter, Shala, has carved a menagerie of animal likenesses from ice, wood, stone, wax, and even chocolate. When *FamilyFun* invited him to try his hand in sand, molding a giant octopus that would inspire our beachgoing readers to try sand-sculpting themselves, his 25-foot creation surpassed our expectations. Zarrella, it turns out, is savvy about octopi. Studying them in the island's tide pools, he has witnessed them change color instantaneously and peered into their eerily humanlike eyes. He has also watched native Hawaiians carry them from the surf, bound for the dinner table. His impression of the new medium? "It's amazing what detail you can create in sand," says the artist. "My wheels are turning." And from what we've seen, the beach is his limit.

Materials

    Cornstarch
    Plastic spray bottle
    Stick or piece of driftwood
    Sand
    Trowel or large spoon

1. Dissolve a bit of cornstarch in fresh or saltwater and pour the mixture into the plastic spray bottle.

Then, use the stick or driftwood to make a simple sketch on the beach. Draw a bulbous body from which eight arms extend and intertwine. Pile and pat down sand atop the outline.

2. Use your hands to shape two rows

of sand domes on a tentacle's underside to resemble the suckers octopi use to trap fish and shrimp. Scoop out the centers of the domes with a trowel or a large spoon.

3. Mist the sculpture frequently with the cornstarch solution to keep it from drying out and crumbling during the process.

4. Finally, bask in the company of your octopus!

Beachcomber Towel

If your beach bums really want to stand out in the crowd, you can help them decorate their beach towels with snazzy footprints. Besides serving a practical purpose, the towel will let your kids compare the size of their feet over the years.

Working outdoors, spread out a beach towel and place stones or other heavy objects along the entire edge to keep it flat. Next, generously paint the soles of your child's feet — don't forget the toes — with nontoxic fabric paint and have him slowly walk across the top of the towel. You can add another coat of paint to each foot just before it's set down, or just let the footprints fade out.

Have a bucket of soapy water ready at the end of the trail. Then, refer to the package for directions on setting the color and washing the towel.

An Octopus Built of Sand

4

Sculpt a Dune Buggy

Here's a beach craft your kids will really get into — a two-seater dune buggy that comes with all the options (sand dollar headlights, a Frisbee steering wheel, a driftwood windshield, and a pebble license plate). To get your assembly line rolling, help your kids pile up a big mound of sand and pack it down firm. Working from the top down, sculpt the car's body, rounding the hood and trunk, carving fat tires into the sides, and digging out a seat for the driver and passenger. Then, add a shell hood ornament and a beach grass antenna, or whatever else your kids dream up.

Beach Comb

Whether your child sculpts his palace on the beach or in a backyard sandbox, this giant cardboard comb can come in handy for clearing and leveling a building site or for swirling designs on or around castle walls. This nifty tool is inspired by *Wacky Cakes and Water Snakes* (Penguin Books), a season-by-season collection of crafts and activities for kids.

Materials

> Corrugated cardboard
> Glue
> Craft knife
> Acrylic paints and paintbrushes
> Acrylic gloss

To fashion the comb, first cut four 6- by 15-inch pieces of corrugated cardboard and glue them one on top of another. Once the glue dries, use a craft knife (parents only) to cut out seven 1- by 3-inch notches along one long edge. Your child can decorate the comb

with acrylic paints (bright colors will be easier to spot against the sand). Finally, seal the comb with a few coats of clear acrylic gloss.

Shell Painting

With rounded frames and smooth, chalklike surfaces that soak up paint, seashells make good palm-size canvases for your children's seascapes.

Materials

> Seashells (chalkier, white shells work best)
> Jar of freshwater (for rinsing shells and mixing paint)
> Watercolor or acrylic paints and paintbrushes

To start, rinse a few shells with freshwater and let them dry in the sun. Your child can paint pictures on the inside of each shell, being careful to let each color dry before adding the next for a crisp picture, or letting the colors blend for an abstract splash of color. Set out in the sun until dry.

Shell Painting

Sea Creatures

Just as a day at the beach seems to fit the bill for various ages and temperaments, so does the following project. The procedure is simple enough: to create a decorative, plaster-cast mask using beachcombed objects. The outcome is another story. Each mask, created facedown in the sand, hides its identity until unmolded and washed in the sea.

Materials

Beach stuff, such as shells, driftwood, sea glass, or feathers
Plaster of Paris
Water buckets for mixing and cleaning up
Stirring tool for the squeamish (a bare hand works best!)
String, about 4 inches per mask

An ideal spot to cast your molds is the moist, hard-packed strip of beach just above the wet tidal sand — but not too close to the water lest the incoming waves wash over your setting plaster.

1. Collect elements for facial features.

2. Dig an oval hole in the sand that measures about 5 to 8 inches tall and 2 inches deep (the sides of deeper molds may crumble while you are putting in your objects).

3. Arrange your beach finds in the hole. Remind your kids to think in reverse since you are seeing the mask from the inside out. Open eyes and mouths, teeth, and hair look great but require engineering, and firm sand, if you want them to hold in place. If you bury feathers, seaweed, or rope in the bottom of the mold so that enough projects up for the plaster to grip, they will dangle or stick out from the mask without being completely embedded.

Next, mix the plaster in your bucket — you can use seawater. (A standard box will make three to six masks, depending on the amount used for each.) Usually, a thick cream consistency works well — too runny, and your plaster can seep beneath objects, so that they are hidden when you uncover the masks; too thick, and the plaster dislodges objects and messes up the mask's shape.

4. As soon as the plaster is ready, slowly pour it over your hand, held just an inch or two above the impression, to break its fall. Keep the plaster layer about an inch thick.

For a hanger, tie a knot about a half inch from each end of the string. When the plaster begins to thicken, push the knots into the back of the mask to harden in place as the plaster dries.

5. Before the plaster becomes too firm, dig the sand away from the mask (rather than yanking the mask out). Then, use ocean water to gently wash away any flaws — you will have a few moments to manipulate the plaster's surface (cleaning off, digging in, rubbing away excess sand) before the plaster hardens completely.

Snow

Neighborhood Snow Bunny

Ice Lantern

Add a little warmth to a cold snap with a glistening outdoor candleholder. Fill the bottom of a bucket with a few inches of water and set it outside to freeze. Next, cut the top off a 2-liter plastic bottle and set the bottom in the bucket, on top of the ice. Place a heavy object in the bottle to weigh it down. Then, fill the bucket (but not the bottle) with more water and let it freeze solid. Pour warm water on the outside of the bucket and slide the ice out. Finally, fill the bottle with warm water to loosen it. Remove the bottle and insert a votive candle.

Neighborhood Snow Zoo

After a snowstorm, the first thing most kids want to do is build a snowman. To expand on this popular winter pastime, try making a zoo full of animals in your backyard.

Materials
- Snow
- Sticks
- Shovels or large spoons

Have the kids begin by rolling together and stacking balls of snow from which they can carve their favorite animals — a bear standing on its hind legs, a sitting bunny, or even an alligator creeping along the ground.

Once they've formed the basic shape, have them carve legs, arms, and faces using the sticks, sand shovels, kitchen tools, or mitten-covered hands.

Ice Castle

When the temperature drops below freezing, you can add a little shimmer to the backyard by building your own ice hideaway.

Materials
- Household containers, such as buckets, pans, and ice cube trays
- Food coloring (optional)
- Large pail
- Spray bottle

To make the building blocks, just fill household containers with water and set them outdoors to freeze. (You can even stir in food coloring for a special effect.) When you're ready to unmold the frozen blocks, fill the large pail with warm water and briefly dip the containers in it. The ice should then slip out easily. Be sure to wear gloves to protect your skin.

To raise the walls of your castle, just spray water on the surfaces to be joined and hold the blocks in place for several seconds until they freeze together.

Ice Castle

Sugar Cube Igloo

Sugar Cube Igloo

Who says you need snow to make an igloo? The polar landscape shown here, inspired by *Wim Kros's Fun Foods* (Sterling), is made from sugar cubes.

Materials

Cardboard
Sugar cubes
2 egg whites
3 cups confectioners' sugar

Cut out a cardboard circle with a 7-inch diameter. Then, lay a base row of sugar cubes around the circle, leaving space for the igloo entrance.

Next, make mortar by mixing together the egg whites and confectioners' sugar. Add subsequent layers of cubes, applying the mortar to the bottom of the new cubes, not to those already in place. Work alternately left and right from the entrance toward the back of the igloo, staggering the cubes the way a builder lays bricks. Gradually decrease the circumference of the igloo with each new row by setting the cubes a little closer to the center each time.

Build a total of ten layers, stopping halfway through the construction to let the igloo dry.

Make the doorway arch and roof separately, working on a flat surface. When they are dry, glue them in place. Allow the igloo to dry completely, then sprinkle with a blizzard of sugar.

SNOW SPRAY PAINT

During winter, the most vibrant sight out your window could just be your kids' handiwork — neon blue snowballs, orange snowdrifts, and rainbow snow people. All they need is some snow paint.

First, make several pitchers of colored water with half a dozen drops of food coloring per container. Experiment to get hot pinks, bright purples, and gaudy greens — the bolder the colors, the better. Choose a variety of applicators for the kids to take outside. Anything with a nozzle will do, including a turkey baster and a watering can. The dye will harmlessly melt away with the next thaw.

Back to Nature

Birds of a Feather

When *FamilyFun* reader Nancy Mendez of Silver Spring, Maryland, and her daughter Maddy (three years old at the time) started going on nature walks together, it was the feathers they discovered along the way that fascinated the youngster most.

To store her finds, the two created Maddy's Feather Book by folding several sheets of copier paper and stapling on a cover sheet decorated with wildlife stamps. Individual feathers are taped in and labeled, by color or by species if they can identify it. The book has turned out to be a fun learning tool as well — mother and daughter have discussed molting, preening, migration, and camouflage.

Recycled Bird Feeder

Recycled Bird Feeder

Backyard birds won't know the difference between a fancy, store-bought bird feeder and one that's homemade, so save your pennies and make one out of an empty milk carton.

Materials

    Cardboard milk carton
    Craft knife
    Glue
    Popsicle sticks
    Acrylic paints and paintbrushes
    Short wooden dowel

Use the craft knife (adults only) to cut openings on opposite sides of the milk carton. Next, your child can glue Popsicle stick shingles onto the roof and then decorate the bird feeder with paints.

For a perch, poke holes below the openings and slip a dowel through each hole. Fill the bottom of the feeder with birdseed. Then hang the feeder with wire from a clothesline or light branch at least 5 feet from the ground to thwart predators.

Encourage your kids to keep track of the birds that stop in by referring to a guidebook. And, remember that once the birds have become dependent on your food, you must continue to replenish it, especially during harsh weather.

Snow Heart for the Birds

While your kids are passing out Valentine's Day cards in February, they can also leave sweet nothings in the snow for their feathered friends and squirrels.

Materials

    Stick
    Birdseed, nuts, or berries

Use a stick to draw an outline of a heart or another shape in the snow. Next, lightly tamp down the design and fill it in with birdseed, nuts, or berries. After sprinkling on the seed, gently pat down your creations so the artwork doesn't blow away in the wind. Soon, the winter wildlife will stop by to pick up their treat.

Snow Heart for the Birds

Jughead

Jughead

Making a scarecrow to adorn the front yard is an excellent way for your family to celebrate fall (and spook some trick-or-treaters!).

Materials

> Plastic milk jug
> Craft knife
> Household broom or feather duster
> Acrylic paints and paintbrushes
> Old clothes, a belt, and gloves
> Rubber bands or twine
> Leaves, straw, or newspaper

Holding the milk jug upside down with the handle turned toward the back, use the craft knife (adults only) to cut an opening through the bottom that measures the same width as the bristle end of the broom (or feather duster). Push the broom handle through the opening and out the pouring spout until half the length of the bristles protrudes (it should resemble a bristly crew cut). Now your kids can paint on bushy eyebrows, a wide grin, big ears, and freckles. Or, cut facial features out of felt and glue them onto the jug.

Now it's time to dress your scarecrow. Use rubber bands to tie off the ends of shirtsleeves and pant legs, then stuff the garments with dried leaves, straw, or newspaper. Secure the pants onto the torso with a belt.

Attach the head to the body by inserting the broom handle through the neck so the jug rests on the shoulders (you may need to shorten the handle). Pull gloves over the scarecrow's wrists and stuff his pant legs into old boots. Add finishing touches, such as a corsage, headband, sunglasses, or even a stuffed lap "pet."

WHAT'S A SCARECROW TO WEAR?

No one says you have to dress a scarecrow in worn-out old clothes. Here are a few suggestions for decking out your porch or garden character in style:

Go formal: Check your closet (or the racks at a local thrift shop) for an out-of-fashion prom dress. Accessorize with costume jewelry and a string-mop wig.

Get scary: Pull out last year's Halloween costume, mask and all.

Call on your child's favorite action hero: Pick up a pair of colorful tights and fashion a cape out of a sheet or beach towel.

Be a sport: Put that outgrown Little League outfit or cheerleading uniform to use — and don't forget a catcher's mitt or pom-poms.

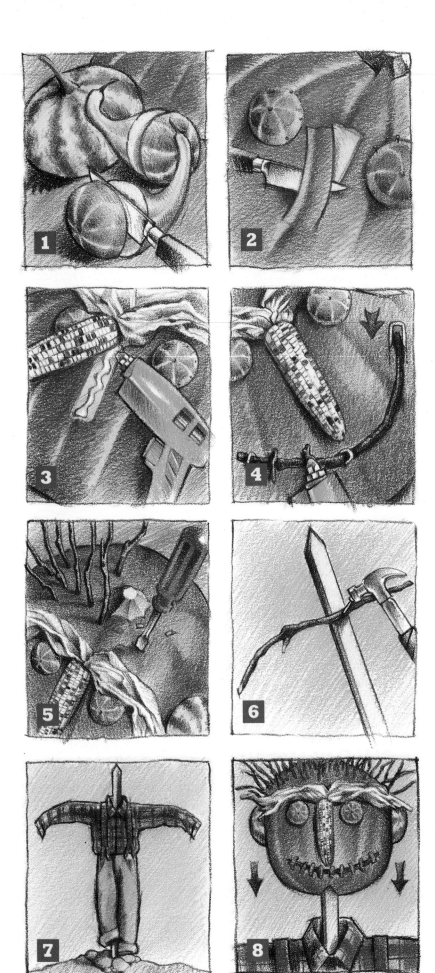

Mister Pumpkinhead

Even if this spike-haired scarecrow fails to scare the birds, so what? Your family will have a lot of laughs putting him together — and he's certain to attract some notice from your neighbors.

Materials

- 2 small gourds and 1 large gourd
- Straight pins
- 1 large pumpkin
- Glue gun
- 1 ear Indian corn
- Florist U-pins (available at craft stores)
- Sticks for mouth, hair, and arms
- Screwdriver
- Nails
- Scary old clothes
- 2- by 3-inch by 6-foot wood stake with pointed ends

1. Slice the small gourds in half and use the bottoms for eyes. Attach them to the pumpkin by pushing straight pins through the outer edges, angling the pins inward for a stronger bond. For ears, cut the large gourd in half and pin the halves onto the pumpkin.

2. Cut away some of the pumpkin skin where the nose will go.

3. Wipe away excess moisture with a towel. Then, using a glue gun (a parent's job), attach the ear of corn to the cut area. Glue the husks over the eyes like eyebrows.

4. Attach an arched stick with U-pins to form a mouth and glue 1-inch sticks across the mouth to create a toothy grin.

5. With the screwdriver, poke holes in the top of the pumpkin and add hair by pushing sticks into the holes.

6. For the body, nail a branch centered on the wooden stake where the arms should be. Push the stake about 1 foot into the ground and support it with rocks.

7 and 8. Dress the body, then push the pumpkin head onto the top of the stake.

Casting Tracks

A wonderful way to discover the presence of animals in the wild is to find and preserve an animal track. Here's an easy project that lets your kids cast a track and take it home.

Materials

> 2-inch-wide strip of poster board
> Stapler
> Plaster of Paris
> Ziplock bag
> Jar of water, with lid
> Stick

To make a mold, use the 2-inch-wide strip of poster board and staple together the ends to make a ring. (Another option is to cut a square, open-ended section, about 2 to 3 inches wide, out of the middle of a cardboard milk carton.) Next, measure 2 cups of dry plaster of Paris (available at hardware stores) into the ziplock bag.

Now you're ready to look for an animal track. Pack up your mold, the ziplock bag, and the jar of water and set out early in the day for a walk through a nature preserve or park. Choose a trail that winds along a running stream with a sandy or muddy creek bed and keep a lookout for prints in the soft mud near the water. If you are among the first people to arrive at the creek bed, you should be able to spot fresh tracks.

Once you've found a track, carefully brush away any debris. Set the mold you made around the track like a collar. Add water to the plaster in the ziplock bag, stirring with a stick, until it is the consistency of pourable mud. Quickly pour the plaster into the cardboard collar to a depth of about ½ inch (see photo below).

Let the plaster set until it hardens (from 10 to 20 minutes) and then peel the collar off. Scrape any dirt from the bottom of the cast and admire your print. At home later, you can try to identify the track by looking it up in a guidebook.

Casting Tracks

Preserve a Spiderweb

Preserve a Spiderweb

Few structures in nature rival the craftsmanship of the spiderweb, and none are both so delicate and so strong. Contrary to popular belief, these silk masterpieces are solely for trapping food — spiders don't live in them. This activity allows you and your children to capture a web and take it home with you.

Materials

Newspaper
Black spray paint that does not contain fluorocarbons, or nonaerosol hair spray
White poster board or mat board

In your backyard or nearby field, search for a web that is abandoned or that has no visible occupant (morning is a great time to go web hunting, because the dew will be clinging to webs). When you find one, look for its anchor lines. Have your child hold up a piece of newspaper behind the web to protect the surrounding plants while you spray-paint both sides of the web. Start at the center of the web and move outward, spraying in a spiral. Holding the poster board firmly, move it toward the web. As it contacts the web surface, hold it steady until the entire web has stuck to the board, then cut the web's "guy" lines to free it. Let the paint dry for several minutes before touching.

Back to Nature

Chapter Seven

The Toy Factory

WHEN *FAMILY FUN* associate editor Cindy Littlefield was clearing her kids' school papers from the table before dinner one night, she came upon a tiny man made of paper. A touch of her fingertip set it cartwheeling across the tabletop. "Isn't it cute?" asked her twelve-year-old daughter, Jade. "Ian made it at school." The thought made Cindy smile. Even with the hefty competition of high-tech store-bought toys, a simple handmade gadget could still amuse her fourteen-year-old son.

That fact is proven over and over again in the Littlefield household, where many of the toys featured in the Family Almanac section of *FamilyFun* magazine are conceived and tested. Ian's acrobatic character turned into the tumbling tots on page 150, while Jade's furry pipe cleaner ponies and woolly poodles became the sculptures on page 135.

"The best part about homemade toys," says Cindy, "is that the excitement begins the instant you and your kids come up with an idea — and it continues throughout the crafting process. That's all before your kids even start playing with the toy."

The next time you're looking for a way to entertain your family — on a rainy weekend or during school vacation — take a tip from the Littlefields and embark on a toy-making adventure. Start by check-

Nadia (Russia)   **Suki (Japan)**   **Duncan (Scotland)**

Worry Dolls, page 138

Paper bat and ball: For the bat, tightly roll a stack of newspaper sheets into a cylinder and fasten the edge with duct tape. Scrunch more newspaper into a ball.

Plastic bowling pins: Set up a bunch of empty liter soda bottles at the end of a hallway and try knocking them down with a rolling rubber ball.

Pasta pick-up sticks: Using red and blue hues, spray-paint some dry spaghetti. Then, drop the pasta and see who can earn the most points by picking up single strands without moving the rest of the pile. Red pieces are worth 5 points, blue ones equal 10 points.

ing out the ideas in this chapter and see where your imaginations take you.

Let your kids call the shots as often as possible. As a parent, you'll want to be in charge of certain toy-making tools (handsaws, drills, and craft knives), but resist the temptation to step in and do the whole project yourself. Remember, if your child has a hand in making his toy, he'll like it more.

Enjoy the toy-making process. There's no need to rush to the finish. Making the toy can be as much fun as playing with it.

Remember, beauty is in the eye of the beholder. If your child is happy with a hairless doll, so be it. On the other hand, if she's determined to fash-ion a wig out of yarn and can't man-age it on her own, offer to help. You can still let her add the finishing touch, cutting the bangs or, say, tying on a ribbon bow.

Turn toy-making into a learning opportunity. If the toy you decide to make has a functional part, such as the blades of a paper helicopter (see page 147), discuss, in simple terms, how the toy is engineered. Encourage your child to use his newfound knowledge to invent a new toy altogether.

Give a homemade toy as a gift. Your child can surprise a friend on her birth-day with a unique gift, such as a set of homemade finger puppets (see pages 139 and 140) or a handcrafted paddle-boat (see page 145).

Juice Can Puppets, page 139

Dolls

Life-size Doll

Older kids tend to like their dolls small, but for the younger set, the bigger the better. Even more so if it's one that bears an uncanny resemblance to its owner.

Materials

- Large sheet of paper and chalk
- White bedsheet
- Straight pins and fabric scissors
- Fabric glue or sewing needle and thread
- Polyester filling (available at most craft stores)
- Broom handle
- Yarn and buttons

Ask your child to lie down on the paper, with her arms and legs outstretched. Use chalk to trace around her entire body. Keep the outline loose, sketching around both hands as if they were mittens. Cut out the pattern and pin it on top of a bedsheet that's been folded in half lengthwise.

Trace around the paper, leaving a 2-inch margin near the head and body and a 1-inch margin for the arms, legs, and feet. Draw a bit closer to the hands. Using fabric scissors, cut through the doubled sheet, 1 inch outside of the chalk line.

The easiest way to attach the doll's front and back is to stick the edges together with fabric glue, but stitching them (allow a ½-inch seam) will produce a sturdier doll. Either way, leave an opening at the top of the head. Turn the figure inside out and stuff with polyester filling. Use a broom handle to push the filling into the arms and legs. Now, stitch the opening closed. Glue on strands of yarn hair and button eyes, and your doll is ready to dress — right from your child's closet.

Life-size Dolls

The Toy Factory

Meet the Beadles

Of all the dolls we've crafted at *FamilyFun*, twelve-year-old Jade Littlefield, a frequent visitor around the office, claims these futuristic figures with their posable bodies and wigged-out hair are the best. They can sit on a windowsill — just bend their knees and straighten their torsos — or move into your child's dollhouse.

Materials

Embroidery floss

Tape measure

Pipe cleaners

¾-inch round wooden bead (with a 5-millimeter center hole)

Felt scraps

4 smaller wooden beads (with center holes you can fit a pipe cleaner through)

fine-tipped colored markers

1. First, create the doll's hair by cutting the embroidery floss into 20 pieces that measure twice the length you want. Fold a 6-inch pipe cleaner in half over the midpoint of the collective strands, as shown. Feed both ends of the pipe cleaner through the center of the large bead. Slide the bead up the pipe cleaner until the fold is hidden in the bead center. Separate each strand of embroidery floss to fashion a thick shock of hair. For curls, dampen the strands with a few drops of water, wind them around a pencil, and let them dry.

2. For the doll's arms, place a 5-inch

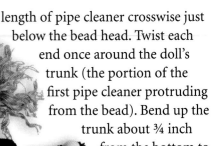

length of pipe cleaner crosswise just below the bead head. Twist each end once around the doll's trunk (the portion of the first pipe cleaner protruding from the bead). Bend up the trunk about ¾ inch from the bottom to form a hook. For legs, fold a 5-inch pipe cleaner in half and hang it on the hook, as shown. Secure the legs by twisting the ¾-inch trunk ends around them.

3. To make a pair of pants, fold a 6- by 1½-inch piece of felt in half, so that the shorter edges meet. Starting from the fold, make a 2-inch cut up the middle, stopping 1 inch from the open end. Make a ¼-inch waist hole ½ inch from one end. For foot openings, make a small slit through the felt fold at the bottom of each pant leg.

4. Slip both legs through the waist opening from the front. Then, push the pipe cleaner tips through the foot openings and match up the short felt edges behind the doll's waist.

For a skirt, cut a 4-inch-long hourglass shape out of felt. Make a waist hole in the center to slide the doll's feet through.

For a shirt, use a 2-inch felt square. Cut two small armholes ½ inch apart and ¼ inch from the upper edge. Wrap the shirt around the doll's chest and over the top of its pants or skirt.

Wind a 3-inch pipe cleaner belt around the doll's waist to secure the clothes. To keep the pants' side seams closed, twist a 2-inch piece of pipe cleaner around each knee.

For hands and feet, slip a smaller bead onto the end of each limb. Bend the pipe cleaner tips to keep the beads in place. Draw on a face with fine-tipped markers, testing the colors on a spare bead first.

Meet the Beadles

Yarn Dolls

On a rainy day, invite your kids to spin yarns — into these cuddly palm-size dolls.

Materials

    Skeins of yarn
    Book

To form a yarn doll's body, loosely wrap yarn around a book, about seventy times, to create a thick hank. Slip a 6-inch piece of yarn between the hank and the book spine and use it to tie the strands together. Slide the hank off the book.

Create the doll's head by tightly tying another piece of yarn around the bundle an inch from the top. Add eyes and a mouth by tying contrasting yarn around single strands in the face and clipping the ends close to the knot. Next, cut the loop at the bottom of the hank.

1. For arms, pull one quarter of the strands to each side and tie them at the wrists, as shown. Trim the yarn ½ inch below the wrists. Then, tie a strand of yarn around the doll's waist, leaving the yarn loose to resemble a skirt. Or, make pants by dividing the strands into two bunches and tying them at the ankles.

2. For a wig, wind another hank of yarn. Tie together one end and snip the other. Feed a piece of yarn through the doll's head and use it to tie on the wig. Then, you can cut bangs, make pony-tails, or add a hair ribbon.

The Toy Factory

Pipe Cleaner Sculpture

Pipe cleaners and twist ties have saved many a parent's sanity on long car trips. Kids can fashion these quiet building tools into endless designs, from stick figures to animals to furniture. Just twist, but don't shout.

135

Apple Gals

Don't let their craggy faces fool you. These little old ladies are sweet-natured and easy to make. And though it generally takes two weeks for the doll's head to dry (longer in humid climates), even kids will agree that it's worth the wait.

Materials

> Apple
>
> Potato peeler and paring knife
>
> Colored markers
>
> Wool yarn
>
> Empty 16-ounce plastic bottle
>
> Bottle cork (available at craft stores)
>
> 10- by 16-inch piece of fabric
>
> Rubber band

When choosing an apple for the doll's head (Red Delicious work especially well), remember that the carved fruit will shrink to about two thirds its original size. Peel and core the apple. Then, carve a face on one side, using the tip of a potato peeler to hollow out deep-set eyes and a paring knife to make a slit for a mouth. For a nose, incise a triangle that extends from between the eyes toward the mouth. Then, carve ears, dimples, and extra creases.

Place the carved apple on a drying rack and store it in a dry spot until it shrinks. (You can speed the wrinkling process by using a vegetable dehydrator.) Once the head is dry, your child can use colored markers to enhance the eyes, lips, and cheeks.

Now, make a wig for your doll. Cut at least ten strands of yarn that measure twice the desired hair length plus 2 inches. Gather the strands together and fold the bunch in half. Tie another strand around the yarn 1 inch from the fold to make a loop that can be stuffed into the top of the head. Let your child braid or trim the wig however she likes.

To make the body, cut the base off the plastic bottle. Plug the top with a cork to serve as the doll's neck. Wrap the fabric around the body so that it extends beyond the top and bottom of the bottle. Secure the fabric around the bottleneck with a rubber band and then fold the cloth down. Tuck excess cloth at the base into the bottle. Now top off the doll by gently pushing the cored apple down onto the cork.

Apple Gals

Corn Dolls

This Native American craft will have your kids grinning from ear to ear.

Materials

  Dried corn husks or tamale
    wrappers (available at grocery
    stores)
  Twine or string
  Colored markers
  Glue
  Construction paper

Soak your corn husks in warm water until they become pliable (about 1 hour). Bunch together several damp husks and tie a piece of twine around them about ½ inch from one end.

1. To make the doll's head, hold the bunch by the tied end and, one at a time, fold the husks down over the twine as if you were peeling a banana. Smooth the husks to create a face, then tie another piece of twine around the doll's neck, as shown.

2. For the arms, tightly roll up a single husk, starting at one long edge. Use twine to tie it off at both ends where the doll's wrists should be.

3. Now, fit the arms up between the husks below the head and then tie off the doll's waist.

4. To fashion a skirt, arrange several more corn husks so that they are inverted around the doll's waist. It will look as if a skirt has blown up over the doll's head. Tie the husks in place around the waist, as shown. Then, fold the skirt down and smooth the husks.

5. For pants, divide the husks below the waist into two groups and tie each one at the ankle with twine.

Now, your kids can draw on facial features and other details. Then, they can glue on a braided twine hairdo and construction-paper clothes.

Worry Dolls

In Guatemala, kids tell their troubles to worry dolls — toothpick-size colorful figures that they tuck under their pillows at night. Your kids can take this tradition worldwide with a multicultural collection of clothespin dolls.

Materials

- Craft stick
- Craft knife
- Straight wooden clothespin
- Glue
- Colored markers
- Yarn
- Toothpick
- Fabric scraps
- Sewing notions

Nadia (Russia)

First, make the doll's arms (a parent's job) by using a craft knife to score the stick 1½ inches from each end and then snapping the ends off against a countertop edge. Smooth jagged edges by rubbing them against a hard, level surface. Position the arms, curved ends down, just below the clothespin head and glue in place.

Style worry doll hair just by drawing on a "do" with a marker or crown your creations with yarn tresses. Cut a bunch of strands that measure twice the desired length, tie them together around the middle, and glue the wig on the doll. Once the glue dries, unravel individual strands for a frizzy look or make ringlets by wrapping wet yarn around a toothpick and allowing the yarn to dry.

You can fashion an outfit for your doll out of fabric scraps and notions from the sewing basket. For inspiration, refer to a cultural guidebook, such as *Children Just Like Me* (Dorling Kindersley Publishing). Create shirts, slacks, and kimonos by wrapping the clothespin with cotton yarn and gluing the ends in place. For robes, kilts, dresses, and ponchos, use bright cloth swatches belted with an embroidery floss sash.

Make a wide-brimmed hat by cutting an *X* in the center of a small felt circle. To wrap a tall turban, make a thimble-shaped dome out of a pipe cleaner and glue it onto the doll's head. Wind and glue a strip of fabric around it.

For jewelry, coil bracelets and necklaces out of craft wire or metallic pipe cleaners. Finally, draw facial features on these tiny confidants with colored markers — the cheerier the better for easing fretful minds.

Rosita (Spain)   **Chinda (Thailand)**   **Kate (U.S.A.)**   **Sesi (Ghana)**   **Meena (India)**

Puppets

Thumbs Up

With a set of these mini puppets at her fingertips, your child can act out a favorite nursery rhyme or make up an incredible tale of her own.

Materials

- Felt scraps
- White glue
- Googly eyes
- Permanent colored markers
- Sewing notions

For each puppet, first cut out a pair of 1¾- by 3-inch felt rectangles to serve as the front and back of the animal. Join the front to the back by gluing together the side and top edges. Leave the bottom edges open for a finger opening. Once the glue dries, use scissors to round the top of the puppet's head. Glue on googly eyes. Now it's time to add distinguishing animal traits.

Woolly Lamb: Attach ears horizontally to the front of the lamb. Glue a bit of cotton "wool" to the top of its head and draw on the face.

Pig Pal: For floppy pig ears, use 2-inch felt circles. Fold them in half lengthwise and glue together the lower edges. Glue the bases of the ears to the back of the puppet. For pig cheeks and a snout, glue on ¾-inch felt circles.

Mr. Horse: For ears, cut out a pair of felt ovals (about 1½ inches long). Attach them as previously described. Add a fringed forelock, white blaze, and rounded muzzle. Use a marker to draw jawlines and nostrils.

Birds of a Feather: Cut out a triangular felt bird beak and glue it in place. Add plumage.

Spotted Heifer: Make cow ears following the same steps used for the pig. Glue on a pink muzzle. Color bold black spots on the ears and face.

Frog Friend: Position googly eyes at the top of the head. Glue webbed frog feet to the front of the puppet.

Thumbs Up

Farm Animal Puppets

If your kids are looking for a way to liven up a quiet afternoon, turn things zooey by shaping up a menagerie of animal finger puppets. For the creatures shown here, use the directions below or adapt them to create characters of your own.

Materials

Construction paper
Glue
Masking tape
Googly eyes, pom-poms, string, waxed paper, and twist ties

To make a basic body, use scissors to shape the puppet's midsection from a 3-inch square of construction paper — perhaps a round potbelly for a pig or a rectangular body for an alligator. For legs, roll and glue four 1½- by 3-inch paper strips into cylinders. Make them wide enough to fit your child's fingers, so she can walk the puppet around. Attach each leg to the midsection with a piece of masking tape, pressing one end inside the cylinder and the other onto the back of the body.

Dog, Lion, Bug, or Deer: Draw a suitable head and ears on a piece of craft paper. Then, cut out the shape and glue it onto the body. Glue on googly eyes and distinguishing details, such as a pom-pom nose, a mane fashioned from snips of string, waxed-paper wings, or twist-tie antlers.

Piglet: With a small half circle, form and glue a paper cone. Flatten the tip of the cone with your thumb to create a pig snout. Glue on big floppy ears and attach the head to the body with tape.

Alligator: Match up a pair of 2½- by 1½-inch rectangles with the shorter edges at the top and bottom. Glue together the very tops, then fold back the glued portion and make a crease. With pinking shears, trim the sides and bottoms of the rectangles to create a tapered, toothy jaw. Glue the folded edge to the back of the body. Finally, glue on a pair of googly-eye stalks.

Farm Animal Puppets

Duck Walk

Duck Walk

Ducks are great swimmers, but these freewheeling drakes, adapted from *Look What I Made!* (TAB Books), are more at home on dry land than water.

Materials

5 9-inch paper plates
Paints and paintbrushes
Clear plastic coffee can lid
Craft knife
Metal paper fastener
12-inch wooden dowel
Tape and glue

Cut a 4-inch circle from the center of one of the paper plates. Draw on rotating duck feet, as shown above, and paint them orange. Once dry, trim along the outer edge of the connected feet. Glue the cutout onto the plastic lid. Then, use a craft knife (parents only) to cut a small hole in the center of the lid.

From the remaining plates, cut two 5-inch circles for the front and back of the duck's body and two 3½-inch circles for its head. Cut wings, tail feathers, and a beak from the plate rims and paint all of the pieces.

To assemble the duck, cut a small hole 1 inch from the bottom of both body pieces. Sandwich the plastic lid between the body, lining up the three holes. Push the paper fastener through the holes and

spread the prongs. (The fastener should be loose enough for the lid to turn.) Then, insert the dowel between the body pieces and tape it in place. Glue the top edges of the body together.

Next, glue together the head circles, except for the lower edges. Slip the head onto the body and glue it in place. Glue on the feathers and bill. To set the duck in motion, grasp the dowel and push.

Sir Frog

He may not be a prince, but this paper frog is charming — and your kids will get a kick out of his flicking tongue.

Materials

Dessert-size paper plate
Green paint and paintbrush
Craft knife
Construction paper (green, white, black, and red)
Tape and glue

Paint both sides of the paper plate green. When it is dry, fold the plate in half and use the craft knife (parents only) to make a 1-inch slit (for the frog's tongue) in the center of the fold. Create a fingerhold on the underside of the body using a 2- by 3-inch piece of green construction paper. Center it on the bottom of the folded plate and tape the shorter edges in place.

For eyes, cut out a pair of 1- by 2-inch green rectangles and round the upper edges. Fold each rectangle in half and glue the lower portion to the top of the body. Glue on white and black paper circles, as shown.

Cut frog legs out of construction paper, a shorter set for the front and a long, bent pair for the back. Tape the tops of the legs to the underside of the body. Cut out a ¾- by 7-inch tongue from red construction paper. Round one end and slip it through the slit. To wag the tongue, jiggle the straight end.

Frog Frolics

When *FamilyFun* reader Cynthia Pegado from Norwood, New Jersey, found out that her son's first grade class would be studying frogs, she thought crafting paper plate frogs would make a perfect group project and volunteered to help. Her one modification to Sir Frog — using party blowers for the tongues instead of paper — made for plenty of lively fun.

Sir Frog

The Toy Factory

Super Sam

Fast Finger Puppets

If your child draws faces on the tips of his fingers, he'll be the hit of your house. Add one of these winning wardrobes, and he'll be ready to costar with Kermit.

Materials

- Felt or fabric scraps
- Tape
- Pipe cleaners
- Glue
- Paper clips
- Needle-nose pliers
- Cotton balls
- Yarn

Super Sam: Wrap a blue felt rectangle into a tube, secure with tape, and slip it on your finger. For a cape, trim the sides of a red felt rectangle, cut a hole in the narrow end, label the back with an S to complete the costume.

Blue Gene: Dress him in a denim tube and make a crepe paper baseball cap. For his red hair, tie 1-inch lengths of yarn together with one piece of yarn.

Piper the Dog: Coil a pipe cleaner around your finger, leaving a tail at the end. Bend a second piece into ears — and don't forget a nose.

Mrs. Pearl: Dress her in a tube of pink felt. Coil a red pipe cleaner into a hat and slip on a string of tiny beads.

Professor Acorn: Bend a paper clip into wire glasses (use needle-nose pliers) and top with an acorn cap.

Ted E. Bear: Make your bear by shaping two ears in the middle of a brown pipe cleaner. Coil the ends into a big circle and shape into a hat.

His Majesty: Craft a purple cape like Super Sam's. Bend a pipe cleaner into a crown; rub with glue and add glitter. Then, glue on a white cotton mustache and beard.

Bikini Bev: Fashion the bikini top and bottom out of ribbons. For a beach hat, cut a doughnut-shaped brim out of felt and tape on a felt top. For sunglasses, add clear tape to the wire glasses and color with markers.

Chill Bill: Wrap masking tape around your finger, sticky-side out, and apply yarn to make a sweater. Make a scarf out of felt and a cap with a red ribbon base and red tape bill.

Doorway Stage

For an instant puppet theater, stretch tension rods across a doorway and hang up curtains. If you don't have spare ones, make them out of red felt. For the valance, cut the felt 18 by 48 inches. Make the two middle curtains 36 by 48 inches and the bottom panel 36 by 48 inches. Sew casings for the rods and hang. Tie string to the tops of the middle curtains and open at showtime.

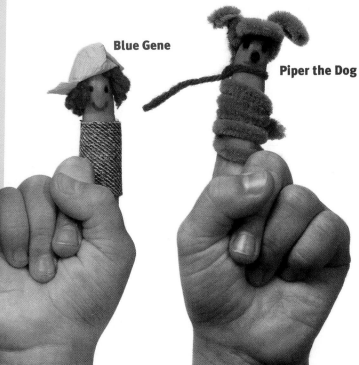

Blue Gene

Piper the Dog

Professor Acorn

Mrs. Pearl

Boats & Planes

Cardboard Canoe

Like the birch bark canoes built centuries ago by the Native American tribes in New England, this lightweight toy craft cuts quickly and smoothly through water. It's adapted from *The Kids' Summer Handbook* (Ticknor & Fields/Books for Young Readers), which features a host of warm weather crafts and activities.

Materials

- Cardboard
- Pushpin
- Large-eye needle and string
- Acrylic paints and paintbrushes
- Box of paraffin wax
- Tall tin can
- Pot holder and newspaper
- Metal tongs

Cut out a 6- by 12-inch piece of cardboard and fold it in half so that the long ends match up. Draw a side view of a canoe on one side of the cardboard, using the fold for the bottom of the boat. Cut through both layers along the sides and top of the canoe, but not the bottom. With a pushpin, make a series of holes in the curved ends, as shown. Then, use the needle and string to sew them together.

For seats, cut two 3½- by 1½-inch strips out of cardboard scraps. Fold in the sides of each strip 1 inch from the short edges and wedge the seats inside the boat. Next, paint the canoe and let

it dry thoroughly.

To waterproof the canoe, put the wax in the can and set the can in a saucepan filled with a couple inches of water. Heat slowly until the wax melts (parents only). Use a pot holder to set the can on newspaper. With tongs, dip the boat, an end at a time, into the wax. (You may have to tilt the can.) When the wax hardens, place a few pebbles in the hull to prevent tipping, and the boat is ready to float.

Cardboard Canoe

Bobbing Buoy

To warn boaters of shallow or rocky spots, the channel markers used by the Coast Guard must stay upright in the roughest waves. You can show your child how a little extra weight can keep a marker from tipping over by helping him fashion a toy buoy.

Materials

Ping-Pong ball
Craft knife
Modeling clay
White glue
Drinking straw
Paper triangle

Use the craft knife to slice the top off the Ping-Pong ball (adults only). Next, cut a hole (big enough for the straw) in the center of the top while your child fills the bottom of the ball with clay. Glue the top of the ball back in place.

Make a slit in the top of the straw and insert the long edge of the paper triangle flag. Push the bottom of the straw through the hole in the ball. Now test the buoy in a sink full of water. Encourage your child to try tipping over the buoy by making waves. Explain that the weight of the clay (called ballast) pulls downward into the water, keeping the buoy upright.

Iceboats

FunFact

Compartments in the bottoms of large boats are also filled with ballast, such as lead or even water, to help keep them stable at sea.

Bobbing Buoy

Iceboats

The rules for racing one of these miniature ice block boats are simple. Instead of crossing the finish line first, the object is to outlast the competition.

Materials

Empty pint-size juice carton
Food coloring
Duct tape
Craft knife
12-inch-long wooden dowel
Cellophane triangle, 6 by 8 by 10 inches
Stapler

Fill the juice carton with 1½ cups of water and several drops of food coloring. Seal the top with duct tape and shake gently. Lay the sealed carton on its side and use a craft knife (parents only) to cut an X through the center of the side facing up. Push the wooden dowel through the opening and set the carton in the freezer overnight.

Next, fold the cellophane triangle along the 8-inch side ¾ inch in from the edge and staple to hold. Cut the carton away from the frozen boat, slip the sail onto the mast, and launch the boat in a wading pool or bathtub.

Puddle Boat

Spring showers bring more than flowers. They set the stage for the type of adventure you can find only in a big mud puddle — like setting afloat a toy boat. The paddleboat shown here is adapted from *Adventures in Art* (Williamson Publishing).

Materials

> ½-inch Fome-Cor (available at craft stores)
> Utility knife
> Glue
> Acrylic paints and gloss
> Paintbrushes
> A few small nails
> Rubber band

Use the utility knife (parents only) to cut a 10- by 5-inch rectangle out of Fome-Cor. Contour one of the shorter ends so that it resembles the bow of a boat. Starting 1½ inches in from the opposite end, cut a 4- by 3-inch opening for the paddle wheel. Use the removed material to make a cabin. Cut out a half circle 3 inches long at the flat end and glue it to the top of the bow, as shown.

To make the paddle wheel, cut two 3½- by 2-inch rectangles from Fome-Cor and make a notch (1 by ¼ inch) in from the center of each of them. Fit the two pieces together to form a cross.

Paint the boat and the wheel and then seal them (top, bottom, and sides) with a coat of acrylic gloss. Tap a small nail partway into the Fome-Cor on both sides of the wheel opening.

Tie an overhand knot at both ends of a rubber band to form two small loops. Slip a loop around each nail. Fit the middle of the band around the center of the paddle wheel. To launch your boat, rotate the wheel until the rubber band is tightly twisted, set the boat in the puddle, and release.

Build a Boat in a Nutshell

If you're not in the mood for heavy construction, try making a fast fleet of little walnut boats instead. Using walnut shell halves, hot-glue a matchstick mast into the bottom of each. Cut out triangular paper sails and use a glue stick to attach one sail around each matchstick. You'll be surprised at how well these boats hold their own on the water. They also do well in private bathtub ponds.

The Toy Factory

Paper Dove

Here's one critter that you won't mind invading your next picnic: a high-flying dove made from paper plates and plastic spoons.

Materials

Paper plate
2 plastic spoons
Pebble
Rubber band
Masking tape
Colored markers

Cut the paper plate in half. Then, cut one of the halves into three equal wedges. Tape one wedge to the bottom of the half of the paper plate that is still intact to form the dove's tail feathers (see above).

Next, sandwich the pebble between the spoon bowls, then bind the spoons with the rubber band.

Tape the joined spoons securely to the bottom of the dove's body so that the bowls extend forward, as shown. Then, use the colored markers to draw on eyes and a bright orange beak.

To fly the dove, throw it like a paper airplane. Adjust the pebble size to improve flight, if needed.

Build a Model Rocket

You don't need to be a rocket scientist to craft a model spaceship — just imaginative. Start by painting a paper towel roll for the fuselage. Next, turn a paper cup upside down and trace the diameter of the paper towel tube onto the cup bottom. Using a craft knife (a parent's job), cut out the circle. Insert the painted tube partially into the inverted cup "launchpad." Then, wrap aluminum foil around the cup.

For a nose cone, cut out a construction paper circle, make a single cut into the center, and then overlap and glue the cut edges to form a cone. Glue the cone onto the top of the tube.

Finish up by using a colored marker to print an official-sounding name, such as *Thunderbird 3* or *Apollo 13*, on the side.

Pasta Planes

Next time your kids are looking for something new to do, let them wing it with a thrifty craft project that turns pasta into a fleet of toy airplanes.

Materials

- Variety of uncooked pasta
- Low-temperature glue gun
- Acrylic paints
- Paintbrushes or cotton swabs

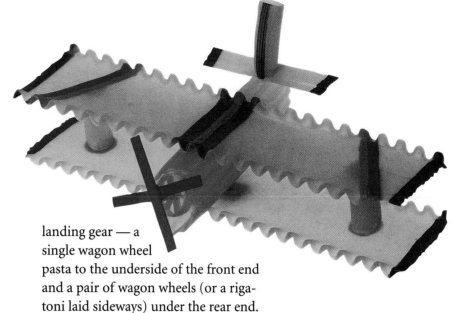

To build an aircraft like either of the ones shown here, just use the following directions, or you can modify the instructions to create a design of your own. In either case, you'll probably want to use lasagna noodles for wings and a manicotti noodle for a fuselage.

To begin, glue the manicotti to the center of a lasagna noodle. If you're building a biplane, glue a second lasagna noodle to the opposite side of the manicotti. Then, for extra support, wedge and glue rigatoni pastas between the wings (see photo). Allow the glue to dry thoroughly.

Next, add a tail wing. Break a fettucine noodle into three equal lengths (about 2 inches) and glue them to the top of the manicotti. Center and glue an upright rigatoni to the fettucine base.

To finish the nose of the plane, glue a pasta shell or elbow macaronis over the open end of the manicotti. Then, fashion a propeller by gluing on two short pieces of fettucine or a single bow tie pasta. Again, let the glue dry thoroughly.

Finally, attach

landing gear — a single wagon wheel pasta to the underside of the front end and a pair of wagon wheels (or a rigatoni laid sideways) under the rear end.

Once construction is complete, paint on distinguishing stripes, numbers, or symbols. When your kids aren't using their plane models, they can display them on a desk or bureau or use fishing line to hang them from a ceiling.

Pasta Planes

MAKE A PAPER HELICOPTER

Invite your child to take a whirl around the backyard with a simple paper gyrocopter. You can make one in five easy steps.

1. Measure and cut out a 6½-inch-long, 1½-inch-wide strip of paper.

2. Starting at the top, cut a 3-inch slit down through the middle of the strip to create a pair of wings.

3. Fold down the wings in opposite directions from one another.

4. For weight, attach a paperclip to the bottom of the strip so that it is pointing straight up.

5. Now your child can drop the finished gyrocopter from an elevated spot, and it should spin to the ground.

The Toy Factory

70944

Toys & Games

The Tortoise and the Hare

Your kids can stage a rematch between the tortoise and the hare with this pair of string-climbing critters — or they can break new ground by facing off with the animals of their choice.

Materials

    Crayons or colored markers
    Paper plate
    Drinking straw
    Stapler
    Paper towel tube
    String
    Two wooden beads

Use the crayons to draw an animal on the paper plate. It can be as simple or fancy as your kids like. Cut out the drawing with scissors and then color the flip side.

Next, cut two 1-inch pieces off the straw. Roll the end of each foreleg over one of the straw pieces and staple the edge of the paper in place.

Next, cut two 4-foot lengths of string and tie them around the ends of the paper towel tube. Thread the strings through the straw pieces. Then, tie a bead to the end of each string.

To make the animal climb, first use a short piece of string to hang the tube overhead — from a cupboard knob, perhaps. Then, slide the cutout to the bottom of the strings. Using the beads as handles, pull the strings gently, alternating from side to side, and the animal will scoot to the top.

The Tortoise and the Hare

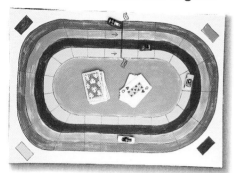

Start Your Engines

If your kids are all revved up with no place to go, let them use their toy dragsters in this grand prix of card games.

Materials

Large sheet of cardboard or
  poster board
Colored markers or crayons
Ruler

Draw a four-lane track on the cardboard sheet or poster board and shade the individual lanes with colored markers or crayons. Measure and mark 3-inch increments along the inner edge of the inside lane. From each mark, draw a straight line that extends to the far edge of the outside lane. Add a start/finish line across one of the straightaways. Place the card deck in the center of the track.

Before the race, ask players to choose a card suit — drivers can even tape a mini heart, club, diamond, or spade on the hoods of their cars. The game starts with one player turning over the top card of the deck. If the suit on the card matches his own, he gets to move his car ahead one space. If not, he stays put. Play continues with drivers alternating turns and moving ahead only when they draw a card with the right suit. The first one to cross the finish line wins.

Audio Bingo

Start off your family's game of bingo with a bang by using noisy symbols instead of numbers.

Materials

Tape recorder and tape
Old magazines
Colored markers
Paper or poster board
Glue
Buttons

First, record eighteen different sounds, such as a dog barking or a door slamming. Then, clip out two magazine photos (or make two drawings) that represent each sound you've recorded. With these depictions you'll be able to make four playing cards. For each card, use a colored marker to divide an 8-inch paper square into nine blocks. Glue a different photo in each block. Be sure no two cards are exactly alike.

To play, give each child a card and nine buttons and turn on the recording. Now, players place buttons on the pictures that match the sounds. The first kid to fill his card wins. For each new game, fast forward or rewind a bit between sounds so that they are played in a different order.

Audio Bingo

SINGING GAME BOARD

To entertain the preschoolers in her day-care center, *FamilyFun* reader Arlene Mayer, from Calgary, Canada, came up with a singing game board. She glued an $8\frac{1}{2}$- by 11-inch piece of plain white paper to a piece of cardboard and then divided the sheet into eight pie-shaped wedges. In each wedge, she drew a nursery rhyme picture (a spider for "Little Miss Muffet," a lamb for "Mary Had a Little Lamb," Barney the dinosaur for his famous "I Love You," and so on). For a spinner, she nailed a cardboard arrow to the game board with a brad. To play, the kids take turns spinning the arrow and guessing the title they land on. Then, everyone gets to sing the song.

70944

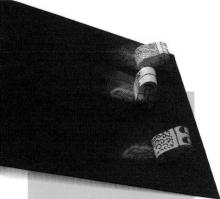

Tumble Tots

These paper dolls put on a good show — jumping and cartwheeling along. To make one, cut out a 5- by ³/₄-inch paper rectangle

and form an oval band by bringing together and gluing the short ends with a ³/₄-inch overlap. For the tumbler's sides, cut out a pair of 1 ³/₄- by ³/₄-inch paper rectangles and round the corners. Glue one of the sides onto the oval band and allow the glue to dry thoroughly. Drop a marble into the tumbler and then glue on the second side. Trim the glued edges so they are flush. Use colored markers to draw on a face, arms and legs. To set the tumbler in motion, simply place it on a slightly inclined cloth-covered surface and give him a gentle poke.

Felt Storytelling Board

Spinning a tale comes naturally for many children, especially when inspired by a storytelling board with movable characters and props.

Materials

> Felt or flannel material in
>   assorted colors
> Shoe box
> Craft glue

First, cut one piece of felt or flannel to fit on the inside of the box lid and glue it in place (sky blue is a good, neutral color for this background).

Next, cut the scraps of felt into figures, which will naturally stick to the storyboard. Try making trees, fish, birds, flowers, stars, and even letters. People and animals can be made up of several shapes, so be sure to cut out circles for faces and eyes, as well as rectangles for arms and legs.

Once you have a variety of characters and props, your child can use them to tell an imaginary story or retell a tradi-tional fairy tale. When the story is finished, clear the board and let your child start a new one. When he's done, pack up the felt figures and store them in the shoe box.

Photo Cutouts Storyboard:

You can also clip magazine pictures, coloring book characters, and real photos to stick on a storytelling board. Glue the cutouts onto cardboard and then trim around them. Glue a strip of sandpaper to the back so they will adhere to the fabric.

Felt Storytelling Board

Dump Humpty Beanbags

Dump Humpty Beanbags

These egg-faced beanbags are adapted from *Prime Time Together ... with Kids* (Discovery Toys, Inc.). Like their fairy-tale counterpart, Humpty Dumpty, they're destined for great falls. Once your kids put together a few, they can line them up and knock them down in a bouncy beanbag toss.

Materials

    Felt
    Fabric glue
    Needle and
        thread
    Popcorn kernels

First, cut out two felt egg shapes for the front and back of the beanbag. They should measure 6 inches high and 5 inches across at the widest point.

Glue together the front and back along the edges, leaving a 1½-inch opening at the bottom (the wider end). To reinforce the glued seam, sew a running stitch ⅛ inch in from the edge. Then, pour about 1 cup of popcorn kernels into the egg through the opening. (Keep in mind that the beanbag will be easier to pose if you don't overstuff it.) Glue and stitch closed the opening.

Next, cut out felt arms and legs and glue the tops of the limbs to the back side of the egg. Glue on felt eyes, a nose, and lips. You can even cut out and glue on felt clothes or fashion a tiny felt baseball cap.

Now your child can perch his finished beanbag on a bench or table edge and see how many pitches it takes to knock it down with a soft rubber ball.

Beanbag Squares

FamilyFun contributing editor Lynne Bertrand, who loves to sew, says this square beanbag is a great starter project for young seamstresses. Once a child has the method down pat, she can try her hand at simple variations, like a treasure pouch or a sachet filled with fragrant herbs.

Materials

    Measuring tape
    Fabric or felt
    Needle and thread
    Dried beans or rice

Measure and cut out two 5-inch squares of fabric or felt. Stitch them together with the right sides facing each other. Leave a small opening to pour in the beans. Turn the bag right side out, fill with beans or rice, and stitch up the opening by hand.

Beanbag Squares

Three Beanbag Games

Play hot potato: Ask everyone to form a circle. Turn on some music and start tossing a beanbag from one person to another as quickly as possible. Whoever drops the bag or is caught holding the "potato" when the music stops is out. The last person left not holding the bag wins.

Sink baskets: Set up a clean wastebasket or bucket across the room and take turns trying to land a beanbag in it. The first to score five baskets wins.

Hold a beanbag olympics: See who can throw a beanbag the farthest and the highest.

The Toy Factory

151

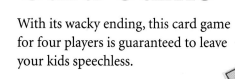

Four Critters Card Game

With its wacky ending, this card game for four players is guaranteed to leave your kids speechless.

Materials

Large sheet of poster board (or unlined index cards)
Ruler
Colored markers

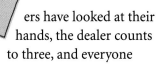

Measure and cut out sixteen 5- by 4-inch rectangles from poster board. With colored markers, draw a pig on four of the cards. The animals need not be identical as long as they are easy to identify. Make similar sets of four using dog, rabbit, and cat images.

Before playing the game, shuffle the deck thoroughly. Deal all the cards. Once all the play-ers have looked at their hands, the dealer counts to three, and everyone passes a card, facedown, to the person on his or her right. Players continue to shift cards around the table in this manner, picking up the pace all the while.

As soon as a player collects four like animals, she discreetly and silently puts her finger on her nose and waits. Anyone who notices instantly follows suit. The last one to touch his nose loses.

Four Critters Card Game

Fish Sticks Hoop Game

You don't need a worm to land a fish in this Native American game of skill — just a little practice catching rings on a stick. The toy shown here is one of the multicultural holiday crafts from *Hands-On Celebrations* (K/ITS Publishing).

Materials

- Cardboard
- Ruler
- White glue
- Craft knife
- Tempera paints and paintbrushes
- 16-inch-long piece of heavy string
- 14-inch stick or wooden dowel
- Four rings with diameters of at least 2 inches (canning jar rims or plastic bracelets work well)

Cut out a cardboard fish that measures about 6 inches long and 4 inches wide. Make a second fish by tracing around the first one and glue the two together to make one sturdier fish. Once the glue dries, use a craft knife (parents only) to cut a 2-inch-wide circle in the center. Then, your child can paint both sides of the fish.

Make a small hole through the mouth of the fish. Thread the string through the hole and knot the end. Tie the other end of the string to the top of the stick. Finally, slide the rings over the bottom of the stick and onto the string.

When your child is ready to reel in his catch, show him how to hold the bottom of the stick and swing the string out in front of him. The object is to catch all of the rings on the stick before "hooking" the fish through the hole in its center. To make the task easier, try shortening the string.

Fish Sticks Hoop Game

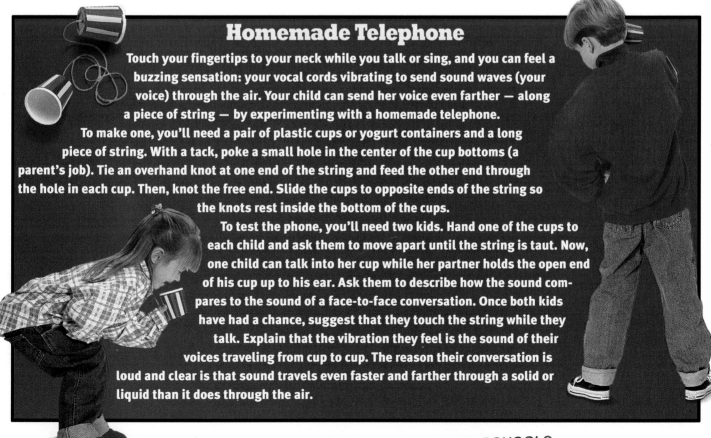

Homemade Telephone

Touch your fingertips to your neck while you talk or sing, and you can feel a buzzing sensation: your vocal cords vibrating to send sound waves (your voice) through the air. Your child can send her voice even farther — along a piece of string — by experimenting with a homemade telephone.

To make one, you'll need a pair of plastic cups or yogurt containers and a long piece of string. With a tack, poke a small hole in the center of the cup bottoms (a parent's job). Tie an overhand knot at one end of the string and feed the other end through the hole in each cup. Then, knot the free end. Slide the cups to opposite ends of the string so the knots rest inside the bottom of the cups.

To test the phone, you'll need two kids. Hand one of the cups to each child and ask them to move apart until the string is taut. Now, one child can talk into her cup while her partner holds the open end of his cup up to his ear. Ask them to describe how the sound compares to the sound of a face-to-face conversation. Once both kids have had a chance, suggest that they touch the string while they talk. Explain that the vibration they feel is the sound of their voices traveling from cup to cup. The reason their conversation is loud and clear is that sound travels even faster and farther through a solid or liquid than it does through the air.

Musical Instruments

COMB IT OUT

This kazoolike instrument will tickle your kids' lips and their funny bones. To make one, wrap a piece of waxed paper around a plastic comb. Hold the covered comb spine down in front of your lips and start humming.

Jingle Bells

Kids love putting on a show, and this paper plate tambourine makes it a cinch. All they need to do is flick their wrist to shake out a tune.

Materials

    2 heavyweight paper plates
    Tempera paints and paintbrushes
    Hole punch
    9 6-inch lengths of narrow ribbon
    9 medium-size bells

First, your child can paint the undersides of two plates with his favorite color. Once the paint dries, help him use a paper hole punch to make nine holes, spaced evenly apart, in the rim of one plate. Make identical holes in the second plate. Match up the plates rim to rim, painted sides out, with the holes lined up. Then, thread a piece of ribbon through each set of holes and loosely tie on a medium-size bell.

Bracelet Bells: For a set of wearable jingle bells, help your child sew bells onto a length of sewing elastic that fits snugly around her wrist (or ankle). Then let her shake away.

Jingle Bells

Rain Stick

If you make only one instrument with your children, a rain stick is the one to try. Not only is it immensely satisfying for kids to hammer nails into a mailing tube, but it also will make your children want to dance up a storm.

When choosing a mailing tube, keep in mind that the sound it produces will vary depending on its diameter. A tube with a 1½-inch diameter works well because the filling (rice or beans) will trickle slowly down through the tube and sound like falling rain.

Rain Stick

Materials

    1 pound 1½-inch nails
      or 3-inch nails
      (depending on the size of your
      mailing tube)
    Hammer
    Cardboard mailing tube
    Mailing tube stoppers or
      colored duct tape (if your tube
      has none)
    Funnel
    Rice, lentils, popcorn, or dried beans
    Con-Tact paper or colored paper and
      tape
    Colored string or embroidery floss

First, let your kids hammer all of the nails into the tube to make an inner maze. Advise them to drive the nails straight through, because the ends will poke out if they are driven at an angle (if this happens, you can simply push the nails back out and adjust their angle by hand).

Seal up one end of each tube, either with a stopper sold with the tube or with duct tape. Then, let your kids experiment with the different choices you've provided for the filling. To minimize spilling, they can use a funnel to pour a test amount of rice or beans (start with about 1 cup) into the tube. Then, they can seal the open end with one hand while they try out the sounds. Once they decide what the contents of the tube will be, seal both ends securely, so that it doesn't rain beans all over your kitchen floor.

To decorate the rain stick, wrap it with Con-Tact paper or use colored paper and tape (this also ensures that the nails will stay in place). Lastly, tie a colorful tassel, made from braided string or embroidery floss, onto one end of the rain stick.

Strike Up a Band

To spark your child's interest in music, you don't need to buy a shiny new instrument. In fact, he'll learn a lot about musical sounds if he makes one of his own. Rhythm can spring from anything, such as a popcorn-filled can shaker to a pair of spoons you click against your knee. Here are two music-making projects that come right from the recycling bin:

Backyard music station: String a series of gongs from a tree or clothesline. Use old hubcaps and sturdy, clay flowerpots, both of which already have holes to thread string through. For strikers, use wooden spoons or chopsticks with rubber bands wrapped around the ends. Get your kids to experiment by hitting different parts of each gong.

Trash can drum: Lay a piece of canvas across the top of a trash can and tape down the edges, pulling the drumhead tight as you do so. Tie string around the can just below the rim for reinforcement. To tighten the drumhead, spray the canvas with water and then let it dry. Play the drum with wooden spoons, sticks, or with your hands.

The Toy Factory

155

70944

Simple Shakers

Paper clip shaker: Fill a plastic box with paper clips and then tape the box securely shut. For a handhold, press together the sticky sides of two pieces of tape. Form a loop and tape it to the top of the box.

Soda can shaker: Pour sand or rice into an empty soda can and then tape paper over the opening for a soft, swishing sound.

For more handcrafted shakers see:

New Year's Noisemakers (page 204)

Giggle Shakers (page 205)

Yogurt Cup Shakers

Enthusiastic percussionists in your household will have no problem keeping a handle on these snazzy maracas.

Materials

2 clean, empty yogurt cups with covers
Popcorn kernels, dried beans, or sand
2 wooden spoons
Hot glue gun
Acrylic paints and paintbrushes

For each shaker, pour various amounts of popcorn kernels, dried beans, or sand into a yogurt cup. Have your child cover the cup with her hand and shake until she finds a sound she likes.

Once she's decided on the type and amount of filling, hot-glue the cover onto the cup (adults only). Next, attach a handle by hot-gluing the bowl of the wooden spoon to the cover. Now your child can decorate the shakers with a bright coat of paint.

FunFact

The first children's rattles (circa 1360 B.C.) were made of clay. Shaped like animals, they were filled with pebbles and then covered with silk to protect little hands should they break.

Yogurt Cup Shakers

Bean Rattles

Box Harp

This box harp inspired by *My First Music Book* (Dorling Kindersley), a guide to making and playing simple musical instruments, operates on the same principles as the real thing. When you pluck the strings, they cause the body of the harp to vibrate, which starts a series of sound waves — the music we hear. The pitch of the notes, high or low, depends on the width and tautness of the strings.

Materials

> Small box and lid
> Wrapping paper
> Colored markers
> Craft knife
> Cardboard
> Glue
> 4 rubber bands of different widths

Use the wrapping paper and markers to decorate the box. Next, cut an oval hole in the lid with the craft knife (parents only). For a bridge, fold a strip of cardboard into a triangular prism and cut four notches along the top. Glue the bridge in place below the hole. Slide the rubber bands over the box (and into the bridge notches) and start plucking.

Bean Rattle

Face the music with a colorful shaker that doubles as a dancing puppet.

Materials

> Colored markers or crayons
> Construction paper
> Plastic liter soda bottle
> White glue
> Twine
> ½ cup dried beans
> Thick 15-inch stick
> Beads and feathers

Have your child draw bold, colorful facial features on pieces of construction paper. Turn the soda bottle upside down and glue on the drawings to create a masklike face. To add hair, gather ten lengths of twine in a bundle, knot the center, and glue the bunch to the front of the bottle above the face.

Next, pour the dried beans into the bottle. Push the stick snugly into the spout and apply glue to hold it. For a finishing touch, tie strings of beads and feathers around the stick.

Box Harp

The Toy Factory

Chapter Eight

Ready to Wear

FOR CENTURIES, Americans have left their mark on fashion. In the 1800s, it was stovepipe hats and laced corsets, and in the early 1900s, flapper dresses and zoot suits. But possibly the most expressive trends of all came from the 1960s when many of us tie-dyed our shirts and embroidered our blue jeans. What freedom we felt back then, tossing our father's staid old white T-shirts into the dye bin or chopping our frayed blue jeans into skirts and pocketbooks. Even if we were only in grammar school, we got to be groovy.

Now our children, growing up three decades later, can express themselves by turning their clothes into works of art. Much to his delight, a preschooler can experience the exhilaration of pressing potato stamps on a jersey (page 161). ("This is okay? I can put paint on my shirt!?") Older kids will be thrilled, and plenty skillful enough, to apply dyes or sew decorations on their clothes. After all, the processes of stamping, gluing, and stenciling make a child's wardrobe truly his own.

The projects in this chapter are largely free of the socio-political commentary of the 1960s — they're mostly just fun. Your child can use them to recycle a tired old pair of overalls into a fabulous new outfit (page 167), turn plain sneakers or shoelaces into wearable masterpieces (page 170), or color up a soft sweatshirt that used to belong to Dad (page 165). Above all, they can use them to celebrate their own creativity.

Pasta Jewelry, page 177

Prep your garments for decorating.

Prewash new T-shirts and garments before

String Stamp Shirt, page 162

Clothes-decorating Supplies

Don't throw away old clothes — save them for a rainy day when your kids can transform them into brand-new styles. Here's a checklist of supplies that will come in handy for decorating shirts, socks, sneakers, or even shoelaces.

✄ **Fabric crayons and markers, fabric paints, and dyes** (just be sure they're designed for fabric use and won't wash out in the laundry).

✄ **Disposable containers** (for paints and dyes), **paintbrushes, stencil brush, and sponges.**

✄ **Measuring tape, fabric scissors, sewing and embroidery needles and floss, thread, sewing elastic, fabric glue, and a hot glue gun.**

✄ **Fabric scraps, felt, ribbon, rickrack, pom-poms, and pipe cleaners.**

✄ **Sequins, beads, buttons, trinkets, and glitter glue.**

✄ **Cardboard, tracing paper, and masking tape.**

applying fabric paints or dyes. In all cases, refer to the manufacturer's instructions for setting color, as well as washing, drying, or ironing the decorated garment. And afterward, never wash them with your whites!

Keep fabric paints on hand. Plan a trip with your kids to your local art supply store to stock up on fabric pens, paints that puff, permanent glitter markers, or other supplies your kids can use to leave their stamp on their clothes.

When in doubt, practice first. When printing with potato stamps or using a medium you've never tried before, experiment first on paper, a handkerchief, or a scrap of fabric.

Dress in old clothes while you work. Fabric markers and paints do stain, so before you set them out to use, be sure your kids are wearing smocks or old clothes you don't care about. When using fabric dyes, it also is a good idea to wear rubber gloves.

Defer to your kids' tastes. Try not to flinch if your kids sew flashy beads or rows of sequins on a garment you think looks good already. Fashion is in the eye of the designer — and we were in our kids' shoes once, if without the sequins.

Have a party! Most of the projects in this chapter lend themselves to festive group activities. Plan a birthday party — or a Scout meeting — around T-shirt decorating or jewelry-making.

Paper Bead Bonanza, page 177

Cool Clothes

Stamped T-shirt

For kids, a colorful design, particularly one they come up with on their own, can turn an ordinary T-shirt into a favorite article of clothing. This simple potato-printing technique lets your child stamp a plain shirt or jersey with a variety of bright, bold shapes.

Materials

- Cardboard
- Prewashed T-shirt
- Masking tape
- Paring knife
- Potatoes
- Pencil
- Nontoxic fabric paints and paintbrushes
- Pie plates or flat bowls
- Scrap paper

To begin, place the cardboard inside the shirt and tape the arms together in back (this provides a flat printing surface and prevents paint from seeping through).

For a printing block, cut a potato in half (a parent's job). Have your child use a pencil to lightly etch interesting shapes on the flat surfaces of the two halves. Then, help her cut away the parts of the potato around her design and blot it with a paper towel.

Pour a shallow layer of paint into the pie plates or bowls and have your child practice printing the designs on scrap paper. Show her how to apply the paint by evenly pressing the potato into the paint dish or by dipping a brush into the color and painting it onto the potato. She then can stamp a pattern of random or repeated images on the shirt.

When your child's design is complete, let the paint dry thoroughly, then heat-set it according to the manufacturer's directions. This usually involves running a very hot iron over each area for about 30 seconds. You may want to iron from the reverse side of the shirt with a rag underneath to protect both the iron and the board. Then, the shirt is ready to wear.

Fruit Stamps

Instead of potatoes, stamp the beautiful shapes of other vegetables and fruits. Cut open the fruits and vegetables and blot the cut surfaces with a paper towel. Your kids can pick their favorite shapes, press them into some fabric paint and then onto a T-shirt. Onions, peppers, and pears work especially well, and an apple cut in half lengthwise will print heart shapes. Remind them not to squeeze the fruits or the paint will bleed. After the shirt is decorated, hang it up to dry before heat-setting the paint.

Ready to Wear

String Stamps

If squiggly lines and wacky spirals strike your child's fancy, these home-made stamps are just the ticket for sprucing up a cotton top or sweatshirt.

Materials

> Corrugated cardboard
> Pencil and ruler
> Glue
> Thick twine
> Prewashed T-shirt or sweatshirt
> Thin cardboard
> Fabric paint
> Plastic dish

1. Cut the corrugated cardboard into several 3-inch squares and have your child draw a design on each one. Next, help him trace the design with an even line of glue.

2. Press a single strand of twine directly on top of the glue. Then, let the glue dry thoroughly so that the twine is secure before stamping.

3. Stretch the T-shirt or sweatshirt flat (but not too tightly) by fitting thin cardboard inside the shirt. Pour some fabric paint in a paper or plastic dish. Place the stamp, twine-side down, in the dish and push it around in the paint until it is evenly covered. Then, press the stamp onto the shirt, applying equal pressure on the stamp before lifting it. One coat of paint should last for two or three stampings.

Your child may choose to cover every inch of the shirt or to print just one row of the design. If he wishes to print a single string shape in a variety of colors, either he can wait for the first layer of paint to dry before applying a second, or he can make a duplicate stamp.

Let the finished design air-dry before setting the color (see the paint manufacturer's directions) and washing and drying the shirt.

Designer T-shirts

FamilyFun crafter Maryellen Sullivan has shirt decorating down to a T. Here are a few of her favorite ideas.

Materials

Prewashed T-shirt
Nontoxic fabric paints and paint-
    brushes, fabric dye, or fabric pens
Disposable paint containers
Pom-poms
Fabric glue

Monster Mania: Paint on a brilliant purple monster with pom-poms glued to the tops of his spiraling antennae.

Identi-Ts: Fill the center of the shirt with your child's first initial and have him paint all of his favorite things around the letter — tiny cars, music notes, pets, sports equipment, or even his favorite foods.

Hanging Out: Paint a zigzagging clothesline across a T-shirt and hang a miniature wardrobe out to dry.

Works of Art: Have your child thumb through colorful art books to find a picture he likes, then help him decorate a T-shirt with his own rendition of the artwork.

Two Tones: Create the sea and sky by dyeing the bottom half of a T-shirt blue and painting in an underwater world. On the top half of the shirt, paint sunshine, seagulls, ships, and leaping fish. For a farm scene, dye a shirt bottom green and paint a field of farm animals. Add a barn, a butterfly, and even a rainbow above the horizon.

Novel-Ts: Children can translate their favorite songs, stories, or poems onto a T-shirt by printing the words with colorful fabric pens and illustrating the piece in fabric paint.

Monster
Mania

Hanging
Out

Works
of Art

Two
Tones

SPLATTER SHIRTS

This free-form splatter technique is especially suited for young T-shirt designers. All it takes is fabric paint and a flick of the wrist to create a wearable masterpiece.

First, hang one or more prewashed white T-shirts outside on a clothesline (be sure the clothesline is far away from unintended targets). If the day is windy, it's a good idea to slip a rectangular piece of cardboard inside each shirt to keep it rigid.

Next, pour nontoxic fabric paints into disposable containers, such as aluminum pie plates, plastic lids, or muffin pan liners, and let your children (dressed in smocks or old bathing suits) dip paintbrushes into the paint and flick it onto the shirts. Don't worry about giving much artistic direction for this part. The flicking will come easily to children and will no doubt be accompanied by dribbling, splattering, smearing, or long-distance slings, so just stay clear.

Leave the shirts on the clothesline to dry thoroughly. If you don't want the paint to run even more, take them down and allow them to dry flat.

Refer to the fabric paint package for specific directions on setting the color and washing the shirt.

Novel-T

Ready to Wear

163

Stenciled Ts

single outline (internal patterns will be lost once you start cutting).

Cut a straight line from the outer edge of the cardboard to the design. Next, carefully cut around the outline and remove the inside shape. Patch up the cut to the outer edge with a piece of tape to complete the stencil. Next, lay the T-shirt flat and slip a piece of cardboard inside the body. Then, your child can tape the stencil onto the cloth.

2. Now, pour some fabric paint into a plastic dish. Dip the stencil brush into the paint, tapping it a few times to remove any excess. Holding the brush upright, gently stamp it up and down inside the stencil until the design is colored in completely. (If you are using a regular paintbrush, apply the paint in strokes from the stencil's outside edge toward the center.)

Move the stencil to another spot and repeat until the design is complete. Once thoroughly dry, heat-set the paint according to the package directions.

STICK-ON STENCIL

FamilyFun reader Lisa Pace, from Salt Lake City, discovered a stenciling method that works even better than cardboard templates. She traces a design onto the dull side of freezer wrap (available at grocery stores), then cuts out the pieces with scissors. Next, she irons the design onto a shirt, waxy-side down so that it will stick to the fabric, and uses fabric paint and a stencil brush to shade all around the edges. Then she carefully pulls off the stencil.

Stenciled Ts

Stenciling is a great method for dressing up a jersey, sweatshirt, or even a baseball cap with distinctive animal figures or geometric shapes. With this foolproof method, kids can cut out easy-to-use templates from empty cereal boxes.

Materials

Cardboard panels from cereal boxes
    or other thin cardboard
Pencil and masking tape
Prewashed T-shirt
Nontoxic fabric paint
Plastic dish
Stencil brushes or paintbrushes

1. Have your child begin by drawing a stencil design on the cardboard. Younger kids can trace cookie cutters or sketch geometric shapes. Point out that the stencil cutouts must have a

164

Crayon Batik Sweatshirts

Wearing your heart on your sleeve is more than a figure of speech with this fashion trick. In fact, this easy batik technique lets kids decorate shirts or hats for a sports team or family reunion by coloring on words and symbols with ordinary crayons.

Materials

Prewashed cotton
    sweatshirt or
    T-shirt
Crayons
Tape
Newspaper
Iron

Before your child draws a design on her clothing, have her sketch out a few drafts on a piece of paper. Encourage her to use bold, basic shapes, such as hearts or stick figures, since intricate patterns tend to lose definition after the garment has been washed a few times. And keep in mind that deep red, blue, or green hues work well on a white background, while pastels are less vivid.

When she's settled on a design, lay the garment on a hard, flat surface and tape it down. Remind your child to press down firmly when drawing on the cloth, retracing and reshading once or twice. To make letters or numbers, form the shapes with cellophane tape, as shown, and shade around the edges.

Once the design is complete, peel off the tape and heat-set the color — place a thick newspaper on top of the ironing board and lay the shirt, colored side down, on top of it. Press the back side of the design (your iron should be on the cotton setting) for a minute or so. Lift the shirt and place it on a fresh spot of newspaper. Press again. Repeat until no color comes off on the paper. Wash the shirt in cool water and tumble dry.

A Gift from the Heart

When her four-year-old daughter, Ravelle, wanted to make a special gift for her babysitter, Amanda, *FamilyFun* reader Toni Kelley thought of the perfect idea — a crayon batik shirt. She used tape to outline the words "I ♥ MY BIG SISTER" on the front of a cotton shirt. Then, Ravelle colored around each letter, and, on the back, she drew a picture of herself and Amanda. "Because there was no messy paint involved, my daughter could do all the work herself," says Toni. "It was truly a gift from the heart."

Crayon Batik Sweatshirts

70944

Snakes Alive!

Here's one reptile that won't give you the willies. Rolled up, it's a cloth snake. Uncoiled, it's a hand-striped T-shirt.

Materials

- Prewashed T-shirt
- Pliers
- 21-inch length of 16-gauge floral wire
- Twist ties
- Heavy-duty thread
- Sewing needle
- Fabric paints and paintbrushes

Lay the shirt front-side down. Use the pliers to bend back the sharp ends of the wire. Then, place the wire diagonally on the shirt back, with one end on the left sleeve and the other touching the lower right corner.

Form the snake's head by folding the corner of the sleeve over the end of the wire. Then, fold over the sides of the sleeve and secure with a twist tie. Using the same method, cover and secure the other end of the wire. This becomes the tip of the snake's tail. Scrunch the rest of the shirt around the wire, applying a twist tie every few inches.

Insert a threaded needle into a fold near the base of the head. Next, wrap the thread firmly around the snake's body, starting at the base of the head and winding your way to the tip of the tail. Remove the twist ties as you reach them. Knot and trim the thread at the tail tip.

Color the snake with bright fabric paints. When your child is ready to wear his creation, snip the thread, remove the wire, and heat-set the paint according to the manufacturer's directions. For more T-shirt surprises, pick up "McCall's Creates" booklet No. 14220 at fabric stores.

Snakes Alive!

Overhaul Your Overalls

Overhaul Your Overalls

With this beginner project, a young seamstress can sidestep intricate dress patterns and use felt cutouts, beads, buttons, and even charms to give an old pair of overalls a new look.

Materials

> Denim overalls
> Fabric pen
> Sewing needle
> Thread or
>   embroidery floss
> Buttons, charms, and
>   beads
> Felt
> Fabric scissors

Before sewing on buttons, mark their placement with a fabric pen. Then, feed thread through a large-eye sewing needle and knot the end. Remind your child to start sewing from the inside of the garment, pushing the needle through the cloth and making an anchor stitch (see right) on top of the mark before adding a button. Now she can stitch repeatedly through the button's holes until the button is firmly attached. Finish with a couple of anchor stitches on the inside of the denim before cutting the thread and sewing on other buttons.

To attach a row of beads, have your child make an anchor stitch and slide one bead over the needle to the bottom of the thread. Push the needle through the denim and back up again. Add more beads in the same manner and end the row with an anchor stitch.

To add felt shapes, pin them in place and sew down the edges with a few strands of embroidery floss. A blanket stitch (see right) works well. When done, denims can be washed on a delicate cycle and hung up to dry.

Ready to Wear

Denim Tote

It's never easy to part with a favorite pair of blue jeans. But this quick sewing project makes it a cinch to recycle them into a cool book bag.

Materials

> Old blue jeans
> Fabric scissors
> Cotton belt

Zip the jeans and turn them inside out. With a pair of fabric scissors, cut off both jean legs 3 inches from the crotch (a parent's job). Next, fold the cutoff jeans, matching up the side seams as you would to press front and back leg pleats.

Using a sewing machine (or a close, even hand stitch), sew closed each leg opening 1 inch from the cut edge. Then, trim the denim ½ inch from the stitching. Turn the jeans right side out. For a handle, thread a cotton belt through the belt loops and tie the ends together.

Denim Tote

Basic Stitches

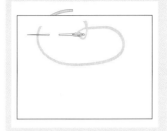

Anchor Stitch: To secure the ends of a seam, pull the thread taut and make a small stitch near the base of the thread. Pull tight (keep the needle tip above the thread) and repeat twice.

Blanket Stitch: This decorative running stitch keeps hem edges flat. Push the threaded needle through the cloth about ¹/₄ inch from the hem. Bring the needle around the hem to the front and again insert the needle through the cloth (³/₄ inch from the first stitch), looping the thread behind the needle. Pull taut. Repeat along the hem.

Socks & Shoes

Slipper Socks

Your kids will get a kick out of this zany slipper craft — it lets them apply puffy designs to their socks. The three-dimensional fabric paint, which is sold at most craft or fabric stores, comes in a variety of colors and costs about $3 for a 1-ounce bottle. It provides plenty of traction on slippery floors.

Materials

> Cotton socks
> Cardboard
> Pencil
> Nontoxic three-dimensional
>   fabric paints

First, prewash and dry the socks, but do not use fabric softener. Next, set a pair of your child's shoes on top of a piece of cardboard and trace around them with a pencil. Cut out the two shoe shapes with scissors. Then, fit the cardboard feet into the socks so that they are pressed flat against the soles of the socks (this will keep the socks flat while decorating).

Now, your child can paint stars, fish, letters, or any other designs he likes on the sock bottoms. Most 3-D paints can be applied straight from the bottle — just press the nozzle gently against the sock to make sure the paint sticks.

Let the paint set overnight before removing the cardboard and wearing the slippers. You'll also want to wait about three days to machine-wash and dry them (refer to the bottle for the proper heat setting).

Fancy Flip-flops

Footwear trends may come and go, but flip-flops have long reigned as the unofficial shoe of summer. Here's how your kids can make their flips truly hip:

✂ **Attach small plastic toys**, such as plastic goldfish, with a hot glue gun.

✂ **Wrap the straps** with colorful embroidery thread.

✂ **Tie on beads** or jingle bells.

✂ **Make a smiley face** by gluing on a pair of googly eyes and painting your toenails red.

Tie-dyed Socks

Although there are dozens of methods for tying socks to achieve bright, bold designs, the circle pattern design is ideal for beginners — it's easy to master and looks great with a single color of dye. You might want to reserve this project for a sunny day and work outside.

Materials

- Plastic bowl or pan
- Nontoxic fabric dye
- White socks
- Rubber bands
- Pennies or buttons
- Plastic spoon

Begin by covering your work area with layers of newspaper or garbage bags. In a plastic bowl or pan, dissolve a packet of nontoxic fabric dye, such as Rit, in hot water according to the package directions. Add more hot water until there is enough to cover a couple of pairs of socks.

Dampen the white socks with clear warm water, then bundle them up in rubber bands. To make stripes, wrap three or four thick rubber bands around the foot and/or top of the sock. To make circles (great for the heels), pinch a section of the sock and tie, about an inch down, with a rubber band. For a pattern of tiny rings, slip pennies or buttons into the socks and wrap bands around them.

When the socks are bound, submerge them in the warm dye and stir occasionally with a plastic spoon. After twenty minutes or so (remember that the color will lighten after the fabric is rinsed and dried), run them under cool water, squeezing until the water runs clear. Remove the bands, smooth out the socks, and rest them flat on layers of newspaper. Let the socks dry overnight. Wash them separately for the first few times to keep any bleeding dye from tinting other clothes.

Tie-dyed T's: Instead of socks, use a prewashed white T-shirt.

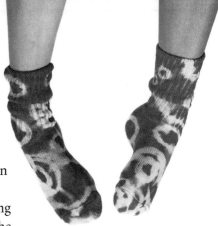

Tie-dyed Socks

Tips on Tie-Dyeing

✄ **Wear rubber gloves when handling dye. If you do get dye on your skin, scrub with soap and a nailbrush — do not use household bleach.**

✄ **To tie-dye with more than one color, use small plastic cups to slowly pour dye onto the fabric. Start with lighter colors and work directly over the central container so that the excess spills back into it. Squeeze out the fabric after each application. When the color is dark enough, rinse the section with cool water and cover it with a plastic bag secured with a rubber band, to protect it from the next color you use.**

When the whole garment is finished, squeeze out any moisture still left in each section before undoing the rubber bands to prevent colors from dripping into each other. Then, lay out the garment to dry.

✄ **When washing tie-dyed garments, always use cold water.**

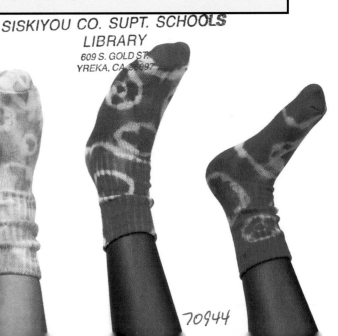

70944

Themed Sneakers

Flower power: Sew on buttons for flower centers, then use fabric paints to brush on colorful petals and leaves.
Zoo life: Dip animal-themed rubber stamps into fabric paints and press them onto the canvas. Or, use a brush to paint on zebra stripes or giraffe spots.
Undersea world: On a pair of blue shoes, paint neon-colored fish.
Night sky: Paint stars, moons, and planets on black shoes with glow-in-the-dark paint.

Rubber-soled Masterpieces

Kids can add a three-dimensional flair — and cool sounds — to their sneakers with buttons, beads, or bells. Keep in mind that flat buttons and beads work best; thicker ones may get lost in kickball games.

Materials

> Canvas sneakers
> Fabric pen or colored marker
> Buttons, beads, or bells
> Fishing line or sturdy thread
> Large-eye needle
> Embroidery floss

First, your child can use the fabric pen or colored marker to mark the spots on her sneakers where she plans to sew on decorations and to draw on designs she will embroider. Then, using a large-eye needle and fishing line or sturdy thread, she can sew the buttons, beads, or bells in place. Next, she can embellish her designs by stitching on colorful lines of embroidery floss.

Hand-painted Sneakers:

Using fabric paint or colored markers, your shoe artist can cover her sneakers with polka dots, stripes, or mini stick figures. To achieve an electric effect, she can brush on fluorescent or glow-in-the-dark, nontoxic paint.

Crazy Laces

To add pep to plain shoelaces, your child can brush on splashes of fabric paint or pens, string beads between the holes as he laces them, or tie small bells or charms onto the tips. Another option is to replace the laces altogether with bright ribbons, braided yarn, or twisted embroidery floss. If your youngster is in the mood for decorative impracticality, have him lace his sneakers backward with bows on the bottom — or invent a new shoe-tying method altogether.

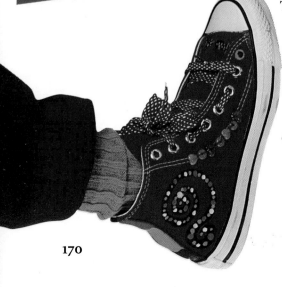

Shades

Cool Shades

There's nothing eye-catching about a pair of plain sunglasses, but touch them up with a few craft supplies, and they're bound to turn heads.

Materials

- Construction paper or colored poster board
- Pipe cleaners
- Glue
- Glitter glue
- Beads, buttons, or pom-poms
- Googly eyes

Flower Power: Cut blossoms (ones that are about 1½ inches wide work well) from construction paper or poster board. Glue the blossoms onto pipe cleaner stems. Then, cut out paper leaves and glue them onto the stems. Twist the stem ends around the frame.

Wing It: Cut a pair of wings from the poster board and brush on glitter glue. Then, glue the wing bases to the sides of the lenses.

Beady Eyes: Glue a row of beads, buttons, or pom-poms along the top of the eyeglasses frame. You can even try gluing together a small pyramid of beads above each lens.

Eyes on You: Stick a pair of googly eyes to the corners of the frame or attach dozens of small ones around the lenses.

Rainy Day Umbrella

In Frostburg, Maryland, nestled in the Appalachian Mountains, it snows and rains more often than not. The inclement weather inspired *FamilyFun* reader Debbie Failinger Buskirk, then a kindergarten teacher in the neighboring town of Cumberland, to cheer her students with an umbrella painting project. She asked each child to bring in an inexpensive umbrella (Debbie suggests looking for them in dollar stores), then set them to work decorating the panels with fabric paints and pens. "Along with waves, fish, and some scribbles," she remembers, "rainbows were a big hit." Tip: Allow the umbrella a full day to dry before closing or taking it out into the rain.

Cool Shades

Ready to Wear

Hats & Hair Ties

Hold On to Your Hats

With this whimsical hat design, your kids might not make headline news, but they'll be wearing it. Fashioning one is simple; all you need is paper and tape.

Materials

Colored tissue paper, crepe paper, gift wrap, or newspaper
Masking tape

Unfold several double sheets of newspaper or cut colored tissue paper, crepe paper, or recycled gift wrap into pieces of comparable size. Place the paper on top of your child's head, fanning out the sheets in different directions. Then, form the crown of the hat, using your hands to gather the paper, all the way around, at eyebrow level. For a brow band, wrap the base of the crown with a long piece of masking tape. Reinforce with a second layer. For taller styles, such as a stovepipe or a Stetson, bundle up the paper so that it rises several inches above your child's forehead before you apply tape.

Once you fashion the crown, remove the hat from your child's head and use scissors to shape the brim. Round the edges to make a floppy bonnet, then decorate with a ribbon sash and silk flowers. To style a derby, trim the brim an inch or two from the brow band and adorn with a feather. For a baseball cap, cut the brim flush with the brow band along the sides and back. Then, round the front brim to create a visor. Another style is a watch cap: merely roll up the brim all the way to the band.

Hold On to Your Hats

Recycled Barrettes

By the time *FamilyFun* reader Lauren MacDonald, from Orlando, Florida, was eleven years old, she had an impressive collection of barrettes. "I have three sisters," says Lauren, "so we have drawers full of barrettes with nothing on them." After gathering up their supply, Lauren and her eight-year-old sister, Kara, adorned them with bows, buttons, balloons, and ribbons.

Materials
Poster board
Ribbons, buttons, shells, and other trinkets
White glue
Plain barrettes
Hot glue gun

Ready to Wear

Cover a large surface with newspaper and have your child spread out all of the items she may use. Next, cut out a piece of poster board that is slightly larger than the barrette back. Have your child sketch a pattern on the cutout and fill it in with buttons, balloons, pins, old puzzle pieces, or miniature bows. Once she's finished the design, carefully push aside the materials and cover the poster board with hot glue (a parent's job). Then, press the collage items onto the glued surface and hot glue the decorated poster board onto the barrette.

No-Sew Scrunchies

There's no such thing as having too many scrunchies. With this no-sew technique, your child can turn out a snappy collection in no time.

Materials
Old necktie
12-inch-long piece of sewing elastic
Masking tape and a pencil
Hot glue gun

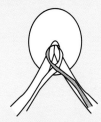

Cut a 24-inch length from the necktie. Thread the sewing elastic through the center of the tie by taping one end of the sewing elastic to the end of the pencil and then pulling the material down over the pencil. Once the elastic is threaded through, remove the tape and tie together the elastic ends.

To complete the scrunchie, pull one end of the tie over the other end and hot glue the loop closed (a parent's job). Lastly, adjust the tie so that the gathered material is evenly distributed around the circle.

Herringbone Braid

This decorative hairstyle, also known as the fishtail, is just right for festive occasions.

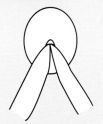

1. Pull your hair into a ponytail and tie with an elastic band. Divide the ponytail into two parts.

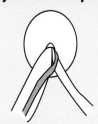

2. Pull out a narrow section of hair from under the right side, cross it over, and add it to the left side, as shown here.

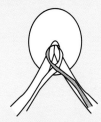

3. Next, pull a small bunch of hair from under the left side of the ponytail and add it to the right side. Repeat steps 2 and 3 until the braid is the desired length.

Jewelry

First, your child will need to draw a pair of either matching or complementary images, such as salt and pepper shakers or a snowman and a snowwoman. Remind her that the images should be small (for a guide, she can mark two 1½-inch squares on the paper and then sketch within the lines). Another option is to cut designs from a magazine or gift wrap.

Next, she should cut around the finished drawings and stick them face-up onto a square of Con-Tact paper. Press another piece of Con-Tact paper tacky-side down on top of the drawings to seal them. Then, trim away the excess Con-Tact paper. For pierced earrings, poke small holes in the tops and attach the hangers; for clip-ons, glue the fasteners to the backs.

Artful Earrings

Snowman Pin

This little snowman looks frosty, but pinned on a child's jacket he's sure to prompt a warm smile. To make one, lay two buttons facedown one above the other. Position the head so that the button-holes resemble eyes; the holes in the body should look like vest buttons. Glue a pin back to the rear of the buttons. Then, glue on a small felt top hat and tie on a ribbon scarf.

Artful Earrings

The secret to designing these hand-made earrings lies at the tip of a pen. With a couple of drawings, your child can make a pair to accessorize a favorite outfit or give as a gift to a friend.

Materials

Heavyweight paper
Fine-tipped colored markers
Clear Con-Tact paper
Earring hangers or fasteners
   (available at bead and craft
   stores)

Jewelry Frames

Instead of stashing jewelry in a box, this decorative screen lets your child hang up her earrings and necklaces and dress up a bedroom wall or bureau top at the same time.

Materials

- Corrugated cardboard
- Craft knife
- Wire cutters
- Metal screening (available by the foot at hardware stores)
- White glue
- Craft paints

For a freestanding earring frame, use a 9- by 18-inch piece of cardboard. Set it on a hard surface with the long edges at the top and bottom and use a craft knife (adults only) to cut a 5- by 6-inch opening in the center.

Measure and mark the bottom of the frame 3½ inches in from both sides. Draw a line from each mark to the top of the frame, slightly angling it toward the center. Then, score the cardboard along the lines (do not cut all the way through) to form foldable flaps. Trim the flaps into L shapes, angling the bottoms a small amount so the frame tilts back when standing.

Next, place a 6- by 7-inch piece of metal screening on top of the opening and glue the edges to the cardboard. Cover the screen edges by gluing on layered cardboard strips. Cut notches in the top of the frame to hold rings or necklaces and decorate the front with paint.

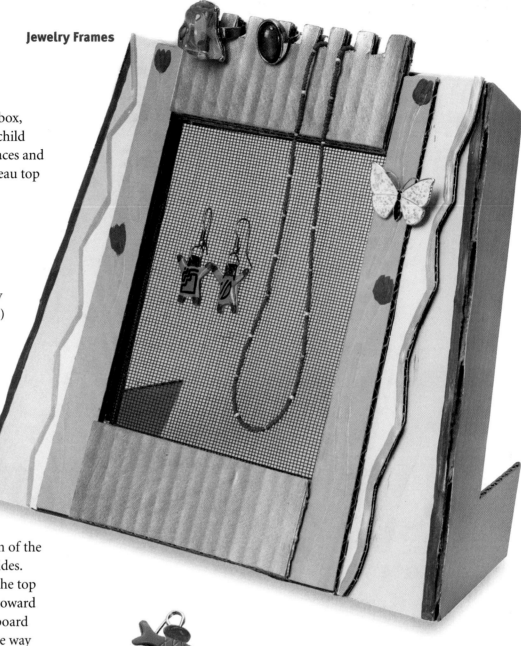

Pin-on Charms

Here's a jewelry-making method that's a snap for kids. First, open up a safety pin, slip a few beads over the point, and close the clasp. Then, use one or more of these charms to make a necklace or bracelet — cut a piece of leather cord to the desired length and tie half of a barrel clasp (available at bead stores) to one of the ends. Next, string on charms by threading the cord through the loop joints of the beaded safety pins. (For a jazzier effect, encourage your child to experiment a bit by tying overhand knots or stringing beads between the charms.) Finally, tie the other half of the clasp to the loose end of the cord. To redesign a necklace or bracelet, simply open the safety pins and slip on a new set of beads.

Ready to Wear

Friendship Bracelet

Friendship Bracelet

Best friends are often inseparable. To prove to each other that their bond will last, your child and her pal can fill up their arms with a batch of friendship bracelets.

Materials

6 24-inch strands of embroidery thread

Tape

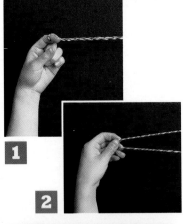

1. Hold the embroidery thread strands together with the ends matched up, then tie an overhand knot 1 inch from an end. Tape the knot to a table-top (or anchor it in a closed drawer). Holding the free end, twist the bunch repeatedly in the same direction until it is tightly wound, as shown.

2. Pinch the twisted band in the center and fold it in half so that the free end matches up with the knotted end. Release the center, and the band will automatically twist back on itself.

Slip the ends through the loop (the pinch point) at the opposite end of the band, tie a knot to secure the bracelet, knot again, and trim the ends.

FunFact

Legend has it that Peace Corps workers first taught Guatemalan children how to make friendship bracelets. Now the bracelets—in bright Guatemalan hues—have made their way back Stateside.

Paper Bead Bonanza

With this bead-making technique, your kids can spin paper and straws into a stash of colorful jewelry.

Materials

- Magazine photos or gift wrap
- Waxed paper
- Glue stick
- Drinking straws

For each bead, cut out a triangular strip of paper that measures about 1¼ inches across the base and 10½ inches from the base to the tip. Lay the strip facedown on a piece of waxed paper or cardboard. With the glue stick (you can also use white glue applied with a small paintbrush), coat the surface of the paper with adhesive.

Stick the base of the strip to the side of a drinking straw. Wrap the paper repeatedly around the straw, applying more glue, if necessary, to stick down the tip of the triangle. (You should be able to fit five or six beads on a single straw.) Once the glue dries, use scissors to cut away the straw on both sides of each bead. Thread the finished beads on cord or string. Or, use craft wire to attach single beads to earring hangers.

Paper Bead Bonanza

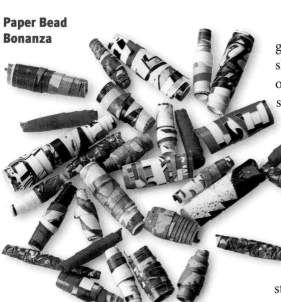

Pasta Jewelry

Pasta Jewelry

The art of making pasta jewelry is no longer limited to stringing macaroni — today's kids can thread wheels, rigatoni, and just about any other type of dried pasta with a hole in the center into bracelets, necklaces, and charms.

Materials

- Pasta
- Acrylic paints, glitter glue, or food coloring
- Paintbrush
- White glue
- String or beading cord

For a bold effect, use acrylic paint or glitter glue to color individual pasta shapes. Or, color a variety of pastas at one time by shaking them in a quart-size jar with a few drops of food coloring and a teaspoon of water. To dry, drain the excess liquid and spread the colored beads on paper towels.

Brush on a coat of glue mixed with a little water to add sheen and strength to the tinted beads. Then, thread them onto string or beading cord, knot the string ends, and wear.

Ready to Wear

Pasta Pets

When you're finished making necklaces, you can use your leftover noodles to make one of these posable toy animals.

First, create the animal's torso by sliding a few pieces of pasta onto the center of a pipe cleaner. (Wagon wheels are perfect for a chubby belly, rigatoni for a lean one.)

Then, bend the pipe cleaner on both sides of the torso to form a neck and a tail. Add more pasta and fold the tips of the pipe cleaner to hold the pieces in place. Bend the neck (between pastas) into a right angle to form a face.

To attach legs, ears, or horns, twist shorter lengths of pipe cleaner around the body and string them with macaroni. You can even glue on miniature soup pastas for a mane or fur.

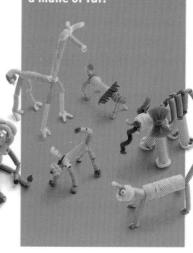

Chapter Nine

Gifts Kids Can Make

E VERY YEAR, *FamilyFun* contributing editor Lynne Bertrand makes a gift for each of her two children. One of six-year-old son Nick's first presents was a stuffed monkey; for her daughter Georgia, age three, Lynne knit a tiny Christmas sweater.

The bulk of Lynne's gift-making is done right by her children's bedside. "While the kids are falling asleep, they want me nearby," she says. "That's when I work on their presents. It means so much more to them when they see me at it, night after night. 'That's going to be for me, right?' they always ask."

As Nick and Georgia are lucky to be learning, handmade gifts are a two-for-one deal. You get the gift itself, of course. But you also get the delicious knowledge that somebody thought about you the whole time he or she was making it. While children may not grasp this concept consciously, they are easily inspired by it. They won't wrestle with dropped stitches until midnight, but they will get excited to make a jaunty button boy key chain (page 185) for a teacher, a hedgehog pincushion (page 195) for a fun-loving aunt, or a picture frame (page 194) for a friend. And just like adults, kids anticipate the gleeful reaction to the gifts they've made.

In honor of that excitement, this chapter is brimming with gifts kids can make. Some take time; others lend themselves to last-minute efforts or mass production. But every single one is a keeper. So let your kids flip through these pages — and make sure they don't skip the last few, which offer up homemade wrapping paper and gift tags for packaging that extra-special present.

Glitter Paper, page 196

Kits for Crafty Kids

Craft kits are thoughtful gifts for a brother, sister, or schoolmate. First, help your child choose a craft the recipient will enjoy making. Then, gather the supplies needed. Pack everything into a box, photocopy the craft directions, and tie with a bow. Many of the crafts in this book lend themselves to a gift kit. Here are a few that beg to be wrapped up:

T-shirt kit: Along with a new T-shirt, wrap up a pile of decorating supplies. See page 160 for ideas.

Doll-making kit: For a doll-lover, give the materials for making the worry dolls (page 138) or all the accessories for finger puppets (page 139).

Sewing kit: This is a great excuse to introduce a child to sewing. For a complete kit, see page 195.

Homemade play clay: Measure out and pack the materials for a batch of clay into a Tupperware container, which can later be used to store clay (add in a few sculpting tools, too). See page 85 for a recipe.

Jewelry box: Into an inexpensive jewelry box, pack the supplies for earrings (page 174), pins (page 175), or a necklace (page 177).

Choose the right gift for the right person: You can enrich the gift-making experience for your child by helping him match his handiwork with the right recipients. First, choose someone who really will cherish something homemade. Next, spend some time talking with your child about what kinds of things that person likes.

Think function. People always appreciate a gift that really works for them. A child's drawing is wonderful, but it's even better (and easier to display) if you turn it into a bookmark or a picture frame with the child's photograph in it.

Over the holidays, take time to craft gifts. Instead of rushing to buy presents for everyone on your holiday list, set aside an afternoon for crafting a few. Not only are homemade gifts more personal, but making them will also give your family the chance to slow down during the busy holiday season — and to get into the spirit of giving.

Mass-produce if necessary. Around the holidays, you may need a lot of little gifts for the people in your daily life. This chapter offers a few ideas for things you can make in large quantities, such as the cutout coasters (page 189), the light switch plates (page 188), and even the birthday calendar (page 185), which

you can duplicate on a copy machine. For more specific holiday ideas, look through the Homemade for the Holidays chapter, which begins on page 200.

Let your child make one for himself, too. Kids are wonderful givers, but let's face it: they're even better receivers. If the gift you're making is something your child might enjoy, by all means encourage him to make two. Plus, your child may get a kick out of having an apron that matches Grandma's or a hand-decorated bedroom clock like the one in Mom's study.

Handprint Apron, page 186

Portable Playhouse

Just for Kids

Lightweight and cheery, this free-standing Styrofoam cottage makes a nice birthday or Christmas gift for a little sister or brother. It's roomy enough for a tea party but also can be folded together for easy storage in a closet or under a bed.

Materials

- 4 3¼- by 4-foot sheets of Fome-Cor (available at hardware stores)
- Utility knife
- Tempera paints
- Paint roller or paintbrushes
- String or thin rope

First, use the utility knife (adults only) to cut out windowpanes and a door from the four pieces of Fome-Cor to create the playhouse walls. Then, cover both sides of the walls with a base coat of paint. Paint on trim and wall decorations.

Now it's time to raise the walls. First, cut holes in each corner and centered on both sides, 1 inch in from the edge. Then, thread string or rope through the holes and tie the walls together at the corners.

To hang curtains, cut holes through the walls above each window, thread pieces of string through, and tie the rods in place. Use the same method to attach a shoe box for a window planter or a cardboard canister for a mailbox.

Easy Indoor Hideaways

Table fort: Pin two sheets together and drape them over a kitchen table. Lift each leg and slide a bit of sheet under it to anchor the walls, leaving a small opening for a door at one of the ends.

Comfort zone: Rearrange the playroom furniture to build a soft and cozy fort. Backs of upholstered chairs or a sofa can serve as one or two walls. Close in the rest of the fort with sofa cushions set on their sides. Then, cover the construction with a sheet or blanket.

Portable Playhouse

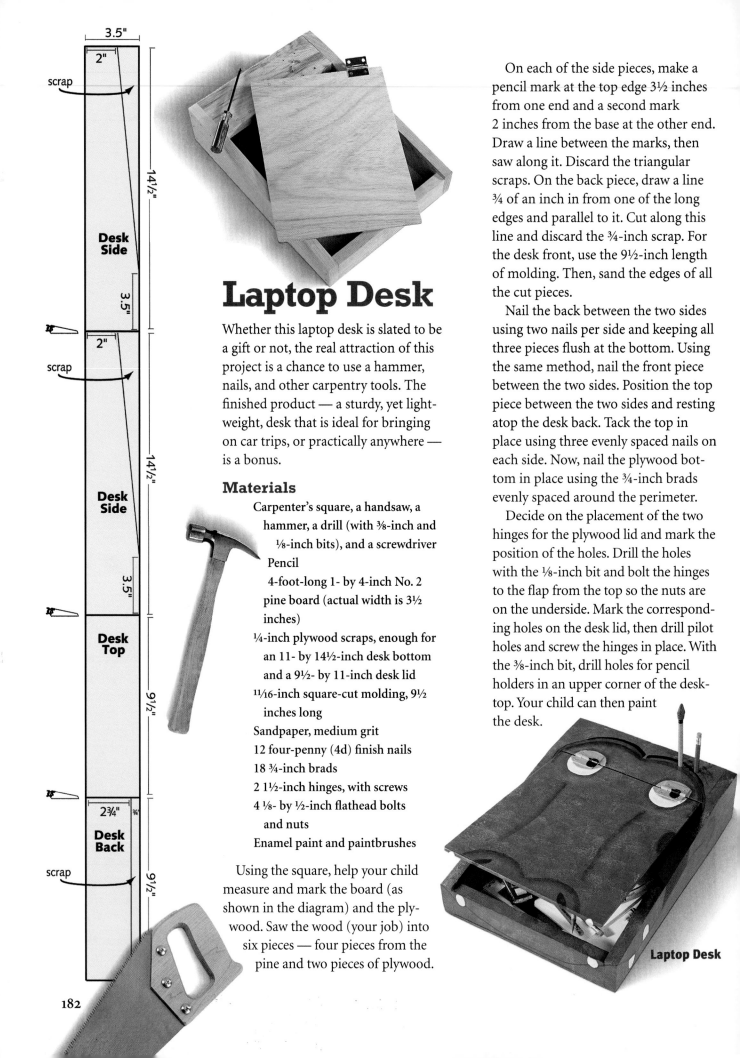

Diagram labels (left side):

3.5"
2"
scrap
14½"
Desk Side
3.5"
2"
scrap
14½"
Desk Side
3.5"
Desk Top
9½"
2¾" ¾"
Desk Back
scrap
9½"

Laptop Desk

Whether this laptop desk is slated to be a gift or not, the real attraction of this project is a chance to use a hammer, nails, and other carpentry tools. The finished product — a sturdy, yet lightweight, desk that is ideal for bringing on car trips, or practically anywhere — is a bonus.

Materials

Carpenter's square, a handsaw, a hammer, a drill (with ⅜-inch and ⅛-inch bits), and a screwdriver
Pencil
4-foot-long 1- by 4-inch No. 2 pine board (actual width is 3½ inches)
¼-inch plywood scraps, enough for an 11- by 14½-inch desk bottom and a 9½- by 11-inch desk lid
¹¹/₁₆-inch square-cut molding, 9½ inches long
Sandpaper, medium grit
12 four-penny (4d) finish nails
18 ¾-inch brads
2 1½-inch hinges, with screws
4 ⅛- by ½-inch flathead bolts and nuts
Enamel paint and paintbrushes

Using the square, help your child measure and mark the board (as shown in the diagram) and the plywood. Saw the wood (your job) into six pieces — four pieces from the pine and two pieces of plywood.

On each of the side pieces, make a pencil mark at the top edge 3½ inches from one end and a second mark 2 inches from the base at the other end. Draw a line between the marks, then saw along it. Discard the triangular scraps. On the back piece, draw a line ¾ of an inch in from one of the long edges and parallel to it. Cut along this line and discard the ¾-inch scrap. For the desk front, use the 9½-inch length of molding. Then, sand the edges of all the cut pieces.

Nail the back between the two sides using two nails per side and keeping all three pieces flush at the bottom. Using the same method, nail the front piece between the two sides. Position the top piece between the two sides and resting atop the desk back. Tack the top in place using three evenly spaced nails on each side. Now, nail the plywood bottom in place using the ¾-inch brads evenly spaced around the perimeter.

Decide on the placement of the two hinges for the plywood lid and mark the position of the holes. Drill the holes with the ⅛-inch bit and bolt the hinges to the flap from the top so the nuts are on the underside. Mark the corresponding holes on the desk lid, then drill pilot holes and screw the hinges in place. With the ⅜-inch bit, drill holes for pencil holders in an upper corner of the desktop. Your child can then paint the desk.

Laptop Desk

Pillow Prints

Pillow Prints

Instead of keeping all of his favorite pictures in an album, your child can display them collage style on a personalized pillow for Grandma or a best friend. Of course, he'll probably want to make an extra one — it can also come in handy for a sleepover. The project involves two steps — first, making a collage, and second, taking it to a photocopy shop to have the image transferred onto a pillowcase (the average cost is about $12).

Materials

Photographs
Sheet of plain paper
Glue
Pillowcase
Trinkets or beads

Once your child has picked the photos he wants to use, ask him to cut out the images with a pair of scissors and arrange them on the white paper. When he is happy with his design, have him glue the cutouts in place, and the collage will be ready to take to the photocopier's.

There, ask the clerk to make a slightly reduced color photocopy of the collage to sharpen the images and then to transfer the photocopy image onto a pillowcase (you'll need to supply your own) or a piece of washable fabric you can sew into a cover. At home, your child can finish off his printed pillowcase by sewing on trinkets or beads.

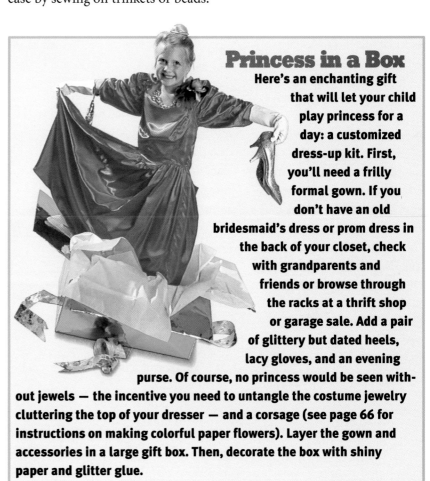

Princess in a Box

Here's an enchanting gift that will let your child play princess for a day: a customized dress-up kit. First, you'll need a frilly formal gown. If you don't have an old bridesmaid's dress or prom dress in the back of your closet, check with grandparents and friends or browse through the racks at a thrift shop or garage sale. Add a pair of glittery but dated heels, lacy gloves, and an evening purse. Of course, no princess would be seen without jewels — the incentive you need to untangle the costume jewelry cluttering the top of your dresser — and a corsage (see page 66 for instructions on making colorful paper flowers). Layer the gown and accessories in a large gift box. Then, decorate the box with shiny paper and glitter glue.

Gifts Kids Can Make

183

For Family & Friends

A Family Flag

GIFT CALENDAR

FamilyFun **reader Susan M. Paprocki of Northbrook, Illinois, recycles her kids' most creative artwork into gift calendars. First, she photocopies the new year's calendar pages. Then the kids choose and sign twelve of their favorite masterpieces. They match each piece of art with a calendar month and paste both onto a large sheet of construction paper. After collating the twelve pages, they bind them together using two key rings (available at discount stores). The calendars make wonderful treasures for family members, and each child's artwork continues to please others throughout the year.**

A Family Flag

Making a felt banner covered with symbols of everyone's favorite things is a terrific way to celebrate family pride. You can make one for a keepsake to hang in your own home or customize a flag to give as a gift to relatives at a family reunion.

Materials

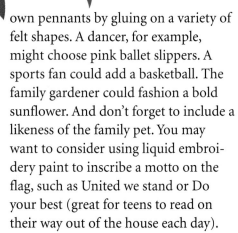

2 yards of 72-inch-
   wide felt
Assorted 9- by 12-
   inch felt rectangles
3½ yards of decorative cording
Glue
Liquid embroidery paint (optional)

Trim the large piece of felt into pennants, one for each family member. Make an extra one for the center of the banner and glue on felt letters cut from a contrasting color to spell your family name. Individuals can decorate their own pennants by gluing on a variety of felt shapes. A dancer, for example, might choose pink ballet slippers. A sports fan could add a basketball. The family gardener could fashion a bold sunflower. And don't forget to include a likeness of the family pet. You may want to consider using liquid embroidery paint to inscribe a motto on the flag, such as United we stand or Do your best (great for teens to read on their way out of the house each day).

To assemble the banner, place the completed pennants on a flat surface, spacing them about 3 inches apart. Run a bead of glue along the upper edge of each one. Lay the cording on top of the glue and press down gently to make it stick. Once the glue is thoroughly dry, you're ready to raise the flag.

> ## FunFact
> **According to *The Guinness Book of Records*, the largest American flag in the world spans 505 by 255 feet and was unfurled over Hoover Dam on May 1st, 1996.**

Button Boy Key Chain

Is your button box bursting at the seams? With this craft project, your child can turn that surplus into a gift for a parent or friend — a colorful doll to use for a key chain or wear as a pendant.

Materials

Heavy-duty elastic thread
(available at fabric stores and
most department stores)
Measuring tape
Buttons

1. Cut two 20-inch lengths of elastic thread. Holding the two pieces together, fold them in half and tie an overhand knot in the folded end to create a 1-inch loop. (When the doll is finished, you can use the loop to attach a key chain or necklace.)

Choose three buttons for the doll's hat. String the hat buttons onto the elastic by dividing the four strands into pairs and thread-ing each of the pairs through a separate buttonhole. Add the widest of the buttons last to create a hat brim. Next, add three medium-size buttons for the doll's head, followed by a couple of slightly wider ones for a shirt collar.

2. For each arm, cut a 6-inch piece of elastic. Thread the ends of the elastic through two different holes of a single button. Slide the button to the center of the strand. String on ten more buttons to form a stack. Knot the elastic just above the top button. To attach both arms to the body, tie the thread ends around the four elastic strands below the doll's collar. Then, add nine new buttons below the collar to create the doll's torso.

For legs, knot the elastic below the torso and, again, divide the strands into two sets. String a dozen or so buttons onto each set of threads, using slightly larger ones at the bottom for the doll's foot. Finally, knot the elastic ends below the feet and trim off any excess.

Button Boy Key Chain

1

2

Leg Threads

JANUARY

1	
2	
3	
4	
5	
6	
7	
8	
9	
10	
11	
12	
13	
14	
15	RACHEL 1969
16	
17	
18	
19	
20	
21	
22	
23	
24	
25	Grandma 1910
26	
27	
28	
29	
30	
31	

Birthday Calendar

Unlike a conventional calendar, a perpetual calendar has no weekday labels, so it can be used year after year. Because it's written in list form, it's a great place for your child to keep track of friends' birthdays and annual events.

For each month, cut a 7- by 17-inch rectangle out of smooth-finish, heavyweight paper (available at art stores). Ask your child to decorate the top of each page. Add the month and a numbered line for each day in it. Then, let him enter his special dates.

Handprint Apron

When her daughter Heather, now eight years old, was in preschool, *FamilyFun* reader Nancy Ojeda of Houston helped the class make a handprint apron for their teacher. The four-year-olds lined up, dipped their hands in saucers of paint, and pressed them on the apron. "It went like clockwork," she says. When they were done, the apron was covered with sixteen little handprints. Nancy appreciated how easy it was to make the gift. What did the kids like? "Oh, the mess!"

Materials

Solid-colored apron
Fabric paints
Paper plates
Fabric pen

Cover your work area with newspaper and lay the apron right-side up. Pour a little paint into a paper plate. Your kids can press their hands into the paint, move them around until the palm sides are covered, then place their handprints on the apron. Continue until the apron is covered with prints. Write each child's name with a fabric pen under his handprint. Let dry for at least 1 day before wearing.

Eight Gift Ideas for Teachers

Box of Chalk
(see page 35)

Brick Bookends
(see page 192)

Creative Bookmarks
(see page 77)

Hand-sewn Blank Book
(see page 76)

Paper Blossoms
(see page 66)

Paper Boxes
(see page 74)

Pencil Toppers
(see page 25)

Personalized Planter
(see page 190)

Tinted Glass

Looking for a memorable end-of-the-year gift for your child's favorite teacher? Try recycling a jar into a hand-painted vase or pencil pot that will add some color to her desk.

Materials

Acrylic or liquid tempera paints
White glue
Clean, clear glass jar
Paintbrushes or Q-Tips
Clear liquid glaze (available at art supply stores)

To make the paints stick to the glass, first mix the colors with some glue. Keep the paint thick so it won't run. Then your child can use brushes or Q-Tips to paint a design on the jar. To erase a mistake, she can use a paper towel to wipe off the paint before it hardens. Once it's dry, she should seal her finished design by brushing on a coat of clear liquid glaze.

Handprint Apron

For the Home

Customized Clock

With a little innovation, your child can turn a plain clock into a masterpiece, just right for hanging in Mom's or Dad's office, or his own bedroom. Dismantling and reassembling the clock may be a project best suited for kids over ten, but even the younger set will find decorating the clock face a breeze.

Materials

> Basic plastic clock (about $7 to $10 at discount or department stores)
> Sheet of sturdy paper
> Pencil and ruler
> Pin or thumbtack
> Assorted craft materials, such as paint, markers, and crayons
> Glue or double-sided tape

First, help your child detach the clear plastic shield that covers the face of his clock. It typically is held in place with plastic tabs or small screws. Trace around the shield onto the paper and cut out the circle, which will serve as the background for the clock face design. Mark the center of the clock face by gently laying the paper circle on top of the uncovered clock and using a pin or thumbtack to make a small hole in the middle.

Next, using a ruler, your child should draw two perpendicular lines through the center of the circle, creating four equal pie slices. The points where these lines touch the circle's edge are where the hours of 12, 3, 6, and 9 will be on his clock. Mark off two equidistant points between each of these four points for the remaining clock hours.

Now, your child can use paint, markers, crayons, or collage materials to customize the clock face. If his mom is a dog-lover, for example, she might like photos of the family pet; a friend who is a stargazer might enjoy a collage of planets and glow-in-the-dark stickers. He also can use cutouts or stickers instead of numerals to mark the hours.

When the design is complete, draw a straight line connecting 6 and 12 o'clock and cut the circle in half along this line. Then, use the knob on the back of the clock to rotate the arms clockwise until they align at 12 o'clock. Following the diagram at right, slip the decorated face into the clock, one half at a time (you may have to cut a small notch in each half to fit around the clock arms). If the clock face fits loosely, secure it with glue or double-sided tape. Finally, replace the plastic shield and reset the clock.

Customized Clock

Gifts Kids Can Make

Jazzy Light-switch Plates

One way to brighten up a child's bedroom or a family room is with a gift pack of hand-decorated light-switch plates.

Materials

> Magazine photos, candy wrappers, postage stamps, or other printed paper
> Light-switch plate
> White glue
> Warm water
> Soft paintbrush

While your child cuts out images she'd like to use from the printed paper, mix together three parts glue and one part warm water. Then, your child can use the paintbrush to coat the back of each cutout before mounting it on the plate (the glue mixture will look white when applied, but it dries clear). Remind her to leave the openings for the screws and switch uncovered.

Fold paper pieces that extend over the edge under the plate to prevent them from curling up. If curling persists when the glue is dry, apply another coat of glue or use strips of clear tape folded over the edges of the plate.

Wallpapered Light-switch Plate:
Place a light-switch plate facedown on a piece of wallpaper. Trace the switch openings with a pencil and draw a ¾-inch border around the plate. Cut around the border and then clip a ¾-inch square from each corner of the cutout. To remove the paper where the switch slot goes, cut an *X* from corner to corner with scissors or a craft knife. The two screw openings can be poked with a sharp pencil. Attach the paper to the front of the plate with an even coat of white glue mix. Fold back the borders and the switch slot flaps to the underside of the plate.

Clay-covered Light-switch Plate:
To create a clay-covered plate, roll out a ⅛-inch-thick slab of Fimo or Sculpey III on a flat working surface. Using a toothpick or plastic knife, carve shapes out of the clay. Bake the shapes on a cookie sheet (be sure they are lying flat while they heat) according to package directions. When cool, the clay can be painted and then attached to a switch plate with a generous coat of white glue mix.

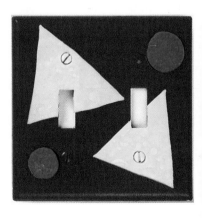

Jazzy Light-switch Plates

Table Linens

rates the top third from the bottom.

Now, pour some orange and yellow paint onto a paper plate. Press each potato stencil into the paint and then onto the fabric. Continue until you've finished your pattern. Air-dry overnight, then put in a hot dryer for about 30 minutes (this sets the paint so that it's machine-washable).

Cup Coasters

Here's a gift that your child can try his hand at making: a stack of handprint drink coasters.

Materials
Tempera paints and
paintbrushes
Construction paper
Clear Con-Tact paper

Stamp handprints (or another design that will fit under a cup) on construction paper and cover the prints on both sides with clear Con-Tact paper. Then, cut them out with enough of a plastic margin to keep fluids off the table.

PLACE MATS

You can turn your child's artwork into a gift set of place mats by preserving it in plastic. Take a set of 11- by 17-inch drawings or paintings to your local photocopy shop and ask the clerk to run it through the laminator (the

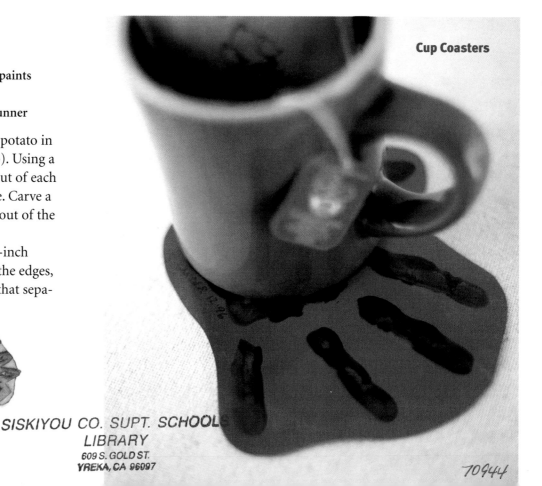

Cup Coasters

fee is generally about $3 each). Or, for a less glossy finish, cover them yourself with clear Con-Tact paper.

Table Linens

Stamped with potato-print acorns and leaves, these hand-decorated napkins and table runner lend a child's imprint to a grandparent's dinner table.

Materials
Potatoes
Craft knife
Yellow and orange acrylic paints
Paper plate
Cloth napkins and table runner

To make a leaf stamp, cut a potato in half lengthwise (a parent's job). Using a craft knife, cut three wedges out of each side of the potato's cut surface. Carve a stem at the bottom and veins out of the leaf's center.

For an acorn stamp, cut a 1-inch square from a potato. Round the edges, leaving a stem, and cut a line that sepa-

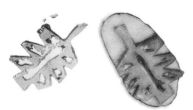

Gifts Kids Can Make

70944

Personalized Planter

FamilyFun **reader Susan Lill from Upper Saddle River, New Jersey, wrote to tell us how the twelve girls in Girl Scout Troop #886 showed their appreciation for the group's three leaders.**

Susan purchased a large terra-cotta pot for each leader. The girls then painted a wide, white strip around each pot. (To keep the painted edges straight, they used masking tape and paper to cover the parts of the pots they did not want to paint.) Next, they divided the strip into thirteen sections, one for each girl plus one for the troop number and year. Each Scout painted a flower on each pot and initialed it. Then, Susan sprayed the pots with a sealer, and the girls filled them with annual flowers and presented them to their leaders.

Gardener's Flowerpot

Using this quick-printing method, your child can create the ideal gift for an indoor gardener — a handsome and colorful planter. Terra-cotta pots look especially nice when printed this way, but plastic ones work well, too. Remember that new pots may be printed on immediately, but used ones should be thoroughly cleaned and dried before applying paint.

Materials

> Small leaves from trees and
>   houseplants
> Acrylic paints and small
>   paintbrushes
> Scrap paper
> Terra-cotta or plastic flowerpot

Your child can begin by choosing a couple of well-formed leaves from one or more types of trees or, with your permission, houseplants. He won't need many, because a single leaf can be used to make lots of prints.

Have him practice printing on a piece of scrap paper before working directly on the flowerpot. After he brushes a thin layer of paint onto the back of a leaf (the side that has prominent veins), he should place it paint-side down on the scrap paper. Have him put a sheet of clean paper over the leaf, then gently press down with his fingers, making sure that the leaf comes into

contact with the printing surface. Remove the sheet of paper and carefully peel back the leaf to reveal the print. If your child is pleased with the print's color and shape, he can repaint the leaf to use on the pot.

It is easiest to print when the flowerpot is on its side and steady, so help hold it in place or have your child wedge it between two heavier objects. Be sure he lets the paint dry on one side of the pot before rotating it to continue printing. Encourage him to experiment with overlapping prints and different patterns and colors (wash off the leaf with a wet paintbrush before switching to a new color).

If your child likes, he can also embellish the flowerpot with stripes, splatter prints, dots, geometric designs, fingerprints, and even his own name. When the printing process is finished, let the paint dry completely, then add the crowning touch — a pretty houseplant.

Gardener's Flowerpot

Tin Can Chimes

Tin Can Chimes

Sometimes scarecrows are just too soft-spoken to intimidate the birds. Your child can solve the dilemma for his favorite gardener with this gift — a clanging noisemaker.

Materials

> Hammer
> Nail
> 2 jar lids
> Empty can
> Twine

Use the hammer and nail (adults only) to poke a hole through the center of the jar lids and the bottom of the empty can. Knot one end of a piece of twine and string on the lids, knotting the twine between them. Tie another knot 1 inch above the upper lid. Next, thread the twine through the hole in the can so that one lid serves as a clapper and the other catches the wind. Tie a loop in the end of the twine, and the can is ready to hang in a garden.

Gardener's Gloves and Apron

Cultivating a green thumb takes practice, patience, and a few handy accessories, like this personalized apron a gardener can use to keep all her tools within reach.

Materials

> Painter's or carpenter's canvas apron and cotton gardening gloves (available at hardware stores)
> Fabric paints and paintbrushes

Help your child design a garden pattern for the apron and gloves, such as a row of bright yellow sunflowers or a bunch of carrots. Then, she can decorate the set using fabric paints. When dry, heat set the paint according to the package directions. Then, fill the apron pockets with seed packets, a garden trowel, and a plastic misting bottle.

Gardener's Gloves and Apron

GARDEN SIGNS

A gardener can stake out the rows of his garden in style with these hand-crafted signs. First, cut out the pictures and names of specific vegetables and flowers from a garden catalog or seed packets. Next, cut 2- by 4-inch rectangles out of corrugated cardboard and fit an end of a small stick into each one (between the grooves, centered along the lower edge). Then, glue on the pictures and names and let dry thoroughly. Waterproof the signs with clear, sturdy tape or Con-Tact paper. Then tie the set together with a green gift ribbon.

Brick Bookends

Not only is this gift project — painting a brick — among the simplest of crafts, it also is good for those on a budget. No special patterns or materials are required. Younger kids can paint on abstract designs, while older kids can try their hand at creating detailed characters, geometric patterns, or landscapes.

Materials

Acrylic paints and paintbrushes
2 bricks
Glue
Felt

Cover a clean surface with newspaper and set out the acrylic paints and paintbrushes. Stand the bricks vertically, so that your child can paint on her designs. Remember that since the surface of the bricks is porous, it can absorb a good amount of paint. Your child may need to apply several layers to create a solid covering. Or, if she prefers a splotchier effect, as is shown here, stop painting while some of the brick's surface still shows through. Once the paint dries, trace around the brick bases on felt and cut them out. Glue the felt squares on the bottom of each brick to prevent the brick from scratching your bookshelf or tabletop.

Decorative Doorstop: To make a fun doorstep, your child should turn a brick on its side, so that it is more stable. Then, he can paint on stick figures, a cityscape, a lounging cat, or any other image that strikes his fancy.

Bookplates

How can you make a collection of storybooks all the more special for a child who loves to read? Personalize them with a gift pack of colorful bookplates.

Materials

Colored markers or paints and a paintbrush
Large self-adhesive postal labels
Stickers or an ink stamp and pad

Using colored markers or paints, print a dedication, such as "This book belongs to," in the center of each postal label. Be sure to leave space for the recipient to write his name. Then, you can embellish the bookplate with a border of stickers or ink prints.

Bookplates

Reading Tree

Here's a gift idea that will make a child's love of reading all the more rewarding. With each new book, enclose a bright paper leaf that he can use to mark his place. Then, when he finishes the book, he can celebrate by posting the leaf on a family reading tree.

Materials

> Colored construction paper
> Brown butcher paper
> Pencil and colored markers
> Glue stick

First, cut out a bunch of maple leaves from orange, yellow, green, and red construction paper. Make plenty so you can keep a supply on hand.

To make the tree, draw a trunk and a few boughs on a large sheet of brown butcher paper. Use a colored marker to trace over the pencil lines and draw on grooves or bark. Then, cut out the trunk and boughs and post them on a door or wall in your home.

Whenever a family member finishes a new book, have him print the title, the author, and his name on a leaf. Then he can glue the leaf on one of the tree limbs. Readers can also set personal goals and decorate the tree with a paper nest or squirrel after reading a certain number of titles.

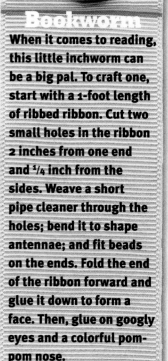

Bookworm

When it comes to reading, this little inchworm can be a big pal. To craft one, start with a 1-foot length of ribbed ribbon. Cut two small holes in the ribbon 2 inches from one end and ¼ inch from the sides. Weave a short pipe cleaner through the holes; bend it to shape antennae; and fit beads on the ends. Fold the end of the ribbon forward and glue it down to form a face. Then, glue on googly eyes and a colorful pom-pom nose.

Gifts Kids Can Make

193

70944

A Shutterbug's Frame

Made from three layers of cardboard, this frame is sturdy enough for any decorating method your child can dream up. When he's done, he can slip in a photo of himself, and he's got the perfect gift for Grandma and Grandpa. The frames shown here fit a horizontal 4- by 6-inch photo, but you can adjust the dimensions to suit any shot.

Materials

- 12-inch-square piece of corrugated cardboard
- Pencil and ruler
- Craft knife
- Glue or rubber cement
- Small piece of ribbon
- Decorating supplies, such as paints, colored markers, puzzle pieces, buttons, or other trinkets

On the piece of cardboard, measure and mark off two 6- by 8-inch pieces, three 1- by 6-inch pieces, and one 2- by 5-inch piece. Cut out the shapes. In the center of one of the 6- by 8-inch pieces, mark off a 3¾- by 5¾-inch opening for your photo and cut it out with a craft knife (adults only).

Lay the frame facedown and collect the three cardboard strips (these will form a pocket that holds the photo). Center, then glue one of the 1- by 6-inch strips about ⅛ of an inch away from the bottom of the frame opening (as shown at left). Glue each of the other two 6-inch strips about ⅛ of an inch away from the sides of the frame opening.

To make the frame's stand, your child should evenly bend the 2- by 5-inch piece of cardboard about 1 inch in from one end. Using glue or rubber cement, attach the folded section against the the second 6- by 8-inch cardboard rectangle (the frame back), 1 inch below the top. To prevent the stand from weakening, glue a short length of ribbon between the back panel and the bottom end of the stand.

Now, your child can embellish the frame front. A map or a collage of stamps makes a nice border for a travel photo or a coat of bright paint enhances a portrait of a good pal. For a three-dimensional look, he can glue on layers of puzzle pieces, buttons, pennies, or seashells. When he's done decorating, your child can glue the frame's back to the pocket strips. The last step is to slip the photo into the frame pocket.

A Shutterbug's Frame

Hedgehog Pincushion

A seamstress needs to keep track of pins and needles, and this little felt hedgehog is up for the job.

Materials

Fabric pen
Felt
Embroidery floss
Large-eye needle
Straight pins
Batting
Googly eyes and a black button

Use a fabric pen to trace a 6-inch circle on a felt square. Cut out the circle and then cut it in half. Thread six strands of embroidery floss through a large-eyed needle and knot the ends.

To form the hedgehog's back, pin together the curved edges of the felt pieces and sew them up using a blanket stitch (see page 167 for instructions).

Next, stuff the body loosely with batting and place it on top of a second felt square. Pin the straight edges to the square and trace around them. Draw a tail at one end of the body, then cut the felt on the traced line.

Stitch the back to the bottom, leaving a 2-inch opening. Fully stuff the hedgehog and stitch up the opening. Glue on googly eyes, sew on a black button nose, and fill with pins.

Sewing Basket

Not only will this gift delight a young seamstress, but it also makes great use of last year's lunch box.

Materials

Plastic lunch box
Fabric scraps or felt
Glue
Plastic or cloth tape measure
Cardboard egg carton

First, decorate the outside of the lunch box by cutting out shapes or letters from the fabric scraps or felt and gluing them on. Cut the tape measure to fit around the box top and then glue it in place. You can even wind and glue a colorful ribbon around the lunch box handle.

Next, furnish the inside of the box with a thread spool holder — trim one end off an empty egg carton so that it will fit inside the box and then place a spool of thread in each cup.

Starting a Sewing Kit

Every starter sewing kit should include pins, a thimble, a pincushion, scissors, a variety of sewing needles, and an assortment of thread (both dark and light colors). Shears for cutting fabric, tailor's chalk for marking fabric, and a tape measure also come in handy, as do buttons, zippers, and fabric scraps.

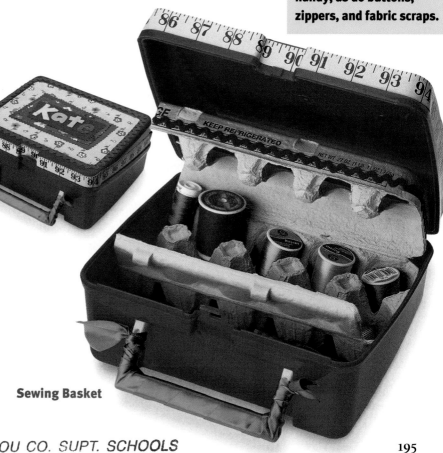

Sewing Basket

Wrap It Up

Plaid Paper

Yarn Paper

Yarn Paper

With this design, you can wrap and decorate all at once.

Materials

> Paper bag
> White glue
> Scraps of yarn

Help your child wrap a gift in a cut-open paper bag. Then, glue the scraps of yarn onto the package. The best method for younger children is to dribble a thin line of glue randomly on the paper and lay yarn along the line. Older kids can try tying the yarn into bows, weaving it into patterns, or making pom-poms. The decorations can then be glued onto the package. Allow the glue to dry thoroughly before presenting the gift.

Glitter Paper: For a dazzling effect, have your child drizzle a pattern of glue onto a flat sheet of brown paper. She can make stars, squiggly lines, and other abstract shapes. Then, sprinkle glitter onto the glue. When the glue is dry, carefully shake the excess glitter back into the jar. Then, use gold or silver markers to outline the designs. Allow the paper to dry thoroughly before wrapping the package.

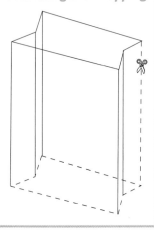

Paper Bag Cutting 101

To turn a grocery bag into wrapping paper, cut along one side seam. Next, cut along all four sides of the bottom of the bag and remove the cut panel. Open the bag up, and it's ready for decorating and wrapping.

Plaid Paper

One way to dress up a package is in stripes or plaids. Here's how you and your kids can turn an ordinary brown paper bag into colorful gift wrap.

Materials

> Paper bag
> Acrylic paints
> Paper plate
> 2- to 4-inch-wide paint roller

Cut open the paper bag, then spread it out on a flat working surface. Squeeze a dab of paint onto the paper plate. Have your child run the paint roller through the paint to coat it, then roll stripes onto the paper. Let each color dry before adding contrasting colors. (To clean the roller, simply rinse it with water.) Once your artist has mastered stripes, it's time to try plaids.

Sponge-print Paper

Using this sponge-printing method, your family can mass-produce rolls of striking wrapping paper and gift tags. Not only are sponges easy to cut into a variety of shapes for printing, but they also can be rinsed out and used again.

Materials

> Tempera or acrylic paints
> Pie plates or bowls
> Kitchen sponges
> Shelf paper, butcher paper, or tissue paper

Cover your work surface with newspaper and pour the paint colors into separate pie plates or bowls. Help your child cut simple shapes, such as trees, stars, diamonds, or hearts, out of clean sponges (slightly dampening a sponge makes it easier to cut). Now, your child can dip a sponge shape into the paint and press it as evenly as possible onto the plain paper. Repeat to create different patterns. Before pressing the sponge into a new paint color, rinse it out in the sink. Let the sponge-print paper dry thoroughly before using it to wrap up your gifts.

More Ideas for Wrapping Your Packages

- Comics or newsprint
- Bandannas, scarves, or handkerchiefs
- Sheet music
- Aluminum foil
- Old maps
- Crepe paper streamers, wrapped mummy-fashion
- Paper bags decorated with stickers
- Unused Chinese takeout containers

Sponge-print Paper

This basic bow is easy to tie, and it will lie flat on packages.

1. After wrapping a length of ribbon around your gift and knotting it, grasp both ribbon ends and bend them into simple loops.

2. Cross the right loop over the left loop

3. Pull the right loop through the hole and pull both loops firmly.

4. Straighten both loops and tails and, if you like, notch the ends of the tails or cut them at an angle.

198

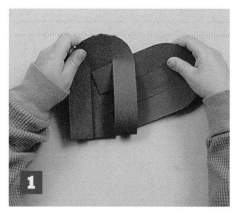

1

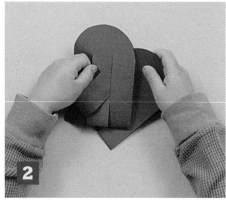

2

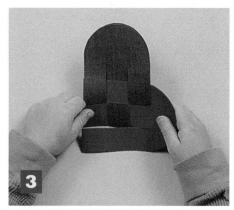

3

Gift Basket

This woven paper heart is handy for kids who want to surprise a friend with fresh flowers or candy. Just fill it up with goodies and anonymously hang it from a doorknob.

Materials

2 3- by 9-inch pieces of
   construction paper
1- by 9-inch strip of
   construction paper
Ruler
Pencil
Glue

First, fold the 3- by 9-inch paper rectangles in half lengthwise (this forms the two halves of the heart). Place them on a table so that the creases are at the bottom. Then, measure 3 inches up from each crease and use a pencil to lightly draw a straight line across the paper. With scissors, round off the top of each half, above the line.

On each half, mark 1-inch increments along the crease. Make a straight cut up from each mark to the pencil line to form three flaps for weaving the two halves together.

1. Now, hold one half of the heart in each hand, as shown.

2. Weave the upper flap of the right half through the flaps of the left half by slipping it through the center of the first one, around the middle one, and through the third one.

3. Next, weave in the middle flap of the right half, this time slipping it around the first flap, through the second flap, and around the third flap.

Finally, weave in the last flap following the same sequence you used with the upper flap. If done correctly, the woven heart will open into a basket.

For a handle, just glue the ends of the construction paper strip to the inside of the heart, and the basket is ready to fill.

Gift Basket

Gift Bags

Not only are these festive gift bags fun for kids to make, but they're also inexpensive, and you don't have to worry about folding perfect corners or running out of tape. To package candy, trinkets, or jewelry, use a lunch bag. Otherwise, a grocery bag (turn it inside out if there is printing on it) can be trimmed to suit most gifts.

Materials
> Paper bag
> Ribbon

First, use scissors to scallop or pink the top edge of the bag. For a more intricate design, cut out a row of trees or candy canes. Next, make a series of holes or vertical snips around the top edge for weaving in a ribbon sash — start about 1 inch from the edge and space them 1 inch apart. For a finishing touch, your child can embellish the bag with shiny stickers, colorful paper shapes, or a crayon drawing.

Gift Bag Tags: Cut out a paper rectangle, fold it in half, and trim the edges. Glue a piece of ribbon or a colored paper cutout to the front of the tag. Punch a hole in the upper right-hand corner (about ½ inch from the fold). Then, thread a piece of ribbon through the hole and tie it to the ribbon sash on the gift bag.

Gift Bags

Gift Bag Tags

THRIFTY GIFT TAGS

Have your child cut out his or her favorite pictures as well as letters from old magazines. Next, fold scraps of construction paper into miniature cards. Let your child play with arranging the cutouts on the cards. The letters can be used to spell out the names of the giver and receiver. When a final design has been chosen, glue the cutouts onto the paper.

Gifts Kids Can Make

Chapter Ten

Homemade for the Holidays

ASK ANY CHILD to describe his favorite holiday memory, and he probably will use the word *always*. We always carve jack-o'-lanterns on Halloween; we always decorate eggs at Easter; we always make ornaments at Christmas. The holiday isn't just one day — it is a tradition, built year upon year, affecting all the senses.

It is in this spirit that we've put together the crafts in this chapter — activities that your family will want to turn to every holiday. This year, you may try crafting the homemade valentines on page 207 with your kids — and sharing holiday hopes and memories while you work with your hands. Next year, that same session at the table will seem familiar — the doilies will come out for the first time since last Valentine's Day. Five years later, you won't be able to imagine the holiday without this ritual.

Crafts add richness and importance to any and all of the calendar's holidays. Taking time to make a mask for Halloween, a card for Mother's Day, an ornament for Christmas, or a noisemaker for New Year's extends the holiday — and ensures that those days will *always*

Fingerprint Hearts, page 209

Holiday Crafts for Kids

Paper chains: For any holiday, you can create paper chains out of construction paper in seasonal colors — pink and red for Valentine's Day, green and red for Christmas, orange and black for Halloween, blue and gold for Hanukkah, and so on.

Quick cards: Cut hearts, Easter eggs, pumpkins, Christmas bells, and other holiday symbols out of construction paper and let your kids decorate them with markers or glitter.

Easy table decorations: Stamp a paper tablecloth with holiday symbols and let it dry before draping over your table. For quick napkin rings, cut cardboard tubes into 2-inch-wide sections, then paint or cover with strips of ribbon, paper, or a collage of magazine clippings.

Decorate your door: Welcome your guests with a holiday greeting — a giant paper jack-o'-lantern with a crooked grin, a paper Santa with a cotton ball beard, or a valentine with a sweet message written in colored glue.

stand out in your family's history.

Look ahead. Pick a craft that you think you and your family will like to do, year after year, such as making an ornament for the Christmas tree or decorating Easter eggs. It won't be quite the same each year; people and crafts both evolve over time. Still, the core activity may become a tradition.

Think back. In this chapter, you'll find many new crafts to add to your holiday repertoire, but be sure to try crafts you did as a child — or ones that are traditional from your ethnic or religious heritage. These activities teach kids about family history and are a special way to connect one generation to the next.

Don't try to do too much. One or two crafts at Christmas are enough, especially if you're also making gifts, baking, or entertaining. If you try to do more, you'll only add to your holiday

stress. You don't need to spend a lot of time on the craft — a holiday decoration you've made in minutes could last for years.

Create a box for each holiday. Store holiday craft supplies and homemade decorations in one box so that the following Halloween, Easter, or Christmas, you'll know just where to find them.

Buy supplies for next year. At the end of every holiday season, stock up on craft supplies, such as holiday-themed stickers, wrapping papers and ribbons, at a discount rate.

Get in the spirit. Play Christmas carols while you make wrapping paper or spooky music while carving jack-o'-lanterns. Munch on jelly beans as you dye eggs at Easter or put on a Pilgrim's hat for crafting Thanksgiving decorations.

Holiday Crafts for Kids

New Year's

Party Hats

For *FamilyFun* reader Gayle Selsback of Minneapolis, New Year's Eve is an occasion for homemade haberdashery. Her family celebrates the last evening of the year with an early supper and a hat-designing extravaganza. The Selsbacks create fancy party hats from colored paper, paper cups and plates, old Christmas ribbons, and whatever else they can find. Then, they don their creations, count down the New Year, and parade through the house banging pot lids together and yelling, "Happy New Year!"

Materials

> Construction paper
> Hole punch
> Elastic cord
> Glue, stickers, or tape
> Colored paper, foil, stickers, feathers, pipe cleaners, and other decorations

1. Fold a large rectangular piece of construction paper in half by bringing together the shorter sides.

2. Turn down the corners along the crease so that they line up (as in paper airplanes), then individually fold up each open edge to create the brim.

3. Make a chin string by punching holes on each side or each end of the hat and threading a piece of elastic cord through the holes.

Now, offer your kids supplies for decorating their hats. Roll up thin strips of paper to make curlicues or cut fringes out of colored foil paper, then attach them with glue, stickers, or tape. As a finishing touch, add feathers, pipe cleaners, or any other odds and ends — the wilder the hats, the better.

Homemade for the Holidays

Party Hats

Cone Hat: Roll a large square or rectangular piece of paper into a cone, staple down the sides, and trim the edges for an even brim. To make a shorter cone, cut a semicircle with a diameter of about 1 foot out of a piece of construction paper. Holding the paper at the midpoint of the straight edge, fold the semicircle into a cone. Staple down the ends and trim around the brim. For both sizes, punch two holes on opposite sides of the hat, and thread a piece of elastic cord through the holes for a chin string (you may want to secure the holes with paper reinforcements).

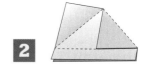

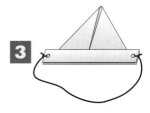

YEAR IN A BOX

Every year, *FamilyFun* reader Ann Van Dort of Rocklin, California, and her family decorate a shoe box with leftover gift wrap and designate it the Good Times box. Throughout the year, whenever the Van Dorts go to the movies, the circus, a fair, a party, or on vacation, they place a memento or ticket stub in the box. On New Year's Eve, they open the box, and family members take turns picking out items and sharing memories of the year gone by.

New Year's Noisemakers

Making noise — from blowing horns to ringing bells to shouting in the street — is an ancient and universal New Year's custom. According to old English tradition, bells are muffled just before midnight to show grief for the dying year, then the wrappings are removed at the stroke of twelve to make a gladsome sound.

For a home-based First Night, the gentle noises made by Native American–style shakers and rattles may be best — taking less of a toll on your nerves. This version has the added advantage of being fashioned from those clear plastic cocktail glasses that folks tend to have on hand during the holidays.

Materials

Dried beans, rice, buttons, or brightly colored beads
2 clear plastic drinking glasses
Colored tape

To make one shaker, pour a handful of beans, rice, buttons, or beads (or a mixture of them) into one of the plastic cocktail glasses. Place another glass on top of it and, matching them rim to rim, tape the two together securely with stripes of colorful tape. Now, shake it up.

New Year's Noisemakers

Giggle Shaker

Giggle Shaker

Kids can decorate this gleeful rattle to look like themselves — with heads of yarn hair and big grins.

Materials

- Markers
- 2 sturdy paper plates
- Hole punch
- Colored yarn
- Beans, rice, or small pebbles
- Glue (optional)
- Tape
- Dowel

Have your kids draw giggling faces on the undersides of two cardboard plates. Place the plates together (top-sides facing) so that the rims line up and there is a pocket of space between them. Then punch holes along the rims and run colorful yarn through the holes.

Before you tie the last piece of yarn, slip beans, rice, or pebbles into the pocket, then secure it (a little glue between the plates will help your rattle to keep from spilling its beans). Tape the noisemaker to the end of the dowel.

Homemade for the Holidays

To make the wand, roll the acetate into a tube about 1½ inches in diameter. Close up one end of the tube by cutting slits in the sides, folding the strips over, and taping them down.

Using a small funnel made from paper, slowly pour the homemade confetti into the wand. Cork the open ends with wads of tissue paper; remove at midnight and wave the wands through the air.

Confetti Balloons: When it comes to making a big bang, popping balloons is unparalleled — and even more thrilling if streams of confetti come pouring out. Prepare your New Year's balloons by setting the kids to work making confetti. Stuff as many confetti pieces as you can into each deflated balloon using a funnel (you can improvise one by cutting a plastic soda bottle in half). You may also want to write fortunes on small pieces of paper and slip them into the mix. Blow up the balloons and hang them high, but still within your children's reach. A few moments before the appointed hour, hand out the pins. When the time is right, let that confetti fly.

Confetti Wands

These sparkling wands are a blast to wave through the air — the only downfall is the cheerful mess they tend to make on the floor.

Materials

6-inch by 1½-foot piece of medium-thickness acetate (available at art supply stores)

Tape

Homemade confetti (see Quick Confetti, at right)

Tissue paper

FunFact

As much as 3,000 pounds of confetti are thrown in Times Square every New Year's Eve.

QUICK CONFETTI

Making confetti is a great way for little hands to join in on the decorating, as well as a quick and inexpensive way to create party magic. When the party's over, these tiny decorations can be vacuumed up.

Grab a hole punch and a collection of colored paper, old gift wrap, mail-order catalogs, and aluminum foil (if you don't have a hole punch, you can simply rip paper into confetti-size pieces). Fill a medium-size mixing bowl about half full with confetti and stir to distribute the color. If you wish, add in a few tablespoons of glitter.

Valentine's Day

Sweet Temptations

Scores of *FamilyFun* readers said their kids couldn't resist these Valentine's Day suitors, who came bearing sweet treats. The idea was inspired by the creative children's craft book *The Best Holiday Crafts Ever!* (Millbrook Press).

Materials

Playing card (hearts, of course)
Thumbtack or straight pin
Ruler
2 8-inch pipe cleaners
Construction paper
Googly eyes
Glue
Markers
Lollipop

First, use the thumbtack to poke arm- and leg-holes 1 inch from the top and ½ inch from the bottom of the card. For arms, fit the ends of one pipe cleaner through the upper holes from the back of the card. Fit the other pipe cleaner through the lower holes for legs. Bend the ends to shape feet.

For a head, cut a heart out of construction paper. Glue on googly eyes and draw on a nose and mouth. Then, glue the head to the card. Finally, wrap one arm around the lollipop. Write a message on a mini card and slip it in the card's free hand.

Bag of Hearts

Bag of Hearts

Need a tote for carrying your cards? This one can be assembled in a flash.

Materials

Colored paper
Brown bag (lunch size works well)
Ribbon
Markers (optional)

Glue a few colored paper hearts onto a medium-size bag. For handles, use two pieces of ribbon. Cut holes in the bag; thread the ribbon through and knot the ends.

Dress in Red

Scarlet, after all, is the order of the day. Help your kids dig up an all-red ensemble from their closets and use ribbons or rickrack for belts, shoelaces, and hair ties. Paint nails with hearts in all the shades of red polish you've collected. You even can tattoo your arms with beet juice, cutting a fresh beet into heart-shaped stamps.

Sweet Temptations

Homemade for the Holidays

My Punny Valentine

Lovebug Brooch

FamilyFun contributor Shannon Summers made one of these ladybugs in first grade for her mother, who decades later, still pins it on. Young kids can make this project nearly independently — and the finished brooch looks more sophisticated than the usual macaroni jewelry many moms get on Valentine's Day.

Materials

> Plaster of Paris
> Plastic spoon
> Safety pin
> Red and black
>   acrylic paints
> Small paintbrush
> Clear varnish (optional)

Help your child mix up the plaster, then fill and level off the spoon. Press the safety pin into the wet plaster so that it opens out. Allow the plaster to harden for an hour. Your child can pop out the brooch and paint it red. Using the black paint and small brush, she can draw eyes, wings, and a head on the lovebug, then cover the wings with hearts, as shown above. If your child makes other brooches, she can decorate them with any simple design, as in the one below. To seal in the colors, a parent can apply a protective coating of clear varnish.

Lovebug Brooch

My Punny Valentine

Why are valentines always filled with puns? We don't know, but we love it.

Materials

> Old magazines and catalogs
> Construction paper
> Glue

Cut out letters and pictures of animals from the magazines and arrange them into punny cards, using a bit of glue to hold them onto the paper. A cat remarking, "I have felines for you," a horse noting, "Bubba, you're my mane man," or a dog sending this sweet nothing to Mama, "I'll hound you till you're mine," are all gems.

Button Hearts

For an easy, handsome addition to any Valentine's Day outfit, dress up your shirt buttons by cutting heart shapes out of a piece of felt.

Materials
Felt
Googly eyes
Glue

Cut romantic shapes out of a piece of felt (they should be about 1 to 2 inches tall and wide). We chose hearts, but you could try flowers, stars, or whatever you like. Cut slits that are the size of your buttonhole in the center of the shapes, then slip them in place. For a goofy-face button slip, glue on googly eyes above the slits.

Fingerprint Hearts

Button Hearts

QUICK VALENTINE CARDS

Lots of kids love glamorous, store-bought Valentine's Day cards. But homemade valentines are the most fun to give, even when you have to mass-produce them. We suggest starting a card-making workshop a few days before the big day. Or, to save time, you can make one card, then color-copy it.

Fingerprint hearts: This is the perfect little-kid card. You'll need a nontoxic stamp pad, scrap paper, and notepaper or postcards. Have your child stamp a V-shaped heart by joining two index-finger prints at the bottoms. Once your kids master the technique on scrap paper, let them add hearts to folded notepaper or postcards or to each frame of a paper accordion card (see below).

Accordion hearts: Cut a long narrow rectangle from a piece of paper, then fold it in four, accordion style. Next, make a heart stencil out of scrap paper. Use the stencil to cut out heart shapes from magazines, wrapping paper, doilies, or old photographs. Children can then glue down a heart cutout on each square.

Chinese New Year

Dragon Mask

In Chinese folklore, dragons guard the earth's jewels, govern the weather, and watch over the rivers. It's no surprise, then, that this mythical creature is also charged with leading the Lantern Festival street processions that cap off the Chinese New Year. With this costume version of the legendary beast, your kids can take turns heading up the traditional Chinese game described below.

Materials

- 6- by 30-inch piece of yellow poster board
- Stapler
- Ruler
- Colored construction paper
- White glue

Wrap the poster board around your child's head with the ends meeting in front of his face; staple them together an inch or two from his forehead. Remove the poster board and make the dragon's face by gluing together the poster board flaps that project from the brow band (the brow band will serve as its neck).

Cut out the dragon's mouth and contour the top of its face. Glue construction paper scales to its neck, face, and chin. Add paper eyes, flaring nostrils, teeth, and horns. Finally, glue the base of a red paper flame to its lower jaw.

Dragon Mask

Chase the Dragon's Tail

This time-honored Chinese game can be played with ten kids or more. One child is the head of the dragon and wears the mask. The other players line up behind him with their hands on the shoulders of the person in front of him. The head has one minute to tag the last kid in line without causing the line to break apart. If he succeeds, he wins; if not, he becomes the tail, and the child behind him wears the mask.

Paper Lanterns

During the Lantern Festival, children carry candlelit lanterns in the street. This construction paper version is wonderfully decorative and doesn't need to be lit — but if you want to, you can rig up a mini flashlight inside.

Materials

> 8½- by 11-inch piece and a ½- by 6-inch strip of lightweight paper, such as gift wrap or decorated newsprint
>
> Ruler

Fold the larger piece of paper in half lengthwise and cut eighteen slits 3½ inches long, into the fold and parallel to the short edges (begin cutting an inch from each edge and leave a half inch between each slit). Unfold the paper and staple or glue the short edges together, then glue the small strip to the sides at the top for a handle.

Stamp Your Name

When a Chinese artist signs his paintings, he uses a carved stone block — called a chop — to print his symbol on the canvas. To personalize her art or stationery, your child can make her own signature stamp out of Styrofoam and cardboard.

Materials

> Pen
> Tracing paper
> Clean Styrofoam meat tray
> Glue
> Cardboard
> Cardboard tube
> Ink pad

1. First, have your child write her initials on tracing paper, making the letters as ornate as she likes or incorporating them into a unique design. Next, place the paper printed-side down on a clean Styrofoam meat tray. Trace over the design with a pen, bearing down to leave an impression in the Styrofoam.

2. Cut out the design, leaving a narrow border all around, and glue it onto a piece of cardboard trimmed to the same size. For a handle, glue a cardboard tube to the back. Then, press the stamp onto an ink pad and stamp it on stationery.

Chinese Calendar

The Chinese calendar dedicates each year to one of twelve animals. Have your kids find the animal that matches their birth years and draw a picture of it.

Rat: 1972, 1984, 1996
Ox: 1973, 1985, 1997
Tiger: 1974, 1986, 1998
Hare: 1975, 1987, 1999
Dragon: 1976, 1988, 2000
Snake: 1977, 1989, 2001
Horse: 1978, 1990, 2002
Sheep: 1979, 1991, 2003
Monkey: 1980, 1992, 2004
Rooster: 1981, 1993, 2005
Dog: 1982, 1994, 2006
Pig: 1983, 1995, 2007

1

2

Stamp Your Name

Homemade for the Holidays

Easter

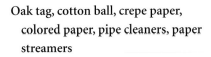

Oak tag, cotton ball, crepe paper, colored paper, pipe cleaners, paper streamers

Easter Bonnets

On Easter morning, your kids can parade around the yard in these fanciful Easter bonnets, made of paper bowls and plates.

Materials

- Paper bowl
- 10-inch paper plate
- Glue
- Tape
- Craft knife
- Tempera paints and paintbrushes

To make either bonnet, set the inverted bowl on your child's head to see if it fits. To make it smaller, cut the bowl into quarters, refit the pieces so the edges overlap (use tape to get it right), then glue the seams.

Rabbit Cap: To make the visor, cut a 7- by 5-inch rectangle from the flat portion of a paper plate. Trace the rim of the bowl along one long edge of the rectangle. Using this line as a guide, cut out a 3-inch-wide crescent shape (see top left). Glue the bowl rim to the inner edge of the visor. Paint the cap and let it dry. Next, cut foot-long ears out of oak tag paper, leaving a ½-inch tab at the bottom of each. Paint the ear backs and front edges to match the cap. Once dry, shade the centers with a lighter hue. Use a craft knife (parents only) to make two ½-inch slits in the top of the hat. Push the ear tabs through and glue them to the inside of the hat. Finally, glue a cotton ball tail to the cap back.

Flower Bonnet: To make the brim, center the fitted bowl rim-side down on top of an upside-down paper plate and trace around it. Cut a circle from the middle of the plate, staying ½ inch in from the line. Glue the rim of the bowl to the inner edge of the paper ring. Paint and dry thoroughly. For a hatband, glue a strip of crepe paper around the hat, above the brim. Next, cut flowers out of colored paper and tape pipe cleaner stems to the backs. To attach, push the stem end through a hole in the hat and secure with tape. For chin sashes, tape an 18-inch paper streamer to the inner brim on both sides of the hat.

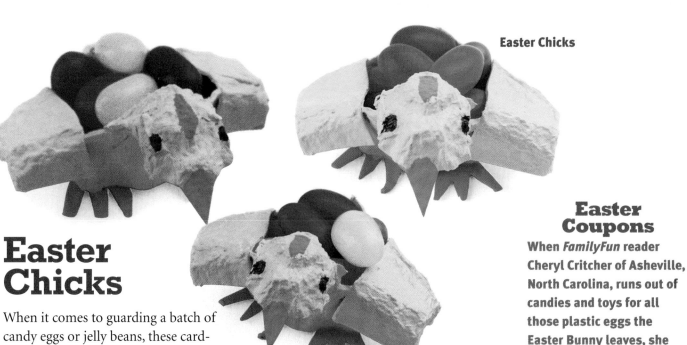

Easter Chicks

When it comes to guarding a batch of candy eggs or jelly beans, these cardboard chicks are made for the job.

Materials

- Cardboard egg carton
- Colored markers
- Glue
- Watercolor brush
- Yellow tempera paint

1. To make each chick, cut a single egg cup from the egg carton for a body. Trim along the top edge, keeping the sides of the cup as tall as possible.

2. Then, with a colored marker, outline a chick's head and neck on the underside of the carton top. (Use the molded portion of cardboard that separates the eggs, as shown.) Cut out the head and glue the base of the neck to the inside of the body.

3. For the chick's wings, cut a second egg cup from the carton, this time trimming the sides about ½ inch from the bottom. Then, cut the cup into halves. Holding the half cups with the bottoms up, fit them onto the sides of the chick's body and glue them into position.

Once the glue dries, brush on a coat of yellow tempera paint. Allow the paint to dry thoroughly. Next, use colored markers to tint the beak orange and draw on eyes.

Finally, cut a pair of feet from carton scraps and color them orange. Glue the feet onto the bottom of the body, and the chick is ready to fill with Easter candy.

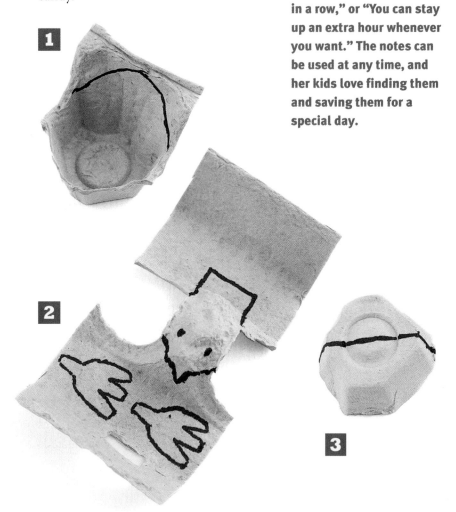

Easter Coupons

When *FamilyFun* reader Cheryl Critcher of Asheville, North Carolina, runs out of candies and toys for all those plastic eggs the Easter Bunny leaves, she fills them with Easter "coupons." These slips of paper say things like, "You can go to lunch at the place of your choice," "You can skip your chores three days in a row," or "You can stay up an extra hour whenever you want." The notes can be used at any time, and her kids love finding them and saving them for a special day.

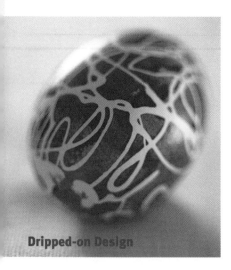
Dripped-on Design

Dripped-on Designs

Kids will get a kick out of letting rubber cement gloop and dribble all over (the egg, that is).

Materials

> Hard-boiled eggs
> Egg dye
> Rubber cement with applicator brush

To start, rest the egg in an empty egg carton lid or on a section of paper towel tube set upright. Next, using the applicator brush, dribble rubber cement over the egg. When the cement has dried, dip the egg into a bowl of dye. When the color is bright, remove the egg and let it dry. Peel off the glue and repeat to add additional colors, if desired.

Sticker Stencils

These eggs are especially fun for little kids to work on — all they need is a few stickers or paper reinforcers.

Materials

> Hard-boiled eggs
> Egg dye
> Stickers (paper reinforcements, store-bought stickers, or designs cut from self-adhesive shelf paper or mailing labels)

Begin with a cooled egg and cooled dye; otherwise, the adhesive gets sticky and difficult to remove. Cover the egg with stickers, then dip the egg until the color is bright enough. Let the egg dry and remove the stickers. If you wish, you can remove only some of the stickers and dip the egg in a second color.

Rubber Band Wrap

Rubber Band Wrap

Twisting rubber bands around an egg can challenge small hands, but the result is a snazzy, colorful creation.

Materials

> Hard-boiled eggs
> Egg dye
> Rubber bands, various sizes

Wrap rubber bands around the egg, covering it completely. When you dip the covered egg, the dye will seep under the bands in some areas and be blocked out in other areas. Remove from the dye when the color is bright enough. Blot dry with paper towels and remove the rubber bands. If you wish, repeat with a new color.

Sticker Stencil

Egg-dyeing Tips

✂ **To make perfect hard-boiled eggs,** cover eggs with water in a saucepan and bring to a boil. Turn off heat, cover the pot, and let sit for 10 minutes.

✂ **To blow an egg,** first shake the egg to break the yolk. Then use a small nail to make a hole in the top and bottom of the egg. Blow gently until the egg is empty. To help preserve blown-egg creations, paint them with craft sealer.

✂ **For extra-rich dye colors,** use food coloring paste (available at craft or cake supply stores). Dissolve a dab of paste in a cup of hot water mixed with $\frac{1}{4}$ cup vinegar.

✂ **Use pasta tongs** for dipping eggs.

✂ **Wear rubber gloves.**

✂ **Make an egg-drying stand** out of a paper towel tube cut into sections.

Sponge-print Eggs

Sponge stamps are easy to use and leave a clean, sharp design. Create your own patterns or just stampede (as it were) at random.

Materials

> Hard-boiled eggs
> Kitchen sponges
> Tempera paints

Cut out shapes, about ½ inch wide, from a sponge (we used a thin rectangle to make our zigzag pattern). Dip the sponge into the paint, dab off the excess, and make a pattern of stamps on the egg. To keep colors fresh, make a sponge stamp for each color.

Sponge-print Egg

Painted Chick

In this particular case, the age-old question is settled: the egg definitely came first.

Materials

> Air-drying clay
> Cardboard or cutting board
> Plastic knife
> White glue
> Blown eggs (see tips on page 214)
> Tempera paints and paintbrushes
> Rolling pin

Painted Chick

Roll out the clay on cardboard. Using the plastic knife, shape the clay into a beak, comb, and feet. Rub a dab of glue onto the clay parts and press into place on the egg. Hold for 1 minute until the glue starts to dry, then set the egg aside to dry completely. Paint on eyes, wings, and feathers. Finally, paint the clay features.

THE EGGHEADS

Have you ever looked at your Easter eggs and wondered what's missing? This year, give the bald ones a head of hair. Use a small nail to make a hole about the size of a quarter in one end of an egg, then drain the egg and rinse out the shell. Draw or paint funny faces on the shells and put them in the egg carton. It's a good idea to use permanent markers so the colors won't bleed when you water the hair. Use a spoon to fill the shells with soil, then plant with grass seeds (follow package directions).

Moisten the soil, cover with plastic wrap, and place the shells in a sunny window until the seeds sprout — it generally takes less than a week. When the eggheads have a thick, green mane, remove the covering and place them on a stand (try using empty film canisters). Style the hair into pigtails, buzz cuts, or Mohawks and water it every day.

Mother's Day

FunFact
If you celebrate Mom with a bouquet of carnations, you'll be right in line with history; carnations have been the official flower of Mother's Day since it was introduced by Anna Jarvis in 1907.

Home Sweet Home Card

With a few art supplies, family photos, and a little adult supervision, your kids can make the picture-perfect Mother's Day gift — a house-shaped photo frame that's modeled after your own home.

Materials
    Crayons or colored markers
    Heavyweight white paper
    Craft knife
    Family photos
    Tape
    Glue
    Cardboard

Use crayons or colored markers to draw your house on heavyweight white paper. Include a window for each family member. With a craft knife (adults only), cut out window openings. Place a photo behind each one, as shown, and tape the photo edges in place.

Use scissors to cut along the house outline. Place the cutout facedown and spread glue along the outside edges. Mount the art on a piece of cardboard and trim the backing so that it is flush with the art. To make a frame stand, cut a 3-inch-wide cardboard strip that is half the height of the house. Fold the strip in half vertically, line it up with the frame bottom, and glue one side to the back of the frame.

Home Sweet Home Card

Jigsaw Puzzle for Mom

To make a photo jigsaw puzzle that doubles as a Mother's Day card, take a family photograph to the copy shop and have it enlarged on a color copier. Then, glue it onto a piece of poster board and trim off any excess border. On the back, write a Mother's Day message in big letters. Using scissors, cut the mounted photo into jigsaw-size shapes — and leave it to Mom to put together the pieces.

Mother's Day Pop-up

Long-stemmed roses may be lovely, but this pop-up bouquet is much more personal — not to mention affordable on an allowance.

Materials

Colored construction paper
Unlined white paper
Colored markers
Glue

Cut a 7- by 4-inch rectangle and a 4-by 1½-inch rectangle out of the colored paper. Position the small rectangle so that the short edges are on the sides and draw a flower vase in the center. On the white paper, draw some flowers with broad stems and leaves. Cut them out and glue the fronts of the stems and leaf ends to the flip side of the

vase. Once they're dry, crease the vase and bouquet vertically. Then, fold back the short sides of the small rectangle ½ inch from the edges, as shown. Fold the large rectangle in half, crease, and reopen. Center the drawing on top of the opened card and glue the side tabs of the small rectangle to the card. Finally, print a greeting.

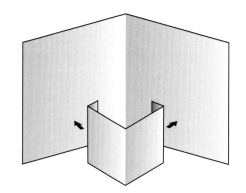

Queen for a Day

On Mother's Day, crown Mom and give her the royal treatment. Cut a strip of construction paper 2 inches wide and about 25 inches long. Tape or staple the ends to make a circle and punch holes around the top edge. Thread flowers (fresh or paper) through the holes and add leaves with staples. For easy Paper Blossoms, turn to page 66.

Father's Day

Desktop Pencil Holder

A Fan of Dad

Dad's admirers can present him with a card that doubles as a fan. Trim a paper plate into a paddle shape on which your child can print a greeting with colored markers. Glue the card to a wooden craft stick or paint stirrer. Once he's read his card, Dad can use it to keep cool.

Desktop Pencil Holder

The next time Dad needs someone to fetch him a pencil, this desktop dog can deliver.

Materials

    4 pinch-style wooden
      clothespins
    Glue
    Felt
    Googly eyes
    Pom-pom
    Craft paints or colored markers
    Pencil or pen

To form the front end of the dog, pinch open a clothespin and apply glue to the inner surface of the opened end. Then, clamp the glued end onto a sec-

ond clothespin, just behind the metal spring, as shown.

For the dog's tail end, glue and clamp together the last two clothespins so that one holds the other wide open. When the glue is dry, fit the opened end of the back half onto the lower end of the front half, as pictured. Apply glue to bond the two sections.

From the felt, cut out floppy ears and circular paws. Glue them, the googly eyes, and the pom-pom nose onto the dog. If your child wishes, he can add spots or other distinguishing details with craft paints or colored markers. Finally, pinch open the dog's mouth and insert a pencil or pen, balancing its weight equally on both sides.

Dad's Reward Jar

FamilyFun reader Lynn Walker of Los Gatos, California, wrote to us that her husband, Mark, loves to work around the house. Since she and her two boys, six-year-old Ben and seven-year-old Jake, are the beneficiaries of many of Mark's projects, they decided to express their gratitude by making Mark a Father's Day reward jar. For every household job that Mark completes, he gets to draw a slip of paper from the jar and collect his reward.

Materials

Empty, widemouthed jar
Stickers
Colored paper
Paint
Glue stick
Colored markers

Decorate an empty jar with stickers, glued-on strips of decorated paper, or paint (see Window Art, page 19, for tips on how to paint on glass). When the jar is done, help your kids figure out what kinds of rewards to offer their dad. One sample from young Jake reads, "Thank you, Dad, for doing all this hard work for us and thank you for being our Dad. I will climb one tree for you." Other ideas might include a breakfast in bed, an afternoon of leaf raking, a big bedtime hug, an evening where Dad gets a story read to him (for a change), or a batch of his favorite cookies. Have your kids write their reward ideas onto strips of colored paper with markers and slip them into the jar, then wrap the whole thing up and tie it with a bow.

Wallet Card

A "World's Greatest Dad" T-shirt may be nice, but this wallet-size collage is a more subtle way to show Dad you care. Cut a credit-card-size rectangle out of poster board. Have your kids decorate both sides with messages, stickers, drawings, and glued-on photographs. To make the card sturdier, cover it on both sides with clear Con-Tact paper or run it through the laminator at your local copy shop (about $2). Dad can keep the card in his wallet and take it with him wherever he goes — a reminder of who loves him best of all.

Dad's Reward Jar

Fourth of July

Firecracker Hats

Kindergarten teacher Jean Alston of Roanoke Rapids, North Carolina, sent *FamilyFun* snapshots (and one newspaper clipping) of six kindergarten classes all sporting these fluttery hats at the same time — apparently, the kids were such an astonishing sight that they made the front page of the local paper.

Materials

- 2 full sheets of newspaper
- Ruler and pencil
- Blue, red, and white tempera paints
- Wide paintbrush
- White construction paper
- Tape and glue

First, unfold the two newspaper sheets one atop the other as if you were reading them. Thereafter, treat them as a single two-ply sheet — this will strengthen the hat and provide a double layer of fringe.

To make the brow band, mark a line 3½ inches from the bottom edge of the sheet and fold up along that line. Roll the band up once more and flatten the fold. Paint the brow band blue. When dry, paint broad red and white stripes on the flip side of the newspaper (this will be the inside of the hat). While waiting for the paint to dry, cut star shapes from the construction paper.

Fit the hat by wrapping the brow band around a child's head and taping the overlap securely. At this point, the hat should resemble a tall cylinder.

Glue the stars to the brow band. Finally, fringe the top of the hat, making cuts an inch or so apart that extend most of the way down the cylinder.

Firecracker Hats

Statue of Liberty Crown

Statue of Liberty Crown

If your bored masses are yearning for a Fourth of July costume, try making this Statue of Liberty headband and Miss Liberty's torch.

Materials

2 sturdy paper plates
Green construction paper
Stapler
Glue
Green paint
Glitter

First, cut 2½ inches from each of the bottom rims of two sturdy paper plates, then cut out their centers, leaving a 2-inch-wide headband (this fits most children's heads snugly, but if it's too tight, carefully trim more away from the edge).

Next, cut six triangles from green construction paper. Each one should measure 4 inches across and 9 inches high. Space these evenly across the front of one headband with the points radiating outward and staple into place. Glue the other headband across the first to conceal the staples. Paint it green, then "oxidize" with glitter.

Miss Liberty's Torch:

Fashion a torch out of a cardboard tube, poster board, and yellow tissue paper. Touch up both to look like Miss Liberty's crown with green paint and glitter.

Star-printed T-shirt

Star-printed
T-shirt

These star-spangled T-shirts are easy to make — whether you use a star fruit (also called a carambola) as a stamp or make your own out of a potato or a gum eraser (see page 161 for directions).

Materials

- Newspaper or piece of cardboard
- Cotton T-shirt
- Fabric paint
- Pie tin
- Knife
- Star fruit (or potato star stamp)
- Paper towel

Insert several sheets of newspaper or a piece of cardboard inside the cotton T-shirt. Then, pour some fabric paint into a pie tin. Slice the star fruit in half and dry both the cut surfaces with a paper towel. Dip the fruit into the paint and use it to press stars onto the shirt. Once the prints dry, follow the fabric paint instructions to heat-set the design.

Margarine
Tub Drum

No Fourth of July parade is complete without a noisemaker (or ten). This one won't quite drown out the firecrackers, but it comes pretty close.

Materials

- Small margarine tub and lid
- Colored duct tape
- Craft knife
- ⅜-inch dowel cut to an 8-inch length
- 2 6-inch pieces string
- 2 wooden beads

First, decorate the tub and lid with shapes cut out of the tape. Use a craft knife (parents only) to cut a ⅜-inch hole through one side of the tub and slide the end of the dowel through it. Poke a small hole in each side of the tub 90 degrees from the dowel. Thread a piece of string through each hole and knot the ends inside the tub. Tie a bead onto the free end of each piece of string. By rolling the dowel back and forth in his hands, your child can make his own one-drum salute.

Uncle Sam Hat

To make the Uncle Sam hat the cyclist is wearing on page 221, start with a 12- by 14-inch piece of poster board. Mark each side with a dot at the halfway points of 6 and 7 inches, respectively. Measure 2½ inches in from each dot and mark an additional dot. Connect the outer dots with a curved line to form an oval; repeat with the inner dots. Cut away the corners of the outer oval, then cut the inner oval sides and rear, leaving the front intact. Raise the inner flap and fold it forward. Trim the top and sides of the flap to square it off and decorate the hat.

Margarine Tub Drum

Halloween

Stack-o'-Lantern

When trick-or-treaters come knocking on your door this Halloween, greet them with our three-story jack-o'-lantern. It's no more difficult to fashion than three conventional ones — in fact, that's really all it is. And its triple glowing power can help keep all those creepy Halloween shadows at bay.

Materials

3 pumpkins (a big one on the bottom with progressively smaller ones above; the top pumpkin should be no less than 9 inches deep)
Paring knife or craft knife
Large spoon or ice-cream scoop

First, cut the tops oV all three pumpkins (adults only). Don't make the openings too wide just yet (leave some room for error) and cut in at a generous slant to provide support for the pumpkins above. Ask your kids to gut the insides with the spoon or ice-cream scoop. The more they scrape, the brighter the pumpkin will glow — but go gently on the bottom.

Test-fit your pumpkins as you go; you may need to trim so upper ones sit firmly in lower pumpkins (see illustration). Once your stack fits together properly, unstack them and carve faces. Light a candle in each pumpkin and carefully restack them.

Say Boo!

Say Boo!

What can you do with four odd-size pumpkins? This solution — making each one a letter of a word — is so clever it's scary.

Materials

    4 small pumpkins

    Pen

    Paring knife, craft knife, or pumpkin
      carving tool

    Large spoon

First, draw the letters and exclamation point in pen on the pumpkins. Cut the tops off with a sharp knife (a parent's job); for best results, carve at an inward angle. Cut a small hole in each cap to allow heat from the candle to escape. Remove the seeds with the spoon and scrape the walls until they are about 1 inch thick. Cut out the drawn letters with the knife or carving tool.

Choosing a Pumpkin

Look for large, heavy, evenly shaped pumpkins. Those that will be lit by candles should be at least 9 inches high. A curly stem can add personality, but it may be delicate and should not be overhandled (remind kids never to pick up a pumpkin by its stem).

Homemade for the Holidays

Pumpkin Painting

Kids who are too young to carve their own jack-o'-lanterns can paint dastardly faces on this seasonal squash.

    Pumpkin

    Tempera paints and paintbrushes

    Plastic yogurt containers filled with
      water for rinsing
      brushes

On a covered surface, set out the paints, brushes, and plastic yogurt containers filled with water. Then let the kids paint goofy, surprised, or creepy faces on the pumpkins.

CARVING TIPS

✂ For stability, work from the center out (nose before eyes, eyes before eyebrows, mouth last).

✂ While huge, gaping features look really cool, they also get mushy quickly. For fine details, use a craft knife or saw through the pumpkin with a piece of thin wire.

✂ For creepy facial highlights, cut trenches just far enough into the pumpkin's skin that the candlelight glows eerily through (in other words, don't cut all the way through the pumpkin).

Pumpkin Painting

Clip-on Paper Bats

and make a sharp crease in the center. Unfold the rectangle and lay it flat so that the short ends are at the top and bottom. Then, form ear tabs. With a pencil, mark both sides of the rectangle 2½ inches up from the bottom. Make a diagonal cut from each mark up to the crease (see above).

2. Refold the rectangle and push up the triangular tabs to create the cat's ears. With the scissors, shape the cat's chin and neck. Then, glue on a black poster board nose and whiskers. Add yellow construction paper eyes. To attach the cat's head to the body, make another cut in the top of the back (this time above the front legs) and fit the lower edge of the neck into it.

Clip-on Paper Bats

If your belfry is looking a bit bare this year, scare up a swarm of these clip-on bats.

For each bat, cut an extended-wings shape from black construction paper. Next, cut out an oblong body with pointed ears and feet and glue it onto the wings. Add round, beady eyes cut from yellow or red paper. Glue a clothespin to the back of the bat, and it's ready to hang onto a curtain.

Black Cats

There's no need to worry about these black cats crossing your path. Bright-eyed and bushy-tailed, they're meant to stand on a table or a doorstep as a surprise greeting for Halloween callers.

Materials

    Black poster board
    Pinking shears
    Yellow construction paper
    Glue

1. First, cut an 11- by 6-inch rectangle out of the poster board. Fold it in half so that the shorter edges meet and make a crease. Using the crease for the cat's backbone, cut out a four-legged body. Trim the bottom of each foot with pinking shears to create toes.

Still using the pinking shears, cut out a bushy, upright tail. With regular scissors, make a small vertical snip in the backbone above the hind legs and fit the base of the tail into it.

For the cat's head, use a 6- by 3½-inch rectangle. Match up the short ends

Black Cats

Gauze Ghosts

It takes practically nothing to make this family of mischievous sprites.

Materials

Assortment of different-size plastic milk jugs or juice bottles
Aluminum foil
White gauze or cheesecloth
Liquid laundry starch

Top each milk jug or bottle with a ball of crumpled aluminum foil. Next, cut the gauze or cheesecloth into 18-inch squares, one for each ghost. Dip the gauze squares into a bowl filled with laundry starch. Pull them out one at a time and squeeze out the excess moisture. Drape a square over each bottle.

To shape the ghosts' shoulders and arms, loosely pile crumpled aluminum foil around the bottle and drape the gauze over it. Flare out the lower edges of the gauze and let dry overnight. (To make the dog, simply drape a small square of gauze over shaped foil.) Once they've dried, carefully lift the ghosts from their bottles. They should stand freely on a flat surface.

Egg Carton Pumpkins

Greet your trick or treaters with a row of mini pumpkins perched along your windowsill.

Materials

Cardboard egg carton
Glue
Orange acrylic paint and paintbrush
Paper clip
Green pipe cleaners or crepe paper
Black marker

Homemade for the Holidays

Gauze Ghosts

Cut two cups from the egg carton. Run a bead of glue along the top edge of one cup. Invert the second cup and position it atop the first, making sure the cut edges align.

Once the glue dries, coat the shell with orange acrylic paint. When the paint is dry, use the end of the paper clip to poke a hole in the top of the pumpkin. Make a stem and curly vines out of the green pipe cleaners or twisted green crepe paper and push the ends through the hole. Use the black marker to draw on a spooky jack-o'-lantern face.

Egg Carton Pumpkins

Ghost Prints

This is an easy party activity for little ghouls. Have kids fold a piece of black construction paper in half, then dribble white paint into the crease. When they briefly press the paper back together, then open it, a ghost will appear.

Mr. Bottle Bones

Start saving your empty plastic gallon jugs — with a snip here and a hole there, you can resurrect a life-size skeleton. Punching holes and tying on bones is a job for little kids; cutting out and gluing together the pieces is a job for older children and parents. If you like, you can paint Mr. Bones a neon color to make him glow.

Materials

  8 or 9 clean, plastic gallon jugs
  String
  Craft knife or heavy-duty scissors, such as kitchen shears
  Hot glue gun
  Hole punch

Head: Choose a jug with a pair of circular indentations opposite the handle and turn it upside down. In the corner, opposite the handle, use the craft knife or scissors (parents only) to cut out a large, smiling mouth, centered under the indented "eyes." Make two small slits in the top of the head and tie a loop of string through them for hanging the finished skeleton.

Chest: Cut a vertical slit down the center of a right-side-up jug, directly opposite the handle. Cut and trim away plastic to make the rib cage. Glue the head and chest together at the "neck" by connecting the spouts of the two jugs with a thick band of hot glue (adults only). Hold the jugs together for a few minutes until the glue cools.

Shoulders: Cut off two jug handles (leaving a small collar on the ends) and attach them to the chest section with hot glue. Punch a hole at one end of each shoulder.

Hips: Cut all the way around a jug, about 4½ inches up from the bottom. Take the bottom piece and trim away a small smile shape from each side to make a four-cornered piece. Punch holes in two opposite corners.

Mr. Bottle Bones

Waist: Cut out two spouts, leaving a ½-inch collar on each. Glue the spouts together and let dry. Then, hot-glue the waist to the bottom of the chest and the top of the hip section.

Arms and legs: Cut eight long bone shapes from the corner sections of three jugs (cut into the curved shape of the jug to make the bones even more realistic). From four of these bones, cut out the center to make lower limbs (forearms and shins). Punch a hole through the ends of all eight bones. Tie two arm sections to each shoulder, and two leg sections to each hip, with string.

Hands and feet: Let the kids trace their hands and feet onto the side of a jug, then cut out the shapes. Punch holes in the hands and feet and tie them onto the arms and legs.

Monster Jugheads

Ever notice that an empty milk jug looks a little like Frankenstein? We did — and we convinced *FamilyFun* reader Rachel Schwartz of Scarsdale, New York, too. She made these monster heads with her whole family — including a three-year-old, a preteen (who thought the project was weird enough to warrant a try), and her husband, whose skills were employed to insert the bolts into Frankie's neck.

Homemade for the Holidays

Monster Jugheads

Materials

- Clean, plastic gallon jug
- Plastic deli container
- Duct tape
- Tempera paints and paintbrushes
- Milk caps
- Aluminum foil
- Pushpins
- Thin piece of cardboard

Turn over a clean, gallon jug and rest it inside a plastic deli container (the deli container helps the monster head stand upright and also makes Frankie's thick neck). Attach the jug to the container with duct tape, then coat both with tempera paint. When the paint is dry, paint on bloodshot eyes, wicked scars, and a head of greasy black hair. To create bolts in the sides of the monster's neck, cover milk caps with foil and attach them with pushpins. Cut a nose from a thin piece of cardboard, then slip it through a slit cut in the monster's face.

Monster Mouth Game

To make this game of skill, cut monster teeth out of the edge of a shoe or cereal box and invert it so the teeth touch the table. Decorate to look like a monster with paint or construction paper, googly eyes, and goofy ears. Place the box on the ground and mark off a masking tape starting line. Offer the kids marbles to flick into the monster's mouth. If you're playing with big kids, give each tooth a score (the smaller the hole, the higher the score). The highest scorer wins.

Spooky Spiders

Here's a bunch of itsy-bitsy spiders that won't take long to hatch.

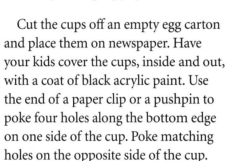

Materials
Cardboard egg
 carton
Black acrylic
 paint and
 paint-
 brush
Paper clips or pushpin
12 black pipe cleaners
Glue stick
12 pairs of googly eyes

Cut the cups off an empty egg carton and place them on newspaper. Have your kids cover the cups, inside and out, with a coat of black acrylic paint. Use the end of a paper clip or a pushpin to poke four holes along the bottom edge on one side of the cup. Poke matching holes on the opposite side of the cup.

To make fuzzy legs, cut four black pipe cleaners into 7-inch lengths. Thread a pipe cleaner through one of the holes, into the cup, and out the corresponding hole on the other side. Make sure the ends protrude an equal length from both sides of the cup and

bend them upward at the base of the spider's body. Fold in the opposite direction midway down the legs to create knees and bend the tips to make feet. Finally, glue on googly eyes.

Turnip Top Flashlights

Carving jack-o'-lanterns is a tradition that got its start in ancient Ireland, where kids used hollowed-out turnips filled with embers to light the way on Halloween night. With these directions, you can make a nonflammable (but still spooky) trick-or-treat lantern.

Materials
Medium-size, purple-top turnip
Paring knife and spoon
Flashlight

Slice off the very top of the turnip and hollow out the inside using a sharp paring knife (parents only) and a spoon. Then, carefully carve facial features in one side, as you would for a pumpkin. Cut a circle in the bottom of the turnip to fit over the end of the flashlight. Finally, turn on the flashlight to give Jack a glow.

Dinner Ghosts

Butternut squash, rather than pumpkin, is the Halloween centerpiece at the Hardy-Johns household in Tampa. *FamilyFun* reader Kimberly Hardy-Johns reported that her oldest daughter, Rachael, came up with the idea. She started by covering three butternut squashes in white paint. To complete her ghosts, she added a mouth and eyes of black construction paper, using straight pins to attach them. (Permanent black marker would work just as well for facial features.) As you can see, each squash took on quite an individual personality.

Turnip Top Flashlights

Thanksgiving

Village People

Setting the Thanksgiving table became an art rather than a chore for *FamilyFun* reader Shelby Powell of Ava, Illinois, and her two children, Neil, age six, and Adi, age four. They had fun creating and naming one placeholder for each of the twenty-six guests at their Thanksgiving table.

Materials

> Cardboard tissue tube
> 4- by 6-inch rectangle of colored paper
> Glue
> Fine-tipped markers
> 2- by 3-inch piece of paper
> Colored paper scraps

For each figure, wrap a cardboard tissue tube with a 4- by 6-inch rectangle of colored paper and glue the paper in place. Draw the facial features on the 2- by 3-inch piece of paper with fine-tipped markers. Glue the face onto the tube. For the hair, cut fringe along one side of a small paper rectangle. Roll the hair around a pen to make curls, trim it, and glue it in place.

Native Americans: Cut and decorate headbands and feathers for the Native Americans and draw a string of beads with a fine-tipped marker.

Pilgrims: Cut and decorate collars for the Pilgrims. To make the Pilgrim girl's bonnet, wrap a 2- by 5-inch paper rectangle around the top of the tube with the ends overlapped and glued at the back. For the Pilgrim boy's hat, cut out a black circle 2½ inches in diameter. Roll and glue a black 2- by 5-inch paper rectangle into a tube shape. Cut slits along one end, fold in the tabs, and glue them to the center of the paper circle. Add a ½-inch band and square buckle and glue the hat to the boy's head.

Native American

TABLE FOR FOUR

When *FamilyFun* reader Eileen Allen of Draper, Utah, hosted Thanksgiving dinner for the first time, her kids were thrilled — until they realized that having all those guests meant they would have to sit with their cousins at a card table. To make this fate more appealing, Eileen suggested they decorate the table. So, Brent and Adam wrapped the table legs with colored crepe paper, made canvas place mats, and even made Pilgrim and Native American headbands. Eileen picked up Silly Straws, candy kisses, and napkin holders in the shape of turkeys. Sure enough, the cousins thought the table was "rad," and nobody complained about not sitting with the adults.

Homemade for the Holidays

Balloon Turkey

Balloon Turkey

FamilyFun contributor Drew Kristofik reports that her kids got a huge charge out of dressing these balloons. If you get ambitious, you might even purchase some helium balloons and let your kids decorate them to float in a mini Thanksgiving Day parade.

Materials

> 2 round red balloons
> 1 oblong yellow balloon
> Rubber band
> Cardboard
> Masking tape
> Acrylic paints and paintbrushes

For the turkey's body, blow up a red balloon and knot the end. To make the head, blow up the yellow balloon about halfway, so that there's an uninflated "nose" at one end, then knot the balloon. Tie an uninflated red balloon to the nose to make the turkey's wattle. Attach the knotted-off ends of the body and the head together by wrapping a rubber band around them. Cut the feet out of one piece of cardboard and attach them to the bottom of the turkey with masking tape. Now your child can dress up her bird, painting on a face and feathers. After you make a few turkey balloons, your kids can hold a race to see who can bop theirs across the room first. The winner gets the real turkey's wishbone.

Balloon Turkey

Gobbler Gloves

Here's a project kids will be happy to lend a hand with — a turkey puppet that doubles as a Thanksgiving centerpiece.

Materials

> Gardening glove
> Felt
> Glue
> Liquid embroidery paint
> Googly eyes

Use the gardening glove for the bird's body. Cut feathers out of felt (make them a bit wider than the glove fingers), fringe the edges, and glue one to each glove finger. Cut a wing shape out of felt and glue it to the palm. Use paint to enhance the plumage.

For a beak, cut a pair of small felt triangles and glue them to opposite sides of the thumb tip. For the wattle, cut a 2-inch-long hourglass shape out of red felt. Drape the wattle over the base of the beak and glue it in place. Glue on googly eyes. To use the turkey puppet as a table decoration, stuff newspaper into the glove and roll up the cuff.

Gobbler Gloves

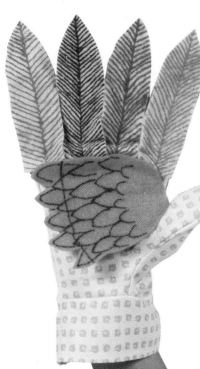

Candy Cobs

Filled with yellow hard candies or after-dinner mints, these miniature corncobs add a sweet finish to your holiday meal.

Materials

  Pair of clear plastic gloves
  Large package of candy
  String or twist ties
  Straw-colored crepe paper

Cut the fingers off the gloves and fill each two thirds of the way with candy. Fasten the ends with string or twist ties, leaving 1½-inch plastic tails. From the crepe paper, cut out a 7½-inch square for each favor. With scissors, scallop the tops and taper the sides to create husks. Place a bundle of candy, tail-side down, on top of each husk. Bunch the lower portion of the husk around the cob's plastic tail and tie both together with a 7- by ½-inch crepe paper strip.

Candy Cobs

Homemade for the Holidays

Apple Candles

While making this unusual table centerpiece, *FamilyFun* contributor Drew Kristofik's daughter Nina delighted in reminding her mom that the Pilgrims weren't crazy about fruits and vegetables. But when Drew pointed out that a few tough winters showed the Pilgrims they needed to supplement their smoked meat habits, the idea of an apple cellar began to seem sensible to Nina. This centerpiece is ephemeral (we recommend composting it the day after Thanksgiving) but beautiful while it lasts.

Materials

  Apple corer
  Large Rome Beauty apples (try to pick ones that stand straight on the table)
  Candles
  Waxed paper
  Potato peeler and lemon juice
  Stickers, paint, or autumn leaves

Using an apple corer, make a straight hole about halfway through the middle of an apple. Remove the core piece. The candle should fit tightly into the hole; if the hole is too large, wrap waxed paper around the candle end. Repeat for as many apples as you'd like. Older kids can decorate apples by carving designs in the skins with the tip of a potato peeler (to prevent the designs from turning brown, rub them with lemon juice immediately). For a base, use a plate or cutting board, or try Nina's method. She decorates aluminum foil with stickers, paint, or leaves and then places the apples in a circle on the foil.

Apple Candles

Pilgrim Hat

To make a Thanksgiving napkin ring, cut a cardboard tissue tube into a 3-inch length to form the top of the hat and cut a 3½-inch doughnut out of cardboard for the brim. To assemble, cut tabs in one end of the tube, slip on the brim, and bend the tabs along the brim. Glue, then decorate.

Stained-glass Hanukkah Windows

Hanukkah

Stained-glass Hanukkah Windows

Brighten the eight nights of Hanukkah and enjoy each other's company by crafting these "stained-glass" candles. Each night, hang another one in your window or door until you have all eight.

Materials

Black construction paper
Craft knife
Colored cellophane or tissue paper
Tape
Cheese grater
Old crayons
Waxed paper
Iron
Glue
String or yarn

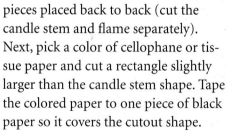

Use the craft knife (parents only) to cut out a candle shape from two black construction paper pieces placed back to back (cut the candle stem and flame separately). Next, pick a color of cellophane or tissue paper and cut a rectangle slightly larger than the candle stem shape. Tape the colored paper to one piece of black paper so it covers the cutout shape.

To make the flame, grate shavings from yellow, orange, and red crayons. Then, cut two squares of waxed paper at least 4 inches square. Spread the crayon shavings across one square, then place the other square on top. Cover both sides of the crayon sandwich with newspaper and press lightly with a dry iron. Let the creation cool, then cut out a

Homemade for the Holidays

piece slightly larger than the candle flame shape and tape it to the black paper. Glue the second sheet of black paper to the back of the first. Punch a hole in the top, thread with string, and hang.

Star of David

Representing David, the Jews' greatest hero-king, the six-pointed star graces the Israeli flag and is Judaism's most recognized symbol worldwide. With some kitchen science, kids can turn pipe cleaners into a crystal star of David.

Materials

Widemouthed jar
Borax (available at grocery stores)
Food coloring
Pipe cleaners
String
Pencil

Fill the jar with boiling water (adults only). Mix borax into the heated water, a tablespoon at a time, until you notice powder settling on the bottom of the jar. Stir in food coloring to add a tint.

Next, bend a pipe cleaner into a six-pointed star. Tie one end of the string to the star and the other end around the pencil. Rest the pencil on the jar lid so that your pipe cleaner is suspended in the solution. Set aside overnight.

As the water cools and evaporates, borax molecules will stack together. By morning, the star will be covered with crystals. Remove it from the jar, let it dry, and hang. To make a three-dimensional star like the one at right, make two six-pointed stars and nest one inside the other before dipping into the borax. (This may look like rock candy, but remind your kids that these are toxic and nonedible.)

Jewish Holiday Crafts

Purim is a joyous celebration, when children dress up in costumes, shake *groggers* (noisemakers), and eat three-cornered cookies called hamantaschen. To make a grogger, place dried beans or rice in an aluminum pie pan and staple a second pan, upside down, on top of the first, and shake.

During the week of Sukkoth, a festival of thanksgiving, people build huts called sukkahs, which are made from branches and leaves and decorated with fruits and vegetables. To make a tiny sukkah, stand a shoe box on its end and glue twigs and leaves to it. Cut out fruits and vegetables from paper and hang them with thread from the top of the box so that they dangle inside the sukkah.

Star of David

SIMPLE MENORAHS

Natural menorah: Find a steady branch, about 10 inches long, then glue or nail metal bottle caps onto it to hold the special menorah candles (melt the bottom of candles to affix them to the bottle caps).

Thread spool menorah: Nail painted wooden thread spools to a board. Widen the holes with a drill (parents only) and be sure to take care as the menorah candles burn down.

Clay menorah: Shape candleholders with clay, poke holes with a menorah candle, then paint when dry.

Felt Menorah

One of the high points of Hanukkah is getting to light the family menorah. This holiday wall hanging features felt candles and stick-on flames, which makes it easy, and safe, for even very young kids to participate in the ritual.

Materials

> White and blue felt (the colors of the flag of Israel)
> Yellow felt
> 2- by 1-foot piece of felt (of any contrasting color)
> Glue
> Velcro
> Wooden dowel
> 2½-foot piece of cord

Cut nine 3½- by 1½-inch candles from the white felt and nine flames from the yellow felt. From the blue felt, cut eight 2-inch squares and one 3- by 2-inch rectangle for candleholders.

Place the felt banner on a flat surface and glue the candleholders along its lower edge. Space them equally apart and put the larger holder in the center for the shammes candle, which is used to light all the other candles. Glue a candle above each holder. For wicks, glue one side of a ¾-inch Velcro strip above each candle. Glue a matching strip to the back of each flame.

Fold over the top of the banner 1½ inches from the edge. Glue the edge to the back of the banner and insert the dowel. Tie the cord to the ends of the dowel, and the menorah is ready to hang.

On the first night of Hanukkah, remind your child to "light" the shammes first and then the candle to the far right. Each night thereafter, he can add a new flame, always starting with the candle to the left of the one he lit last.

Kwanzaa

Kwanzaa Mobile

From December 26th to January 1st, African American families can pay tribute to their heritage by celebrating Kwanzaa. This simple holiday decoration will help teach your kids the seven principles of Kwanzaa — Unity, Self-Determination, Collective Work and Responsibility, Cooperative Economics, Purpose, Creativity, and Faith.

Materials

    Red, black, and green felt (the three
      colors of Kwanzaa)
    Glue
    3 wooden paint stirrers
    Tempera paints and paintbrushes
    Pushpin
    Fishing line

With your kids, brainstorm symbols that represent the seven principles of Kwanzaa (a drum for Creativity, say, or a star for Purpose). Cut the shapes out of felt and glue on the first letter of the principle each stands for.

To form the hanger, paint the paint stirrers red, black, and green. Stack them so their tips fan out like the spokes of a wheel and glue in position. Once dry, use a pushpin to poke a hole 1 inch in from each of the ends. Make a seventh hole through the hub. Thread a 1-foot piece of fishing line through each hole and tie a knot at the top. Poke small holes through the tops of the felt shapes and tie them to the fishing lines.

To suspend the mobile, thread three 2-foot pieces of fishing line under the crossed stirrers. Gather the six ends above the stirrers, secure with a knot, and hang.

Homemade for the Holidays

Kwanzaa Mobile

Felt Kufi

Get into the Kwanzaa spirit by crafting this classic Kufi hat, adapted from *The Kids' Multicultural Art Book* (Williamson Publishing).

Materials

    Red, black, and green felt
    Stapler
    Masking tape or duct tape

Cut and staple a 2-inch-wide brow band of red felt. Next, cut a pair of 1- by 12-inch strips out of red, black, and green felt. With each pair, form an X and staple together in the center. Pile the X's on top of one another so the felt strips extend out like the spokes of a wheel. Attach to the band by folding up the ends and stapling in place. Finally, cover the staple prongs by lining the inside of the brow band with masking or duct tape.

Cowrie Beads

With pasta shells, kids can make beads that resemble cowrie shells, symbols of good fortune in Africa. Hold a shell with the inside facing you with the curled flap at the top. Apply glue to the inner edge of the lower flap. Hold a second shell as if it were a bowl and slide its open flap behind the curled flap of the first shell. Once set, paint with black, red, and green acrylics and let dry. String the beads in alternating colors on cord.

Felt Kufi

Christmas

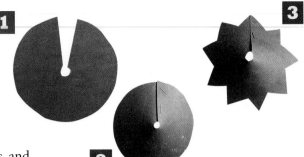

Paper Tree

Decking your halls, doors, mantels, and tabletops with homemade decorations will put your family in the holiday spirit, especially if the crafts are quick, like this miniature Christmas tree.

Paper Tree

Materials

- Green poster board
- Stapler
- Acrylic paints and paintbrushes
- Cardboard tissue tubes
- Large Styrofoam cup
- Styrofoam block
- 18-inch wooden dowel
- Glue
- Construction paper
- White puffy paint

1. Using a dinner plate as a guide, draw a circle on the poster board and cut it out. Cut out five more circles, each an inch or so smaller than the previous one. Make a cut from the edge into the middle of each circle and cut a hole in the center.

2. Tuck one cut edge under the other so that the circle becomes slightly cone-shaped.

3. Staple together the edges. Cut out small triangles around the edges of the circles.

Paint the outside of the cardboard tissue tubes green and cut them into 1½-inch sections. Turn the Styrofoam cup upside down and push the dowel into it, using a Styrofoam block in the cup to hold it secure. Start with one tube ring for the trunk, then stack the green circles on the dowel, separating each one with another ring. Put glue on the top and bottom rims of each ring to secure it. Paint the base and glue a construction paper star on the treetop. Use puffy paint to tip the branches, glue on paper ornaments, and if you like, twine around a store-bought gold garland.

Reindeer Gear

The kids can begin this year's Christmas party by decking themselves out with the latest in North Pole couture: easy-to-make reindeer antlers. The headbands double as a party souvenir — or as a crowning touch to a Rudolph costume.

Materials

Brown poster board
   or construction
   paper
Pencils
Stapler
Glue
Glitter
Face paint (optional)

Before the party, you and your kids should cut the brown poster board or paper into 1½-wide by 24-inch-long strips for the headbands and also into 6- by 9-inch rectangles for the antlers (two for each child). Put out pencils, scissors, a stapler or two, glue, glitter, and, if you like, some face paint.

When the guests arrive, help each of them wrap a strip around his or her head for a comfortable fit, remove it, and securely staple the ends. On the 6- by 9-inch rectangles of poster board, each child can draw the outline of a pair of multi-pronged antlers and then cut them out. Kids who want spiffier antlers can add glue and glitter; less patient reindeer simply can staple the antlers to the front of the headband. Use the face paint to finish off each reindeer's costume with a bright, red nose.

Skirting the Issue

When her son Jon turned one and her daughter Allison was three and a half, Janna Kuklis of Cozad, Nebraska, started making a Christmas tree skirt. She cut it out of muslin and quilted her children's names on each side. Each Christmas, before Janna puts the skirt under the tree, the kids print their handprints onto it in a bright color. Allison also writes her name — pretty soon, Jon will be writing his, too. It's a lot of fun, and it makes a wonderful keepsake (once, when they unpacked it, Allison discovered she'd spelled her name wrong the year before). The only problem is that the skirt is filling up — the kids are growing too fast.

Homemade for the Holidays

Growing Tree

This felt Christmas tree is a true evergreen that can serve as a visual record of your family's growth from year to year. After measuring it, your kids can print their heights on felt ornaments and add them to the tree.

Materials

  2 yards each of red and green felt
  Fabric glue
  Two plastic 6-foot tape measures
  Felt scraps, assorted colors
  Wooden dowel
  20-inch piece of yarn
  Fabric paint

Cut a 6- by 2-foot piece of red felt and lay it on a flat surface. Apply glue to one long side. Press a tape measure onto the glued edge, with the 1-inch mark at the bottom of the banner. Glue the second tape measure to the opposite side.

Cut out a 7- by 5-inch tree trunk from the felt scraps. Center it on the banner 2 inches from the bottom and glue it in place. From the green felt, cut five triangles that measure 20 inches tall and 17 inches across the base. Glue a triangle onto the banner, overlapping the top of the trunk by an inch or so. Glue on a second triangle over the top half of the first one. Add the other triangles in the same manner. Top the tree with a felt star.

Fold over the top of the banner and glue the edge to the back. Insert the dowel, then tie the ends of the yarn to the ends of the dowel.

Finally, cut out a bunch of colorful 3½-inch circles on which your kids can note their heights and the year with fabric paint. When gluing the ornaments onto the tree, line up the tops of the circles with the appropriate marks on the tape measures.

Growing Tree

Poinsettia Napkin Rings

Because there's no sewing involved, this craft lets young kids make something elegant with little fuss. It will seem magical to them that three pieces of felt, folded properly, can become a napkin ring so pretty it wins a place at the table.

Materials

  Poster board
  Red and green felt

Measure and cut out poster board templates for the shapes pictured above: a four-pointed leaf (about 5 inches across), four rounded petals (about 3½ inches across), and a dog

Poinsettia Napkin Rings

240

bone shape (about 9 inches long and 4 inches high). Trace around the leaf template on the green felt and around the petals and dog bone on the red felt.

Cut out the shapes and then cut 1-inch slits in the center of the petals and leaf. Lay the red petals over the green leaf, fold the dog bone shape in half, pull the ends up through the slits, and open the felt into a flower.

Gingerbread Garlands

String these cheery garlands along your mantel, on the front door, or across a special present. Made from old grocery bags, this project is an easy one to whip together at a moment's notice.

Materials

Brown paper bags
Construction paper
Glue
White puffy paint (for the
    gingerbread "icing")

Cut a 5- by 16½-inch strip from a brown paper bag. Fold up the rectangle, accordion style, five times. On the top layer, draw a gingerbread person, either by hand or by tracing around a cookie cutter. Make sure the hands and feet extend out to the folded edges.

Now cut through all the layers of paper *except* where the hands and feet touch the fold, as shown below. (If you have young kids, you may want to do this and leave the decorating to them.) Cut scarves, hats, boots, mittens, and skirts out of construction paper and glue them in place. To put the "icing" on the "cookies," use puffy paint. Squirt on buttons, hair, smiles, and eyes. To make a long garland for hanging on the tree, tape together a few chains.

Tabletop Santa

For a Santa decoration (or an angel, reindeer, or elf), simply adapt the Village People on page 231. For Santa, wrap a cardboard tissue tube with a 4- by 2-inch sheet of red paper and glue in place. To make the face, use a 3-inch-wide circle of pink paper; for Santa's beard, glue on layers of white paper circles. For the hat, wrap a paper rectangle around Santa's forehead and glue the edges together. Finish off with a belt, facial features, and a paper pom-pom.

70944

Merry Christmas to Ewe

Artful Ornaments

FamilyFun contributor Vivi Mannuzza of Stockbridge, Massachusetts, has two children (ages six and a half and eight) who return home from school and summer camp loaded with art projects. To make good use of the smaller items, Vivi turns them into ornaments for their Christmas tree. Marked with each child's name and the month and year created, the god's eyes, shell clusters, cut-paper lace, clay baubles, and even paper dreidels are hidden in a box until it's time to "do the tree." At Christmas, when the family opens their box of ornaments, everybody gets to admire the kids' work and remember the time (and circumstances) when they created their treasures.

Merry Christmas to Ewe

In a season full of new purchases, tree ornaments, like this roly-poly sheep created by *FamilyFun* editor Ann Hallock, stand out as distinctly homemade. That's precisely why her mother has saved a few similar ornaments from Ann's childhood to hang on the tree every year.

Materials

　　White yarn
　　3- by 4-inch cardboard rectangle
　　Rubber band
　　Black felt square
　　Small gold bell
　　Black pipe cleaner
　　Red ribbon and embroidery needle

To make the body, loosely wrap the yarn around the width of the rectangle until you have covered it at least three times. The more yarn you use, the fluffier the sheep's coat will be. Next, slide the yarn onto your fingers, gathering all the loops together. Using your other hand, put a rubber band around the loops, cinching them in the center like an hourglass. Cut through the loops on both ends and

fluff up the pom-pom. If the yarn pieces are uneven, "shear" the sheep with scissors. After cutting a face shape out of the felt, glue it and the bell onto one end of the sheep. Cut the pipe cleaner in half and thread the two pieces through the center of the sheep's body, so they stick down on each side like legs. For a hanger, cut a 10-inch length of ribbon, fold it in two, and knot the two ends together. Thread the unknotted end of the loop through an embroidery needle, then pull it up through the center of the sheep.

Felt Tree

Looking for a new way to spruce up your Christmas tree? With little more than felt and buttons, your family can whip up a collection of ornaments that outshine even the fanciest store-bought bulbs.

Materials

　　Felt
　　Embroidery floss or doubled thread
　　Needle
　　Buttons
　　Batting

To craft a miniature Christmas tree, cut a matching pair of 5-inch-tall trees out of felt. With embroidery floss or doubled thread, sew buttons to the front of the tree. Using a running stitch, sew together the two tree shapes ¼ inch from the edges, but leave a 1-inch opening in one side. Stuff batting through the opening, then stitch it closed. To ready the ornament for hanging, thread a 6-inch piece of floss through the top of the tree with a needle and knot the ends together.

Felt Tree

Pasta Angel

We've all heard of angel-hair pasta, but a pasta-haired angel? This one has a mess of jaunty curls and will brighten up any Christmas tree.

Materials

Dried lima bean
Glue
Markers
Assorted dried
pasta (tiny soup
pastas, rigatoni,
noodle, wagon wheel, elbow
macaroni, bow-tie pasta wings)
Thread

To create a pasta angel, start with a dried lima bean for the head. For curls, let your child brush glue on one side of the bean and press it into a pile of tiny soup pastas. Then, she can use markers to draw on a face. Use a rigatoni noodle for the body. Glue on a wagon-wheel pasta collar, elbow macaroni arms, and bow-tie pasta wings. Glue the head onto the body. For a hanger, tie on a loop of thread below the bean.

Pasta Angel

Air Santa

Air Santa

A high-flying Kriss Kringle, complete with billowing white silk scarf, pilots this old-fashioned biplane. Children who love miniatures and model-making enjoy inventing cool trimmings for this clothespin flying machine.

Materials

Old-fashioned clothespin
2 Popsicle sticks
Wooden coffee stirrer
Fine-point marker, paint, and small
paintbrushes
Small wooden bead
Glue
White yarn and ribbon
Gold-colored thread

Before your child glues his plane together, he should paint its body (the clothespin), its wings (the Popsicle sticks), and its propeller (the stirrer). With a paintbrush or marker, he can decorate the wooden bead with a Santa face and hat. Next, glue one wing on top of the clothespin and one wing to the bottom of it. Glue the pilot's head in place just in front of the wings. Snap the stirrer in two and affix one half onto the plane for a propeller.

Decorate the biplane with stripes, numbers and letters, polka dots, or holiday designs. Poke a piece of white yarn into the top of the bead to make the pom-pom on Santa's hat and tie a short length of ribbon around Santa's neck for his aviator's scarf.

SHOOTING STAR

Brighten up your Christmas tree with this two-tone star. Draw a five-point star (about 3 inches across) and a slightly smaller star on thin cardboard and cut the shapes out. Trace the larger shape onto purple felt and the smaller shape onto red felt; cut out both stars. Next, cut three 8-inch strands of one color ribbon and three 8-inch strands of another. Gather the ribbons, making sure the ends are even, then staple them together across one end. Lay down the purple star, place the stapled end of the ribbons in the center, squirt with glue, and center the red star on top of the purple one. Once dried, poke a hole in the top and thread a ribbon through it to hang.

70944

Dress-up Cards

Last year, *FamilyFun* reader Susan Wieser of Lima, Ohio, incorporated one of her daughter Diana's favorite activities — dressing up — into their annual card-making extravaganza. Diana and her brother, John, dressed up as snowmen, wearing long white sweatshirts and putting crib sheets over their heads and hair. Susan stuffed the sweatshirts with fiberfill and cinched them at the waist with white tights. After the kids finished off the costumes with scarves, gloves, paper buttons, and a broom, Susan took a photo of them and had extra prints made. When they came back, Susan cut the background away from the photos, and Diana glued the snapshots onto blank cards she had decorated with paint and holiday confetti.

Sock Full o' Nuts

Part of the point of sending a family Christmas card is to give your relatives a picture to hang on their fridge, right? With this silly greeting, you can give them the giggles, too.

Materials

> Family photo
> White card stock
> Rubber stamp and ink
> Red felt
> Glue stick or Tacky Glue
> Cotton balls
> String

To take the photo, ask everyone to stand behind a table (the table represents the top edge of the stocking). Wave and act silly, but be sure to keep your arms above the tabletop.

Next, cut out an 8½- by 11-inch piece of card stock and fold it in half. Use a rubber stamp and ink to make a background for the card. Then, cut the background out of the photo and cut off the bottom along the tabletop. Cut out a red felt stocking wide enough to hold the photo. Glue the photo and stocking onto the card, then add cotton balls and a string loop.

Snowman Surprise

This wintry greeting puts your child in the starring role of Frosty the Snowman.

Materials

> Card stock
> Craft knife
> Felt and glue
> Double-sided tape
> Ribbon, buttons, and a pipe cleaner
> Photo of your child

Fold the card stock in half lengthwise and, using the craft knife (parents only), cut a circle in the card's front, about three quarters of the way up. Glue on two circles cut out of white felt to create the snowman's body. Glue a ring of white felt for the snowman's head. Add a felt hat, a ribbon scarf, three buttons, and pipe cleaner arms.

Help your child affix his photo inside the card with double-sided tape so his face can be seen through the hole, as well as on the inside of the card when it is opened.

Snowman Surprise

Homemade Stamps

When you're ready to write out your holiday greetings this year, let your kids add their stamp, too — by hand-printing wreaths, reindeer, and stars on your cards and envelopes.

Materials

Ink pads
Notecards, envelopes, or holiday stationery
Markers and pencil
Cotton ball

Thumbprint Reindeer: Even younger children will find it easy to print this cute and quick reindeer head. Press your thumb onto an ink pad and then, with the tip pointing down, make a thumbprint on a card or an envelope. Use colored markers to draw on ears, eyes, a mouth, and antlers, finishing up with a bright red nose.

Cotton Ball Wreath: Press a cotton ball onto a green ink pad. Lightly dab the cotton onto holiday stationery, forming a circular pattern. Using the same method, apply another layer or two of green ink. Next, add holly berries by pressing the tip of a pencil eraser against a red ink pad and using it to print dots on the wreath. Or, draw on berries with a red marker or colored pencil.

QUICK CARDS FOR BUSY ELVES

Hand-colored photos: Make black and white photocopies of a favorite photograph; let your kids embellish them with stamps or stickers, or color them with markers or fluorescent highlighters.

Sidewinders: Make paper chains of angels, snowmen, or gingerbread men and attach them to a sideways-opening card. When  the chain is extended, each figure bears the letter of a Christmas greeting. Recipients can detach the chain and drape it on their tree.

What's cookin'? Along with your season's greetings, include in your card a favorite holiday recipe.

A banner year: Accordion-fold a long piece of card stock and write your seasonal message — using markers, cutout letters, or stamps — across succeeding panels.

Yule be famous: Position cutout heads of family members among a group shot of a favorite sports team, music group, sitcom family, or crew of astronauts.

Inscribe the photo with "Three cheers from our team!" or "Merry Christmas from Travis Tritt!" or "Season's greetings from out of this world!"

The combo card: To make a card that serves double duty as its own envelope, fold card stock into two and a quarter panels. Round the quarter panel so that it makes an attractive envelope flap.

Deep sea-son's greetings: Draw a fishbowl or aquarium shape on the front of your card, cut out an opening within it, and tape blue cellophane over the opening from inside the cover. Pose for your photograph in bathing suits (and even face masks) or dress up like pirates. Decorate the card with fish stamps or paper fish cutouts.

Funny foldouts: Cut out a tall Christmas tree (about 18 inches high) from green construction paper. Make horizontal accordion folds about every 3 inches down its length. Tape or glue the tip of the tree inside a card and decorate with shiny star stickers, paper ornaments, and tinsel.

Glossary

acetate: This lightweight plastic comes in a variety of colors and is sold at art supply stores.

acrylic gloss: An acrylic paint that dries to a high-gloss finish. Clear acrylic gloss can be used for a final, "sealer" coating on some craft projects. It can be sprayed or painted on. Available in craft, hobby, and art stores.

acrylic paint: Use this water-based, quick-dry paint for wood, papier-mâché, plaster projects, and other crafts you would like to last. Available in tubes, tins, and paint sets at art, craft, stationery, and hardware stores for about $2 for a 2-ounce bottle.

balsa wood: Because it's soft and light, this wood is easy for children to handle in simple carpentry projects. Sold at craft stores.

batting: Otherwise known as fiberfill, this stuffing material comes in cotton and polyester. A medium-size bag costs about $2.50 at fabric and craft stores.

beeswax: Used to make the candles on pages 102 and 103, beeswax comes in a honeycomb pattern and is sold in rolls and sheets in a number of colors (a 12-sheet package costs about $12). Be sure to store in a cool place.

block plane: One of the smallest planes, usually about 6 inches long, this is used to trim and smooth wood surfaces. Available at hardware stores.

butcher paper: Great for large-scale paper projects, this heavy-gauge paper comes in wide rolls and many colors. Available at school supply and craft stores.

cake decorating paste: This concentrated food coloring paste is brighter than the ordinary liquid type. Available in tubes and jars at baking supply and grocery stores.

card stock: Somewhere between construction paper and poster board in weight, card stock makes a good canvas for greeting cards. Available at stationery and photocopy shops.

carpenter's square: Used to mark right-angle cuts, this tool is required for the simple woodworking projects in this book. Available at hardware stores.

construction paper: This craft staple is available in a wide range of colors and sold most everywhere — supermarkets, drugstores, craft stores, and stationery shops.

Con-Tact paper: You can use Con-Tact paper, the brand name for clear adhesive shelf paper, to laminate paintings and drawings you think are keepers. Available at crafts, hardware, and stationery stores.

cording: Look in the curtain section of your fabric store for these decorative ties, which come in an assortment of colors and designs (some have pom-poms).

craft knife: Commonly referred to by its brand name, X-Acto, this knife has a razor-sharp screw-in replaceable blade. It's available in craft, hobby, hardware, and art stores for about $4.

craft sticks: Otherwise known as Popsicle sticks, these smooth-finish hardwood sticks can be found in packages of 150 for about $3. Available in assorted colors from craft, discount, and hobby stores.

crazy scissors: This is the common name for any scissors that produce a designed edge rather than a straight one. Each cut repeats a pattern, such as a zigzag, scallop, or Victorian scroll. Fiskars's crazy scissors cost about $4 at craft and hobby stores.

darning needle: Not as sharp as other needles, this long needle has a large eye that is easy for kids to thread. Available at craft and sewing stores.

decorating wax strips: About 8 inches long, these wax strips are sold in packages that include a range of colors. If you can't find them at your local craft store, call The HearthSong Catalog (800-382-6778) to order packages of 12 strips.

double-sided tape: Sticky on both sides, this tape comes in clear and foam styles. Available at stationery, art, and hardware stores.

electrical tape: Commonly used to wrap wire couplings and as a temporary electric line insulator, this tape comes in bold colors, has a very sticky adhesive, and can be used to add color to crafts. Available in hardware, discount, and grocery stores.

embroidery thread or floss: Heavier and sturdier than your average thread, this comes in bright colors and can be woven into a Friendship Bracelet (see page 176).

fabric glue: This glue is specially designed to bond fabric and is available at craft, sewing, and fabric stores. Most brands are nontoxic, including Elmer's Craft Bond Fabric Glue.

fabric paint: Use this paint when you want your kids to permanently mark T-shirts, sweatshirts, aprons, and table linens — once the paint is heat-set, the designs won't wash out. Available in a variety of colors at craft, fabric, hobby, and sewing stores. Look for a nontoxic brand, such as DecoArt So-Soft.

fabric pen: Like fabric paint, this permanent ink pen leaves marks on fabric that won't come out in the wash. Available in a range of colors at craft, hobby, sewing, and fabric stores. Most brands are nontoxic.

fabric scissors: Heavier and sharper than regular scissors, these allow you to make clean cuts through fabric and should be reserved for this purpose only. Available at fabric, hobby, and craft stores.

Fome-Cor: Fome-Cor is the brand name for Styrofoam that is reinforced by poster board. It comes in 20- by 30-inch sheets and costs about $4 at stationery, hobby, and craft stores.

glitter glue: A squirt of this glitter-filled glue won't hold two pieces of paper together, but it will add sparkly color. Three tubes of .5 ounce each cost $2.99 and are available in craft, hobby, and art stores.

glue gun: This appliance delivers hot liquid glue that firmly bonds together woods and other materials. However, because the glue gun produces hot glue, it should be used by parents only (older kids can use low-temperature glue guns). Both the gun and replacement glue sticks are available at craft stores.

glue stick: This solid cylinder of glue allows for a mess-free application. Either white or clear types dry transparent and are nontoxic. Available at craft, hobby, discount, and grocery stores for about $1.

googly eyes: Essential for puppets and dolls, these small plastic domes with colored disks make whimsical eyes. Available in many colors and shapes, they're sold in bags at craft and hobby stores.

heavy-duty elastic thread: Great for making homemade scrunchies (see page 173), this stretchy elastic thread is sold at fabric stores.

iron-on seam binding: When ironed, this fabric adhesive bonds pieces of material together. Brand names include Stitch Witchery and Wonder-Under. Sold at craft and fabric stores.

light-gauge craft wire: Available at craft stores, this lightweight but sturdy wire can be cut with wire snips or scissors.

liquid embroidery paint: This fabric paint comes in a fine-tip squeeze bottle and is used for highlighting and defining cross-stitches. Available at sewing supply stores for about $2.50.

Lycra: This is the brand name for spandex, a stretchy fabric available in solid colors and patterns at fabric stores.

mat board: This heavy paper board, which is used to frame a picture, comes in a variety of colors and finishes, such as plain, flat, antique, crackle, marbleized, and crimped. Some mat board is pH neutral to preserve fine photos and other delicate prints and materials. Available in craft, hobby, and art stores.

metal screening: Generally used to screen outdoor patios, this material can also be adopted for the jewelry frame on page 175 and paper-making frame on page 68. Sold by the foot at hardware stores.

molding: Strips of this decorative wood, used to add trim or ornamentation to woodworking projects, are sold by the foot at lumber stores. Molding comes in dozens of designs, and the prices vary accordingly.

muslin: This woven cotton fabric comes in textures from sheer to coarse; can be used in Flower Pounding on page 115, Table Linens on page 189, and other craft projects. Available at fabric stores.

nontoxic: A description applied to any substance that does not give off dangerous fumes or contain harmful chemicals in sufficient quantities to endanger a person's health. Always read the label to be sure the materials you use are nontoxic.

nylon fabric: An elastic synthetic fabric, this is available in a wide variety of colors and weights. Sold by the yard at fabric stores.

oak tag: This poster-size tan-colored paper is heavier than poster board and available in craft, hobby, and art supply stores.

origami paper: These small square sheets of fine paper are used in the ancient Japanese art of folding paper into recognizable shapes and figures. From *ori* (fold) and *kami* (paper), it is sold in many textures and colors. A package of sheets imported from Japan costs $2.29 to $4.99. Available in craft, hobby, art, toy, and discount stores.

paper drop cloth: These large lightweight sheets of paper protect furniture and carpets from splattered paint. Available at hardware and paint stores.

paper fastener: Made from brass, this fastener has a rounded top and two prongs at the base. When pushed through a hole and pressed down, it will hold paper in place. Available at stationery and craft stores in both small bags and boxes.

paraffin: Easily melted on the stove top (parents only), paraffin wax provides the basis for many of the candlemaking crafts in this book. Sold in blocks at craft, candle, and hobby stores.

permanent markers: These quick-drying, waterproof pens come with a fine or broad tip in myriad colors; average price is $1.29 each. Read the labels and make sure you buy nontoxic varieties — and don't confuse them with washable markers, which are made specially for children. Available in craft, hobby, art, grocery, stationery, and discount stores.

pine board: Go to your local lumber store for this reasonably priced wood, which comes in a variety of lengths and thicknesses and is sold by the foot.

pinking shears: Fabric- and paper-cutting scissors that produce a uniform zigzag edge. Available in craft and fabric stores.

pipe cleaners: Commonly used to form dolls and animals, these fuzz-covered wires are the crafter's version of the brushes used to clean the inside of tobacco pipes. Fabricated with long and short nap, pipe cleaners come in all colors and are sold in packages of 100 for about $3. Available in craft, hobby, art, discount, and stationery stores.

Tips for Buying Nontoxic Materials

If you're not sure whether an art or craft material is nontoxic, read the label. The Art & Creative Materials Institute, which is based in Boston, certifies nontoxic materials and runs a product seal of approval on the label. For a complete list of brands of nontoxic art supplies (and toxic products to avoid), write or call the institute at 100 Boylston Street, Suite 1050, Boston, MA 02116; 617-426-6400.

Supplies on a Shoestring

Looking for inexpensive or free art materials? Check your area businesses. Local paper companies may offer free rolls of newsprint, a potter may sell wholesale clay, or a fabric factory may be ready to unload fabric scraps. If you live in a city, look for a recycled material store that sells foam strips, fabric, ribbons, Con-Tact paper, and a range of other products donated by local businesses.

Great Craft Books

Art and craft books are excellent resources for learning new techniques and sparking ideas. There are scores of them available, but here are a few favorites:

Adventures in Art, Kids Create!, and *EcoArt!* are just a few of the many terrific children's craft books put out by Williamson Publishing Company. This series is packed with "art and craft experiences" for kids of all ages.

Bright Ring Publishing offers *Scribble Art* and *Mudworks,* two craft books by award-winning children's art book author and elementary school teacher MaryAnn F. Kohl.

Sticks & Stones & Ice Cream Cones (Workman Publishing) and *Cups & Cans & Paper Plate Fans* (Sterling Publishing) contain a wealth of unique ideas on how to turn ordinary around-the-house items into creative crafts.

The Best Holiday Crafts Ever! by Kathy Ross (Millbrook Press) is another extensive collection, with 175 full-color pages of craft and decoration ideas for special occasions, from Earth Day to Hanukkah.

plaster of Paris: In powdered or premixed form, this calcium sulfate mixture supplies a quick-drying (it sets in an hour) and nonshrinking medium to create molds and sculptures. Available in craft, hobby, and hardware stores.

plywood: This lumber is made from thin layers of wood glued on top of each other and pressed when dry. It comes in a variety of thicknesses and is normally sold in 4- by 8-foot sheets at hardware stores and lumberyards.

pom-poms: These soft acrylic balls make a fine head for a doll or other creature sporting googly eyes. A bag of 40 of the 5-millimeter size costs $.49; two of the large size sell for $.49. Available in craft, hobby, toy, and discount stores.

poster board: This heavyweight paper is sold in large sheets and many colors; you can substitute shirt cardboard. Available at craft, stationery, and hobby stores.

poster paint: See description of tempera paint, below.

puffy paint: This washable acrylic paint creates a three-dimensional design on fabric. It is usually sold in small squeeze bottles with fine applicator tips. Prices start at $.99 for 1 ounce, and colors run from metallic and glitter to neon and pastel. Available in craft, hobby, art, toy, and discount stores.

rickrack: These wavy ribbons are primarily used as decorative trim. They come in assorted colors and widths and are available at most notions departments and sewing and fabric supply stores.

rubber cement: Use this adhesive with caution, since many brands are toxic (Conros makes a non-toxic rubber cement). The real advantage to rubber cement is that it's quick-drying and easily cleaned off most surfaces. Available at craft, stationery, art, hardware, and hobby stores.

Sculpey III: A brand name for modeling clay, this hardens quickly in a low oven and makes colorful figures to populate dollhouses and model villages. Sold in small packages at craft stores.

sealer: Also called spray-on glossy varnish, this sealer lends a shiny finish to projects you'd like to hold on to for a while. It comes in aerosol cans and should always be used in a well-ventilated area with adult supervision (most varieties are toxic). Available at hardware, hobby, and craft stores.

spray paint: This enamel paint packaged in an aerosol can allows for fast and convenient coverage to crafts. It comes in glossy, satin, or flat finishes and is not washable. It is toxic, so work in a well-ventilated space and look for a "low-odor" type. Parents only. Available in craft, hobby, hardware, and discount stores.

stamp pad: Used to apply color to rubber stamps, these ink-filled pads are available in bright colors, metallics, pastels, and stripes for about $2 at craft, hobby, stationery, and discount stores. Ink replacement bottles are also available.

Styrofoam molds: These lightweight Styrofoam shapes come in spheres, domes, cones, cubes, rings, rectangular sheets, and other shapes. Available at craft, hobby, and art stores.

tapestry needle: These short needles with big eyes work well with embroidery thread and thin, lightweight wools. Available at fabric stores.

tempera paint: Many painting projects in this book call for this thick, brightly colored paint, which is water-soluble and comes in both liquid and powdered forms. The liquid is sold in jars and bottles, as well as gallon jugs. The powdered type is sold in jars and should be mixed with water according to package directions. You can also find glitter, fluorescent, neon, and pastel tempera paint. Available in craft, hobby, discount, toy, art, and grocery stores.

tissue paper: This thin paper comes in a variety of colors and strengths; it makes pretty paper blossoms and the stained-glass hangings on page 66. Available at craft, stationery, and art stores.

utility knife: For use by adults only, this knife has a razor-sharp, retractable blade. Available at craft and hardware stores for about $10.

Velcro: This simple closure device consists of a piece of fabric with small hooks that sticks to another piece of fabric with small loops. Comes in both self-adhesive and sew-on varieties and is available at sewing, fabric, craft, and hobby stores.

watercolor: When you dip a wet brush into these dry cakes, you activate the paint. Available in a variety of colors, which blend easily, the paints are sold in palettes as well as individually at craft, art, school supply, and hobby stores.

white canvas: This heavy cotton fabric is closely woven and resists tears and snags. Sold by the yard at fabric stores.

white glue: This nontoxic adhesive (the most common brand is Elmer's) is the perfect glue for kids: it dries clear, is easy to use and clean up, and washes out of most fabrics. Available at craft, art, hardware, school supply, stationery, toy, and hobby stores.

wicking: This material is used to make the wicks for the candles on pages 98 to 103. It comes in both waxed and unwaxed varieties and is available at craft and hobby stores.

wooden dowels: Usually about 3 feet long, these round rods are sold in diameters from as small as ⅛ inch up to about an inch or more. Available in craft stores.

X-Acto knife: See craft knife, above.

Index

Index

Art & Photography Credits

Special thanks to the following *FamilyFun* magazine photographers and stylists for their excellent work.

PHOTOGRAPHERS:

Dean Abramson: *95 (top & bottom right).*

Animals Animals/Earth Scenes: *124 (top left).*

Robert Benson: *52, 227 (middle right), 229.*

Paul Berg: *77 (bottom right), 128, 218 (bottom left), 234, 235 (middle).*

John Burke: *130, 156 (bottom).*

Michael Carroll: *26 (bottom left), 159, 177 (middle right), 228.*

Susie Cushner: *76, 161 (top).*

Ron Dahlquist: *118 (right), 119, 121.*

Faith Echtermeyer: *109 (top right).*

Peter Fox: *20 (top left), 35 (bottom), 116 (top), 120 (bottom left), 145 (bottom), 146, 161 (bottom), 168 (left), 173 (bottom right), 176, 189 (top left & bottom left), 192 (top), 200-201, 208 (top left & bottom left), 209, 219 (top right), 221 (bottom right), 222, 238, 240 (top right & bottom right), 241 (top & bottom middle).*

Susan Fox: *171 (bottom).*

Jim Gipe: *84, 90-91, 122 (top left), 167 (top middle), 224, 244 (top).*

Tom Hopkins: *24, 30, 32 (top left, bottom left & bottom right), 33 (top), 81, 106, 110 (top), 113 (top & middle), 127, 137 (top & middle), 232 (top left & bottom right), 233 (top right), 239 (top right & middle).*

Ed Judice: *16-18, 20 (top right & bottom right), 21 (bottom), 22, 25, 27 (middle, bottom middle & bottom right), 28-29, 34, 35 (top), 36, 39, 41 (top left), 42 (bottom), 43 (top left & bottom), 46, 53 (top right & middle right), 55 (bottom), 56, 57 (bottom), 58-61, 63, 64 (bottom right), 67 (middle & top right), 69 (bottom), 70 (top left), 73 (top left & bottom left), 78, 80 (bottom), 86 (bottom), 88-89, 92, 94 (bottom), 108, 109 (top left), 114-115, 120 (top left & middle), 132, 134, 135 (top & bottom left), 137 (right), 139-140, 141 (top left), 143-144, 145 (middle), 147, 148 (top right & bottom), 150 (top left), 151, 152 (top right & middle), 153, 154 (top left, middle & bottom), 156 (top left), 157 (bottom & right), 160, 165 (top left & bottom), 166 (middle & bottom), 167 (bottom right), 171 (top right), 172, 173 (top left, middle left & bottom left), 174, 175 (top), 177 (bottom right), 178, 180-181, 183 (top), 185 (top left, top middle & bottom), 186, 189 (bottom right), 191 (top & bottom left), 193 (bottom right), 195 (top right), 198-199, 207, 211 (bottom left & bottom middle), 212 (bottom left), 213-214, 215 (top middle & middle left), 216, 218 (top & bottom right), 223 (bottom), 226, 230 (bottom right), 233 (top left & bottom left), 235 (bottom right), 236, 240 (left), 242 (bottom), 243 (top left & bottom left), 245 (top & bottom left).*

Brian Leatart: *157 (top left), 203, 205-206, 220.*

Lightworks Photographic: *8-9, 19 (top), 21 (top), 23 (top right & middle), 31 (top left & middle), 32 (top middle & top right), 37, 41 (bottom), 44, 45 (middle & bottom), 47 (top left & bottom), 48, 49 (bottom), 50 (bottom), 51, 54 (bottom right), 55 (top left), 62, 64 (top left), 65, 68 (left & bottom right), 69 (top right), 70 (middle right), 72, 73 (right), 74-75, 77 (top left), 79 (top left), 82, 87 (bottom right), 93, 94 (top left), 95 (bottom left), 96, 105, 110 (bottom left), 111, 112* (bottom right & middle right), 116 (right), 117, 123 (top), 124 (middle), 131, 133, 135 (bottom right), 136 (top right, middle, middle right & bottom), 138, 141 (bottom right), 142, 149, 150 (top right & bottom), 163 (bottom), 167 (middle [buttons]), 169, 170 (top & bottom left), 175 (middle & bottom), 179, 182, 183 (bottom), 184, 185 (right), 188, 189 (middle right), 191 (bottom right), 193 (top), 195 (top left), 196, 208 (top right & bottom right), 210, 211 (top), 215 (bottom right), 221 (top), 227 (top & bottom), 230 (top), 231, 232 (bottom left), 237 (top right & bottom), 241 (bottom right).

Marcy Maloy: 107, 168 (top middle & bottom).

Tom McWilliam: 87 (top left & top right), 118 (top left), 204.

Todd Powell: 122 (middle left & bottom).

Marc Romanelli/Image Bank: 193 (bottom left).

Russell Photography: 40, 97, 100 (bottom), 104, 120 (bottom right),123 (bottom right), 124 (bottom right), 145 (top).

Jim Scherer: 190 (bottom).

Joanne Schmaltz: 217.

Shaffer/Smith: 10-15, 31 (top right & bottom [crayon shades]), 38, 57 (top right), 66, 68 (background), 70 (bottom), 79 (middle left & right), 100 (top right), 154 (top right), 155, 156 (middle), 170 (middle right), 173 (bottom middle [scrunchies]), 177 (top & bottom left), 192 (bottom left), 195 (bottom), 212 (top left & middle), 219 (bottom), 225, 233 (bottom right).

Silver Photography: 197.

Brian Smith: 23 (bottom right), 27 (top right).

Steve Smith: 98-99, 101-103, 113 (middle right [mushroom prints]), 158, 162, 164 (top, middle right & bottom right), 187, 194, 202, 242 (top), 243 (top right & bottom right), 244 (bottom right).

Tony Stone Images: 129.

Sync Associates: 83, 85, 86 (top).

Jake Wyman: 237 (top left).

Chip Yates: 67 (bottom left), 125.

STYLISTS:

Fazia Ali, Bonnie Anderson/Team, Grace Arias, Laurie Baer, Suzanne Boucher/Ennis, Margo Brumme, Catherine Callahan, D.J. Carey, Carol Case, Bill Doggett, Katia Echivard, Erica Ell/Team, Susan Fox, Ron Garnica, Scott Gordon/Ennis, Jacqueline Lemieux-Bokor, Karin Lidbeck, Barbara Jo Metcalfe, Amy Malkin Pearl, Jillian Rahm, Hilda Shum, Lisa Smith/Ennis, Nan Whitney/Ennis.

ILLUSTRATORS:

John Hart: 48.

Katherine Mahoney: 211.

Donna Ruff: 52, 126, 224.

John Ursino: 113.

Pencil Toppers, page 25

Credits